50 Hikes in Arizona

50 *Hikes*

In Arizona

Walks, Hikes, and Backpacks through Sky Islands and Deserts in the Grand Canyon State

First Edition

MARTIN TESSMER

The Countryman Press
Woodstock, Vermont

AN INVITATION TO THE READER

Over time trails can be rerouted and signs and landmarks altered. If you find that changes have occurred on the routes described in this book, please let us know so that corrections may be made in future editions. The author and publisher also welcome other comments and suggestions. Address all correspondence to:

Editor, 50 Hikes™ Series
The Countryman Press
P.O. Box 748
Woodstock, VT 05091

LIBRARY OF CONGRESS CATALOGING-IN-PUBLICATION DATA

Tessmer, Martin.
50 Hikes in Arizona : walks, hikes, and backpacks through the Sky Islands and deserts in the Grand Canyon State / Martin Tessmer.–1st ed.
    p. cm.
  Includes index.
  ISBN 0-88150-599-4
    1. Hiking–Arizona–Guidebooks. 2. Trails–Arizona–Guidebooks. 3. Arizona–Guidebooks. I. Title: Fifty hikes in Arizona. II. Title.

GV199.42.A7T47 2004
796.51'09791–dc22

                              200409423

Cover and interior design by Glenn Suokko
Composition by Blue Mammoth Design
Cover photo © Kerrick James.com
Interior photographs by the author
Maps by Mapping Specialists Ltd., Madison, WI, © The Countryman Press

Copyright © 2004 by Martin Tessmer

First Edition

Published by The Countryman Press, P.O. Box 748, Woodstock, Vermont 05091

Distributed by W.W. Norton & Company, Inc., 500 Fifth Avenue, New York, NY 10110

Printed in the United States of America

10 9 8 7 6 5 4 3 2 1

DEDICATION

To "Uncle Denny Blue Eyes."
No better brother born.

50 Hikes at a Glance

Hike Name	Nearest Town	TOTAL MILES	DIFFICULTY	TRAIL WATER?
1. Echo Canyon Loop	Wilcox	3.2	M	S
2. Ed Riggs–Heart of Rocks Trail	Wilcox	7.3	M	S
3. Fort Bowie Loop	Wilcox	6.2	M	Y
4. Atascosa Lookout Trail	Nogales	4.8	D	N
5. Juan Bautista de Anza Trail	Tumacacori	9.0	E	Y
6. Florida Canyon Trail	Green Valley	9.0	S	Y
7. Brown Mountain	Tucson	4.8	M	N
8. Douglas Spring Loop	Tucson	7.2	M	Y
9. Romero Pools	Tucson	5.6	D	Y
10. Aravaipa Canyon Trail	Mammoth	24.0	M	Y
11. Barnhardt	Payson	12.0	D	S
12. Boulder Canyon	Mesa	14.4	M	N
13. Peralta Trail	Mesa	11.8	D	N
14. Lookout Mountain	Phoenix	1.2	M	N
15. Alta-Bajada Loop	Phoenix	8.1	M	N
16. Waterfall Canyon–Black Rock Loop	Phoenix	3.1	M	Y
17. Bell Trail	Camp Verde	6.6	M	Y
18. West Clear Creek Trail	Camp Verde	15.2	D	Y
19. Fossil Springs	Payson	8.2	D	Y
20. Horton Creek	Payson	6.8	M	Y
21. Highline Trail	Payson	51.0	D	Y
22. Thumb Butte Loop	Prescott	2.0	M	N
23. Granite Mountain Trail	Prescott	7.6	D	N
24. Parsons Spring	Clarksdale	7.4	M	Y
25. Boynton Canyon Trail	Sedona	4.8	E	N

E	Easy	S	Strenuous	Hb	Horseback Riding	Xc	Cross country
M	Moderate	Bk	Biking	Sw	Swimming		skiing
D	Difficult	F	Fishing	Tr	Trail running	P	Poor; high clearance

CAMPING OPTIONS	AUTO ACCESSIBILITY	ACTIVITIES	COMMENTS
CG	E	––	The habitats are as varied as the hoodoos.
CG	E	––	See why this area is called the "Wonderland of Rocks."
––	G	Tr, Hb	A trek through Wild West history.
B	G	Hb	Edward Abbey once lived and worked at the lookout.
––	E	Hb	Follows a desert river from one historic site to another.
B	G	Hb	Why don't more hikers take this dramatic trail?
CG	E	Bk	Leads to the can't-miss Arizona Sonora Desert Museum.
––	E	Tr,Hb,Bk	Everything from saguaro forests to waterfalls.
B	E	Sw	Scenic trail ends at rock-walled dipping pools–fun!
B,CG	G	Sw	Staggeringly beautiful hike through a wilderness canyon bottom
B	F	––	Dependable water source at trail's end (Chilton Spring).
CG,B	E	Tr, Hb	Lots of volcanic rock formations and vistas near Phoenix.
CG,B	G	––	Staggering views of Weaver's Needle from the saddle.
––	E	Tr, Hb	A 360-degree overlook in the heart of the Phoenix metropolis.
––	E	Hb, Bk	Wilderness and city panoramas on this suburban trail.
CG	E	Tr, Hb	Petroglyphs and a waterfall.
CG, B	G	F,Sw,Hb,Bk	A popular recreational trail, lots of trailside water.
CG, B	F	Sw,F, Tr,Bk	Large red rock sunbathing platforms.
CG, B	G	Sw	This pellucid spring has a million-gallons-an-hour output.
CG, B	E	Hb, F	Wonderful during fall changes.
CG, B	E	Tr, Hb, F	Can be day-hiked in sections.
CG	E	Hb	Outstanding views. Wheelchair accessible for a mile, hiking clockwise.
CG, B	E	Tr, Hb.	Very good overlooks and rock formations–cool in summer.
B	F	Sw, F, Hb	Some wading required on this lovely streamside ramble.
B	E	Tr, Hb, Xc	Check out the energy vortex sites in this beautiful canyon.

F   Fair–bumpy   E   Excellent   S   Seasonal
G   Good–   Y   Yes   CG Campground
       some bumps   N   No   B   Backcountry (primitive)

50 Hikes at a Glance

Hike Name	Nearest Town	TOTAL MILES	DIFFICULTY	TRAIL WATER?
26. Brins Mesa Trail	Sedona	6.2	E	S
27. Secret Canyon Trail	Sedona	10.0	M	Y
28. Sterling Pass–Vultee Arch Trail	Sedona	5.0	S	N
29. West Fork Trail	Sedona	6.5	E	Y
30. Escudilla Mountain	Alpine	5.0	M	S
31. KP Trail 70	Alpine	18.8	D	Y
32. Foote Creek and Clell Lee Cabin	Alpine	2.5	E	Y
33. White House Ruins Trail	Chinle	2.4	M	N
34. Buffalo Park Loop	Flagstaff	2.0	E	N
35. Heart Trail	Flagstaff	7.6	D	N
36. Kachina Trail	Flagstaff	10.0	D	N
37. Mount Humphreys	Flagstaff	9.4	S	N
38. Sandys Canyon	Flagstaff	7.6	E	S
39. Bill Williams Mountain	Williams	6.0	D	N
40. Potato Patch Loop	Kingman	4.3	M	Y
41. Red Butte	Grand Canyon	2.4	M	N
42. Bright Angel Trail	Grand Canyon	19.2	S	Y
43. Rim Trail	Grand Canyon Village	11.9	M	Y
44. East Rim, North Canyon, and Arizona Trail Loop	Fredonia	6.9	D	Y
45. South Canyon	Fredonia	5.0	S	N
46. Mount Trumbull	Fredonia	5.2	D	N
47. Horse Crossing Trail #20	Heber	2.8	M	Y
48. Rim Lakes Vista Trail	Heber	6.6	E	N
49. Buena Vista Trail	Show Low	7.5	M	N
50. Long Logs and Agate House Trails	Holbrook	2.2	E	N

E Easy	S Strenuous	Hb Horseback Riding	Xc Cross country
M Moderate	Bk Biking	Sw Swimming	skiing
D Difficult	F Fishing	Tr Trail running	P Poor; high clearance

CAMPING OPTIONS	AUTO ACCESSIBILITY	ACTIVITIES	COMMENTS
B	F	Tr, Hb, Xc	Outstanding overlooks. Water in spring months.
B	G	Tr, Hb	Excellent backpacking sites 2 miles in.
B	E	Hb	One of the best Sedona trails for solitude
B	E	Sw, F	River sandals are useful for the multiple stream crossings.
CG, B	G	Xc	Wonderful views. Shorter hike than described in many books.
CG, B	E	Hb, Xc	Solitude and beauty in the Arizona that few tourists ever see.
B	E	Xc, Tr, Hb	Iris-covered fields and an Old West homestead.
CG	E	Tr	This Canyon de Chelley hike does not require a guide.
----	E	Tr, Bk, Xc	A pretty suburban hike that accesses a backcountry trail network.
CG, B	E	Tr, Bk, Hb	Great views without the crowds of other Flagstaff trails.
CG, B	E	Hb	An overlooked gem with lots of meadows and views.
CG,B	E	----	Magnificent views from Arizona's highest peak.
CG, B	E	Tr,Bk,Hb,Xc	"Honey, I shrunk the Grand Canyon!"
CG, B	E	Hb	Bikes and cars can take FS 111 to the scenic mountaintop.
CG, B	G	Hb, Bk	Lots of overlooks on this Hualapai Mountains hike.
CG, N	F	Hb	Wonderful vistas of the Coconino Plateau.
CG, B	E	Hb	One of the most famous hiking trails in the world.
CG	E	Tr, Xc	Magnificent overlook tour of Grand Canyon's depths. Trail segments are wheelchair accessible and open to pets.
CG, B	E	F	A spectacular summer sojourn from canyon bottom to rim.
CG, B	G	Hb	Hike into Marble Canyon via this nonmaintained trail.
B	F	Hb	Solitude and vistas in an almost prehistoric landscape.
CG, B	P	F, Sw, Hb	Backcountry camping spots next to a stream, in a canyon.
CG, B	E	Tr, Hb, Bk	Spectacular views overlooking the Mogollon Rim.
B	E	Tr, Bk, Hb	A forest ramble with four different overlook points.
--	E	Tr	A stroll among the agate logs of the Petrified Forest.

F	Fair–bumpy	E	Excellent	S	Seasonal
G	Good–some bumps	Y	Yes	CG	Campground
		N	No	B	Backcountry (primitive)

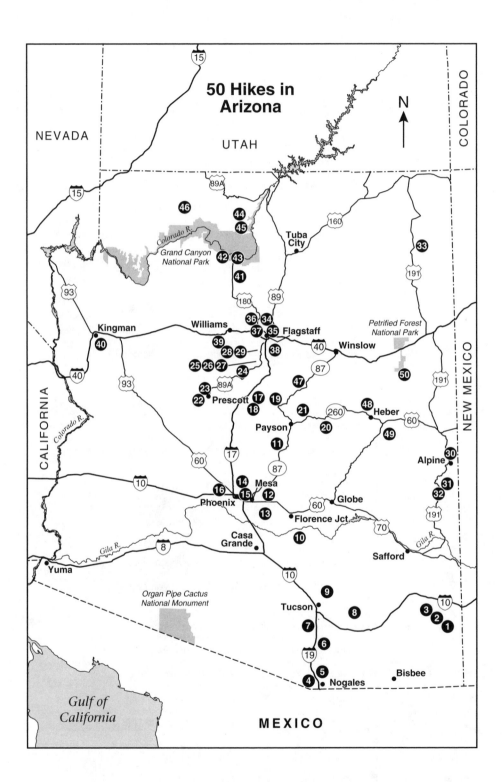

50 Hikes in Arizona

N

NEVADA

UTAH

COLORADO

CALIFORNIA

NEW MEXICO

Grand Canyon
National Park

Petrified Forest
National Park

Organ Pipe Cactus
National Monument

Gulf of
California

MEXICO

Kingman

Williams

Flagstaff

Winslow

Prescott

Payson

Heber

Alpine

Mesa

Phoenix

Globe

Florence Jct.

Casa
Grande

Safford

Yuma

Tucson

Nogales

Bisbee

Tuba
City

CONTENTS

Acknowledgments

To assure that my trail details are accurate, I have compared my hiking trips to the trail details in a dozen fine Arizona hiking books. Chief among these are Scott Warren's *100 Classic Hikes in Arizona*, Tom Dollar and Jerry Sieve's *Guide to Arizona's Wilderness Areas*, and Betty Leavengood's *Tucson Hiking Guide*. All are well written and have been immensely helpful to me.

Identifying the rocks and vegetation of desert trails is a tricky business, and I was greatly helped by using Halka Chronic's *Roadside Geology of Arizona* and Anne and Lewis Epple's *A Field Guide to the Plants of Arizona*. These two books are my constant trip companions.

I have been very fortunate to work with an excellent editing team at The Countryman Press. Jennifer Thompson has been a dream of a production editor: prompt, organized, and caring. Bill Bowers, my manuscript editor, has been both perspicacious and judicious in his changes to my base text; this a much better book for his work upon it. And Kermit Hummel, my managing editor, has my enduring gratitude for offering me this assignment, and for taking a chance with me on my first outdoors book, *Weekend Wilderness*. You guys made it a lot easier than it could have been.

Scott Grabinger, my University of Colorado boss and friend, was remarkably supportive of my efforts to balance my trail writing and instructional technology careers, often telling me to "go home and write" if I spent too much time at university work. Scott, maybe I could have done it without you, but it would surely have been a lot more difficult—thanks so much.

My writing style is unconventional, to say the least, for trail guides. Without the support of my friends to stay the course on my writing voice, I might have drifted off to mere trail reporting. John Lofty, thanks for your invaluable, one-writer-to-another support. And I'll always follow your advice to "never scrimp on the scholarship" when doing my research.

And Ellen, your support was as constant as the Northern Star, and your advice more illuminating. All trails do lead to you.

Marty Tessmer
Evergreen, Colorado
2004

Introduction

"You're doing a hiking book on Arizona? Isn't it all just deserts and cactus? What will you write about?" A number of my out-of-state hiking companions have asked me those questions. Having been no farther into Arizona than a Tucson or Phoenix conference center, they fell prey to the popular stereotypes about the Grand Canyon State perpetuated by the media: flat, dry, open spaces punctuated with the occasional butte or mesa, just like you see in the Western movies.

Little did my friends know it, but Arizona has more topographical and habitat variety than almost any state in the union. With elevations that range from 70 feet near Yuma to 12,700 feet near Flagstaff, a six-hour drive from one elevation point to another is, as Tom Dollar noted in *Arizona's Wilderness Areas*, the environmental equivalent of a drive from Mexico to Alaska—there is that much diversity in the climate, geology, flora, and fauna. You start out in flat desert drylands studded with cactus and palo verde and end up in arctic tundra among jagged peaks covered with snow-loving spruce and firs. And on the way you could stop off at any of the scores of springs and creeks that vein the Central Highlands.

To portray all this scenic diversity, I set out to write a myth-busting Arizona hiking book. I've included trails with waterfalls, lakes, springs, snowfields, subalpine mountaintops, boreal forests, and stream-lined canyons. I've also included a number of the state's desert trails, but these are hardly—as my friends have implied—barren: Arizona's Sonora Desert is one of the most verdant deserts in the world, alive with saguaro and organ pipe cactus forests that have an understory of all manner of desert plants, including some of the most beautiful flowers in America. Barren, indeed.

To showcase Arizona's diversity of topography, habitats, and history, I have selected a range of short and long trails that characterize each region's outstanding features, as described in the next three sections. Let's start with Arizona's most desert-like region.

SOUTHERN ARIZONA

The Sonora Desert sprawls across much of the southern Arizona landscape around Tucson. Studded with tall cacti, it's also home to a wide range of birds and animals. For example, hiking along the Douglas Spring Loop (Hike 8) is like touring a desert arboretum and zoo. But the desert is only one of southern Arizona's outstanding features. The fascinating Chiricahua Mountains (Echo Canyon and Ed Riggs trails) are among the most rugged and biologically diverse mountain ranges in America. The Chiricahua region not only features fascinating rock shapes, it also contains Old West forts and battlegrounds from the time when Cochise and Geronimo roamed the land (see Fort Bowie Loop, Hike 3).

The precipitous "sky island" mountain ranges around Tucson seem to vault straight from the valley floor. Within sight of the Mexican border, these precipitous peaks are high enough to be shawled with subalpine forests and crowned with snow-capped peaks. And there's no better way to experience them than to hike the rigorous Florida Canyon Trail (Chapter 6) thousands of feet up into the Colorado-like Mount Wrightson Wilderness. If you are in the mood for a less elevated hike with cooling waters, you'll find many of them in southern Arizona. Within a short drive of downtown Tucson you can find waterfalls (Douglas Spring Trail), wading pools (Romero Pools), historic rivers (De Anza) and the paradisiacal, stream-filled Aravaipa Canyon (Hike 10). Do these routes sound like barren drylands to you?

CENTRAL ARIZONA

Phoenix's Superstition Wilderness is one of the most popular wilderness areas in America, and for good reason. Home to a rugged landscape of 4,000-foot-high trails, craggy peaks, and bouldered canyons, it's only a two-hour drive from the city, making it the perfect weekend wilderness getaway for Phoenix hikers. The Superstitions contain the famous Peralta Trail (Hike 13), which leads up to the solitarily spectacular Weaver's Needle pinnacle, one of the Southwest's most-photographed rock formations. Those seeking a little more trail solitude often approach The Needle from the scenic Boulder Canyon Trail (Hike 12) on the north side of the wilderness by Canyon Lake. For hikers looking for trails even closer to Phoenix, the Lookout Mountain Trail (Hike 14) offers vistas in the heart of the metropolis, while the Alta and Waterfall trails (Hikes 15 and 16) lead to petroglyphs, waterfalls, and unspoiled wilderness.

Folks who think that central Arizona is all desert should take the hour's drive up I-17 north of Phoenix to the Campe Verde

area in the Central Highlands. Here, some 5,000 feet above Phoenix, they would find a cool wonderland of bell-clear streams cutting deep into multicolored wilderness canyons, accessed by rambling trails such as the Bell and West Clear Creek routes (Hikes 17 and 18). These are great trails for sunbathing, swimming, or wilderness walking. Or they might drive up to thick forests around Payson, and hike down the Fossil Springs Trail (Hike 19) to its million-gallons-an-hour namesake spring, in a riparian habitat thick with cottonwoods, alders, and all manner of birds.

Although the Grand Canyon is the most magnificent canyon in the state, many hikers prefer the eye-level panorama of Sedona's red rock country, whose rainbow canyons and buttes are easily accessible to all levels of hikers. Every year, a host of calendars are produced with photographs of Boynton Canyon (Hike 25), Brins Mesa (Hike 26) and the West Fork Trail (Hike 29). For a change of spectacle, hikers need only drive down the road to tramp Prescott's rock-menagerie Granite Mountain Trail (Hike 23) or visit verdant Parsons Spring (Hike 24) in the Sycamore Canyon Wilderness.

From the more balmy Sedona climes it's less than an hour's drive up US 89A into the snowy forests and canyons of northern Arizona, which has its own host of unique habitats and geologic attractions.

NORTHERN ARIZONA

Two famous geographic features dominate northern Arizona: the Grand Canyon and the Mogollon Rim. The spectacular Grand Canyon is known throughout the world, with routes such as the Bright Angel and Rim Trails (Hikes 42 and 43) featuring fabulous canyon overlooks. Amazingly, most

Grand Canyon visitors stay along the South Rim portion of the Great Hole, neglecting to visit the wilder and more forested (but equally scenic) North Rim, which offers solitary trails such as the North Canyon and South Canyon routes (Hikes 44 and 45) or the remote and primitive Mount Trumbull Trail (Hike 46).

The Mogollon Rim is a 50-mile-wide escarpment (long cliff) that runs for hundreds of miles across most of northeast and north central Arizona. Although it's well known to geologists and geographers across the world, few hikers visit these pine-covered and lake-filled highlands, other than to make a pilgrimage to the see the agate logs of the Petrified Forest (Long Logs Trail). Yet there are few vistas that compare to looking down from the Rim to see all of Arizona below you (Rim Lakes Vista Trail), and the Rim Country has many trails that lead to cliff-lined streams and pools, such as the Horse Crossing 20 Trail (Hike 47).

Flagstaff is the center city of northern Arizona, and it has its own unique trail attractions. The city is surrounded by one of the largest volcano fields this side of Hawaii, and a hike up the suburban Heart or Kachina Trails (Hikes 35 and 36) shows off the many cinder cones in the area. Or climb up into the alpine regions of Arizona's tallest mountain, 12,633-foot Mount Humphreys (Hike 37), passing through Canadian Zone firs and aspens to top-of-the world views of the lava cones and the Coconino Plateau.

North-central Arizona, near the New Mexico border, is the most unexplored portion of the state. This is ski and snowmobile country, home to the wolf and elk that live in the wilds of the Blue Range Primitive Area. It's also a summer haven for Arizona cognoscenti who seek out its solitary stream-filled wilderness canyons (KP Trail), high-country meadows and mountaintops (Escudilla Mountain Trail) and flower-filled meadows (Foote Creek). A hiker could spend a month in the backcountry here, and not take the same trail twice.

In short, hikers have a wealth of varied scenery and climates to explore in Arizona. The trails in this book capture much of that diversity. But before you set out on any of these entertaining paths, a few words of advice.

HIKING TIPS

Arizona's weather is as diverse as its scenery. With little humidity to hold the heat in, the difference between sunlight and shadow temperatures is abrupt and dramatic. You can start out comfortably cool on a hike at sunrise, only to have the same trail turn into a desiccating inferno by early afternoon, then drop to jacket-wearing temperatures when the sun sets. Wise hikers will heed these five basic backcountry rules:

1. Pack plenty of water. Take at least a gallon of water per person for hot summer day hikes that exceed a couple of miles, and pack at least a half gallon in other seasons. Drink at least a pint of water or sports drink every hour you are on the trail, and up to a quart an hour on hot days. Tote a filtered water bottle for those trails that have springs or streams. Trying to hike without drinking enough water isn't macho, it's stupid—as *Backpacker* magazine notes, a 2- to 3-percent loss in body water can reduce performance by 10 percent. And drink water in small, regular doses—some hot-weather hikers have suffered from hyponatremia (inadequate sodium levels, which causes nausea and decreased alertness), drinking so much

water that they deplete their body salts when they perspire.

2. Eat regularly. As you hike, you perspire; as you perspire, you lose body salts. If you don't replenish them with an occasional salty snack; you'll lose electrolytes and become more exhausted than you need to be, and run the risk of hyponatremia (see above). So pack those peanuts, Payday candy bars, or nut-filled gorp. This is no time for dieting!

3. Pace yourself. If you can't comfortably carry on a conversation while you are hiking, you're going too fast. When it comes to wilderness hiking, the race does not go to the swift, but to the enduring—those who conserve their energy for the long haul. If you are hiking up a steep trail such as Mount Humphreys or the Romero Pools (Hikes 37 and 9, respectively), stop every now and then and take 20 breaths, enjoying the scenery. You'll be able to sustain a steadier pace in the long run.

4. Weather the weather. Layers are a must for hiking in the West, where the weather can change at the drop of a ten-gallon hat. A waterproof windbreaker and a hat are requisites for any season. If you find yourself cooking in the sun, slow your pace and douse your cap and shirt with some water—all the more reason to bring extra aqua!

5. Pack the hiker's 10 essentials. Even if you're only going a couple miles, you should pack these basics for unforeseen circumstances:

a.) Map and compass (and know how to use both).

b.) Sunglasses and sunscreen.

c.) First aid supplies, including splints and blister treatments.

d.) Extra food.

e.) Hydration—you might find that others need a drink, including dogs.

f.) Whistle. Everyone should have one, especially children.

g.) Flashlight or headlamp.

h.) Multipurpose knife.

i.) Extra clothing—socks, gloves, etc.

j.) Emergency shelter, in case you are stranded overnight.

A cell phone is a new, 11th addition to this time-honored list. Most work well in high, open country near metropolitan areas. For example, my cell worked well in the saddles of the Mount Humphreys and Peralta Trails, as well as on the Alta's high ridges. Portable global positioning system (GPS) devices (for example, Garmin or Magellan units) are also handy; they have backtrack features that can guide you back in the direction from which you came.

Hiking poles are not a trail requisite, but many experienced hikers, myself included, wouldn't leave home without them. Poles reduce the shock to your knees, especially on those jarring rocky descents. They also act as a "third leg" to stabilize your steps over steep or slippery terrain. And for the calorie conscious, note that a 170-pound hiker will burn more calories hiking with a pole (640 per hour without a pack) than without (524 per hour). That's because poles make you use your arms more, moving like a cross-country skier.

For more hiking tips, go to *Backpacker* magazine's informative web site at www .backpacker.com/technique.

CHAPTER TERMINOLOGY

Each trail chapter has an information block about trail characteristics. The main headings are explained here.

Trail sections. One of the unique features of this book is that it reports the distance, elevation gain, and difficulty between portions of each trail. These segments are mainly identified by significant geographical landmarks (e.g., a saddle or pinnacle) along the trail, as well as junctions with other trails. For those who don't want to hike the entire 51 miles of the Highline Trail (Hike 21) or all of Aravaipa Canyon (Hike 10), there are several trail segments that are worthy hikes in themselves. So use the trail segments to plan a hike that suits your distance and scenery requirements.

Overall distance is the round-trip distance to hike the trail. In cases where a shuttle hike is possible, I have noted that distance in parentheses. To measure trail distances, I have used a pedometer as my base measure, and compared that measure with my GPS distance measures, my hiking time, trail maps, and other trail reports. Where several sources indicate my pedometer measures may be a little high or low, I have adjusted my estimates. In general, however, I have found pedometer measures to be the most reliable source, and that measure is my major standard.

Hiking time is based on my time on the trail—I walk at a measured pace that allows for conversation and observation.

Total elevation gain. In cases where the trail is a constant ascent or descent, elevation gain is the difference between the low and high points on the trail, as measured by my GPS system. A number of trails will swoop up and down, descending into valleys before climbing back up to ridges. This type of trail adds hundreds of feet of elevation gain to your hike, and extra effort. For these roller coaster trails, I have accounted for the elevation gains en route. Thus, the total elevation gain for a trail may exceed the difference between the high and low points on the trail.

Difficulty is my estimate of the degree of effort a moderately fit hiker would expend to complete the trail in season. Bear in mind that this is a subjective estimate, one based on my experience hiking the trail. Elevation gain and distance are factors in my estimation of difficulty, but so is the elevation gain distribution—Mount Humphreys has such a gradual distribution of elevation that it has an "easy" 3,300-foot elevation gain. The trail terrain is also a factor—rocky trails can be more punishing to the feet and knees. The degree of comfort also factors in—the shady North Canyon Trail near the Grand Canyon (Hike 44) is more comfortable in summer than the wide-open Peralta Trail, making it easier to hike.

Auto accessibility. Over the years, many hikers have asked me about road conditions on the way to a favorite trail of mine. There are many hardy trekkers who don't own trucks or SUVs, and they don't want to wreck their cars trying to reach the trailhead. As a result, almost every trail I've chosen for this book can be accessed in season without a high-clearance vehicle or four-wheel drive, and every chapter contains an estimate of the difficulty of using a regular-clearance auto to reach the trailhead.

Comments are my personal impressions and advice about the trail. At the end of the day, returning to the trailhead, I think about what impressed me most about this path, or what counsel I would give to those who would hike it.

Nearby trails. Figuring you might want to hike another trail while you are in the area, I've included at least one trail near the trail detailed in that chapter. In some cases it will even be another trail in this book.

Benson and Wilcox Area–
Land of Cochise and Geronimo

1

Echo Canyon Loop: Rock Concert

Location: Chiricahua National Monument in southeast Arizona near the New Mexico border, 41 miles south of Wilcox.

Total distance: 3.2-mile loop

Hiking time: 2.5 hours

Total elevation gain: 450 feet

Difficulty: Moderately difficult

Best months: October through April

Auto accessibility: Excellent

Maps: USGS Chiricahua Peak. A park map with trails and distances is available free at the Chiricahua National Monument Visitor Center.

Rules: $6 park entry fee. Pets prohibited on trails except for those between Bonita Canyon Campground and Faraway Ranch. No bikes on trails.

Comments: Enjoy an incredible variety of rock formations, vegetation, and wildlife along this trio of trails. Many folks come here for the August wildflowers and the fall changes to the trees and shrubs.

"I see the Chiricahuas as the biological Grand Canyon of the United States. As near as we can tell, it has the highest degree of biological diversity in the United States."
    –Dr. Wade C. Sherbrooke, in "The Violent Chiricahuas" by Peter Aleshire. *Arizona Highways*, November 2002.

With its multifaceted rock formations and widely varied life zones, Chiricahua National Monument is one of Arizona's premier outdoor attractions. Hiking the Chiricahua trails, you'll negotiate arid cactus lowlands that are a colorful mix of Sonoran and Chihuahuan desert vegetation, which transitions to chaparral shrubs and trees on the upper ridges. Then, as you move into the cooler, moister canyons, you'll enjoy the Douglas fir and Arizona cypress groves that frame the hundreds of erosion-carved hoodoos (eccentric rock formations) that earned this area the pioneers' nickname Wonderland of Rocks. It's as if someone compacted the intriguing features of Mexico, Colorado, and Utah together into this 12,000-acre park. Small wonder that this small wonder has been featured in outdoor publications from *National Geographic* to *Arizona Highways*. The only surprise is that more Arizona travelers don't make the pilgrimage to this crown jewel of the southwest mountains. The popular Echo Canyon Loop trail is one of the best park routes for sampling its many birds, plants, and rock formations.

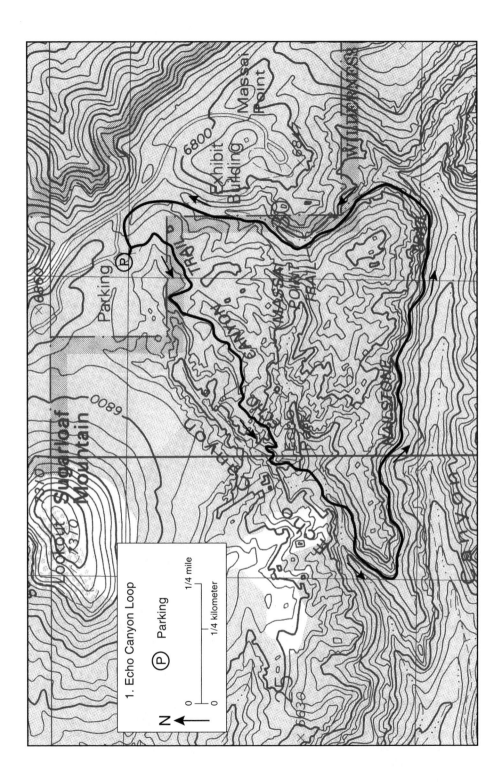

1. Echo Canyon Loop

Ⓟ Parking

N

0   1/4 kilometer

0   1/4 mile

Getting There

From Tucson, drive 88 miles east on I-10 to turn right (south) off exit 340 onto AZ 186. Drive 35 miles south on AZ 186 and AZ 181 to the Chiricahua National Monument park entrance, where there is a $6 entry fee. From the entrance, drive 5.7 miles to the Echo Canyon parking lot.

The Trail

Echo Canyon trailhead to Hailstone trailhead, 1.5 miles, 450-foot elevation loss, moderately difficult.

From the Echo Canyon trailhead (elevation 6,780 feet), follow the rocky but well-marked trail along the ridge of a shallow canyon on your right, passing through a mixed-habitat population of pines, alligator juniper, oak, Arizona cypress, and manzanitas. The first fantastical formations appear just 0.25 mile into your hike, as you gradually descend into a captivating rock garden. Here you'll gape at the groves of goblinlike turrets that line up alongside the trail, marching over to the distant canyon walls opposite you. Composed of ancient volcanic ash, these buff and gray columns have a patina of green-yellow lichen that almost glows in the bright desert sunlight. Hike here in the morning, and you'll see the sun frame these bright spires in angular black shadows, adding yet another dramatic touch to this striking rockscape. As you hike along the trail, you'll slide through an area known as Wall Street, negotiating 2-foot gaps in sheer rock walls vaulting some 50 feet above you.

After a mile, the sunny and rocky trail gradually switchbacks down and morphs into a shady dirt trail surrounded by Arizona cypress, some over 60 feet tall. You have now entered Echo Park, where you might find some pools of water for bottle refills. The trail continues down and along the canyon bottom until you come to the trail junction with the Upper Rhyolite and Hailstone Trail (elevation 6,330 feet). Continue straight to start on the Hailstone Trail.

Hailstone trailhead to Ed Riggs trailhead, 0.8 mile (2.3 total miles), 90-foot elevation gain, easy.

This trail segment is open, level, and sunny. Here you'll have continuous views of Totem Canyon 0.5 mile over on your right, where you'll see islands of rocky turrets rising from the sea of conifers flowing along the canyon bottoms. These wide and flat-sided turrets have faces reminiscent of the Easter Island monoliths. Kids of all ages will love searching for familiar shapes in these columns.

The Hailstone Trail is named for the rounded rocks that litter the trailside. Some 27 million years ago, a series of volcanic eruptions rained molten rock down from the sky, cooling it into the rhyolite "hailstones" scattered around the trail. These are the same eruptions that formed the numerous mountains and the rock grottos of the scenic Chiricahua region. The Hailstone Trail also features many plants of the Chihuahuan desert habitat: agave, manzanita, and yuccas are interspersed with woodland pines and oaks. After 0.8 mile you reach the end of the trail and the junction with the Ed Riggs and Mushroom Rock Trails (elevation 6,420 feet), where you bear left to start the Ed Riggs Trail.

Ed Riggs trailhead to Echo Canyon trailhead, 0.9 mile (3.2 miles total) 360-foot elevation gain, moderately difficult.

The Ed Riggs Trail transitions from a sunny desert trail with rock hoodoos to a path shaded with oak, pine, and cypress. From the trailhead (6,420 feet) you gradually climb up this trail to return to your starting point. Keep your eye out for some of the many birds that populate this area. Many of them are Mexican imports, more likely to be found in the Sierra Madres than the United States: Mexican chickadees, sulfur-bellied

Near Wall Street

flycatchers, and the resplendent elegant trogon. The birds are another reason to take your time on this hike: There's just so much to see.

After 0.7 mile on the Ed Riggs Trail, make a right and trek up a short 0.2-mile switchback to arrive at your starting point. And congratulate yourself for being smart enough to choose such a pretty little hike.

Nearby Trails
The Echo Canyon hike can be made longer and even more scenic by adding on a trip to the amazing Heart of Rocks grotto (see Hike 2). This 9-mile round-trip trek will show off a gallery of famous rock formations: Balanced Rock, Duck on a Rock, Punch and Judy, and a dozen other named displays. To access this area, turn right at the junction of the Hailstone and Ed Riggs Trails, venturing forth onto the Mushroom Rock Trail.

Camping
There is no backcountry camping on the trail. The Bonita Canyon Campground is 0.5 mile from the park visitors center. This tree-shaded facility has 24 tent and RV (up to 26-foot) sites available on a first-come, first-served basis, many with a scenic backdrop of canyon walls. The fee is $12 per night, per site. Pets are permitted on leash. There are no hookups or showers. For more information, contact the national monument visitors center at 520-824-3560. For updated information on the park and its trails, go to www.nps.gov/chir.

2

Ed Riggs, Heart of Rocks Trail: Tuff Love

Location: Chiricahua National Monument in southeast Arizona, 41 miles south of Wilcox.

Total distance: 7.3-mile loop

Hiking time: 4 hours

Total elevation gain: 1,410 feet

Difficulty: Moderately difficult

Best months: October through April

Auto accessibility: Excellent

Maps: USGS Chiricahua Peak. A park map with trails and distances is available free at the Chiricahua National Monument Visitor Center.

Rules: $6 park entry fee. Pets prohibited on trails except for those between Bonita Canyon Campground and Faraway Ranch. No bikes on trails.

Comments: This extended day hike will fascinate you with the array of rock shapes that are scattered among its varied trailside habitats. Take the 1-mile side trip to Inspiration Point—it's worth it. And pack your own water.

Almost 30 million years ago in the Chiricahua Mountains, a series of volcanic eruptions exploded torrents of thick, molten rhyolite (a light-colored, silica rock) into the air, which fell as clouds of white-hot ash. As the fiery ash fell upon the steep mountainsides, it slid down into the open lowlands and cooled into 1,000-foot-thick walls of tuff, a rock composed of compacted volcanic ash. As these stone ramparts chilled out, vertical cracks veined their faces, and eons of wind and rain penetrated the cracks to carve a Disneyland of stony animals, people, and plants. The Chiricahuas' premier collection of rock sculptures lies in the 1-mile Heart of Rocks Loop, reached by trekking a trail trio that starts with the Ed Riggs Trail at the Echo Canyon parking lot.

Getting There

From Tucson, drive 88 miles east on I-10 to turn right (south) at exit 340 onto AZ 186. Drive 35 miles south on AZ 186 and AZ 181 to the Chiricahua National Monument park entrance, where you are charged the $6 entry fee. From the entrance, drive 5.7 miles to the Echo Canyon parking lot.

The Trail

Ed Riggs trailhead to Mushroom Rock Trail, 0.9 mile, 360-foot elevation loss, easy.

Starting from the Echo Canyon parking lot (at 6,780 feet), head east (left) for 0.2 mile, switchbacking down to the junction with the Ed Riggs trailhead and the Massai Point Nature Trail, going left along the Ed Riggs Trail. The rest of the trail is an easy 0.7-

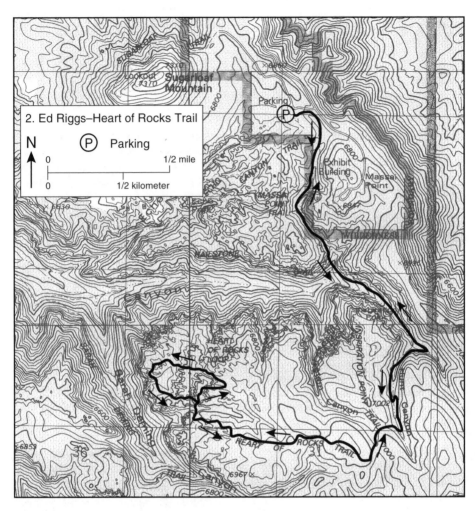

2. Ed Riggs–Heart of Rocks Trail

N (P) Parking

0   1/2 mile

0   1/2 kilometer

mile decline along a well-marked, forested path that has several interesting pastel pinnacles, an opening act for the rock concert you will see at Heart of Rocks. The sunny trail ends at a junction, where you take the Mushroom Rock Trail (elevation 6,420 feet), heading southeast to the Heart of Rocks.

Mushroom Rock trailhead to Big Balanced Rock trailhead. 1.2 miles (2.1 total miles), 610-foot elevation gain, moderately difficult.

The first segment of this trail is a scenic hybrid of Utah-type hoodoos and Colorado subalpine forests. Near the 0.25-mile point, you'll see Mushroom Rock standing alone up above the trees on your right, looking like a buff-colored flying saucer parked on top of a stone turret. From here you'll gradually ascend via a series of long, shady switchbacks. This surprisingly verdant trail segment is more woodland than desert, with pines, alligator juniper, and shrubby oaks populating the trailside drainage. Here you might see a pileated woodpecker, only one of the myriad birds that hop among the dense trailside foliage.

Balanced Rock

At 1.2 miles you come to a trail junction (elevation 7,010 feet) with the Inspiration Point route, but you go straight to start up the Big Balanced Rock Trail.

Big Balanced Rock to Heart of Rocks trailhead,1 mile (3.1 total miles), 150-foot elevation loss, easy.

The Big Balanced Rock Trail is an elevated ridge route with expansive overlooks that will give you a different point of view than the rest of the trail. Here you'll see the craggy Chiricahua Mountains off in the distance, row upon row, snaking south to Mexico. From your 7,900-foot vantage point you can also study the southeast Arizona valley sprawling below you on your right. The trail has inspirational sweeping views all around you, and it's a good place to pull out the binoculars and study one of the most unique and diverse ecologies (and geologies) in North America, the Chiricahua region.

After 0.6 mile along the Balanced Rock Trail, you'll pass by an intriguing gallery of turrets and pinnacles: some look like stacks of coins, others with mushroom tops, and still others with faces. At 0.7 mile you start to see some ghostly size 10 footprints on the trail, beige-colored outlines branded into the rocky path. No one seems to know where these mysterious prints came from, my inquiries about them at the ranger station met with little success.

Soon after you start following these footsteps, you arrive at the trail's namesake, a 1,000-ton, 22-foot-wide boulder balanced on one rocky toe. Balanced Rock signals your entry into a showcase of some of the most captivating rock sculptures you'll ever see, as you arrive at the Heart of Rocks trailhead junction, at 6,860 feet.

Heart of Rocks trailhead loop, 1.1 miles (4.2 total miles), 300-foot overall elevation gain, difficult.

From the trailhead you gradually descend into a shady depression and then start stairstepping up to the main body of shaped stones. As you clamber up and down this loop, you'll enjoy close-ups of some of the most intriguing rhyolitic rock arrangements in the Chiricahuas, so unique that many of them have their own names: Duck Rock, Old Maid, Kissing Rock, Punch and Judy, Thor's Hammer, and others. This up-and-down trail is a bit hard on the knees, but it's not to be missed. Completing the Heart of Rocks Loop takes time, especially if you stop to study the formations and take photos, so don't expect to rush through this route.

As you exit the trail loop back at the Heart of Rocks trailhead, make sure you turn left to return along Big Balanced Rock Trail—don't go right onto the Sarah Deming Trail, which goes back near the park visitors center. While daydreaming, I made the wrong turn and had to backtrack a quarter mile!

Heart of Rocks trailhead to Echo Canyon parking lot, 3.1 miles (7.3 total miles), 360-foot elevation gain, easy.

The return to your starting point will be an easy downhill for most of the way until you join the Ed Riggs Trail, which inclines some 360 feet up to the Echo Canyon parking lot. Maybe you'll be a little tired at the end, but considering all you've done and seen, wasn't it worth it?

Nearby Trails

If you have the time and energy, take the 1-mile side trip up and back to Inspiration Point—you'll be glad you did. The oft-photographed point has a spectacular overview of spire-studded Rhyolite Canyon. Inspiration Point can be reached from the Mushroom Rock–Balanced Rock trail junction, so it's right on your way to or from the Heart of Rocks.

Camping

Bonita Canyon Campground is 0.5 mile from the park visitors center. This tree-shaded facility has 24 tent and RV (up to 26-foot) sites available on a first-come, first-served basis, many with a scenic backdrop of canyon walls. Fees are $12 per night, per site. Pets on leash are permitted. There are no hookups or showers.

For more information, contact the national monument visitors center at 520-824-3560. For updated information on the park and its trails, go to the web site at www .nps.gov/chir.

3

Fort Bowie Loop:
A Trail with a History

*Location: Fort Bowie National Historic
site, 29 miles southeast of Wilcox, 113
miles southeast of Tucson.*

Total distance: 6.2 miles

Hiking time: 3 hours

Total elevation gain: 920 feet

*Difficulty: Easy on the way to the fort;
moderately difficult on the return via the
Overlook Trail.*

Best months: October through April

*Auto accessibility: Fair. The dirt access
road is bumpy but is negotiable by car.*

*Maps: USGS Cochise Head. Free park
map available at ranger station on trail.*

*Rules: Dogs on leash. Horses permitted.
No camping.*

*Comments: Take a walk through history
on a route frequented by Cochise,
Geronimo, and the US Cavalry.This 3.1-
mile stroll is more like an open-air museum tour than a hike. Allow extra time to
read the trail's en route history signs and
to visit the fort ruins.*

Hiking along the Fort Bowie Trail is like
walking into the set of a 1950s Western
movie: This is rugged desert countryside,
sprawling across the junction of the
Chihuahuan and Sonora Deserts. The wavy
grassland bottoms are flanked with hillsides
of yucca and cactus that slope up to
rounded mountains and craggy little pinnacles: You almost expect John Wayne to
come riding down the side of a hill, leading
a band of cavalry.

One hundred fifty years ago, this lonely
grassland was a busy center of activities re-
lated to the white men's relentless westward expansion. Apache Spring was one of
southeast Arizona's few dependable water
sources, so the spring became a popular
trail stop for stagecoaches, westering mi-
grants, homesteaders, and prospectors.
With this infringement into the Chiricahua
Apaches' hunting grounds came the in-
evitable conflict between the two nations,
starting with the 1861 capture (and subsequent escape) of Apache chief Cochise on
false charges of kidnapping. The resultant
battles between white man and Apache led
to the creation of Fort Bowie, used as a
base to pursue Cochise and Geronimo during the Apache Wars. With its many nineteenth-century ruins and battle sites, the
Fort Bowie Trail takes you back in time to
depict soldiers' and Native Americans' life
on the western frontier, including the
tragedies that befell each group during their
conflicts.

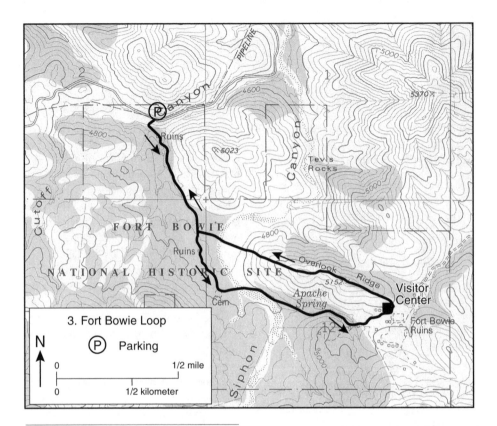

Getting There

From Tucson, drive east on I-10 84 miles to Wilcox. From Wilcox, drive south 21 miles on AZ 186, turning left onto Apache Pass Road at a brown sign directing you to the Fort Bowie site. Go 8 miles east along this dirt road to the Fort Bowie Trail parking lot. There are several rest rooms and a picnic area near the trailhead.

The Trail

Fort Bowie trailhead to Fort Bowie, 1.6 miles, 230-foot elevation gain, easy.

From the trailhead (elevation 4,770 feet) you drop downhill into sunny grasslands, surrounded by views of the rolling hills and round-shouldered mountains of this northwest terminus of the Chiricahua Mountains. The soft earthen trail has small mileage posts

every 0.25 mile to track your progress, along with nameplates for many of the Arizona plants that populate desert grasslands: alligator juniper, cane cholla, desert sumac, saltbush, rose-colored prickly pear, Arizona white oak, and sandpaper oak. There are also a dozen historic site markers along the trail, explaining Apache life, the stagecoach business, historic battles, and fort structures. This trail segment is an excellent way to learn about southeast Arizona's desert foliage and frontier history.

As you hike, you'll be accompanied by scores of birds that swoop through the Fort Bowie grasslands and hills. Some permanent residents are the western bluebird, eastern meadowlark, goldfinch, and red-tailed hawk. Many migrating birds also visit the area, so you can count on enjoying

Fort Bowie ruins

some birdwatching along with your historical sightseeing anytime of the year. With all these attractions, this is a trail best enjoyed at a slower pace, the studied stroll of a museum tour.

At 0.5 mile you will pass the ruins of the Apache Pass stage station, built in 1858. Then, in the middle of the trail, you arrive at a historic marker about the Butterfield Overland mail route. Twice a week, the Butterfield stagecoaches made the 2,800-mile journey from Memphis, Tennessee to San Francisco, California within 24 days—not exactly FedEx, but impressive for that day and age. The historic marker is for one of the 240 stage stops scattered along this route. From the marker you turn left and follow the sign marked RUINS to head for Fort Bowie.

After 0.75 mile you arrive at the fort cemetery, one of the highlights of this hike. You'll notice that most of the gravestones are epitaphs for men in their twenties—killed by Apaches—and for infants: mute testament to the harshness of the "romantic" western frontier life. In the southeast corner is the tombstone of Geronimo's two-year-old son, Little Robe, who was taken from his family and brought by the US Cavalry to Fort Bowie, where he died.

At the 1-mile mark you will come to the ruins of the Chiricahua Apache Agency. Look above you and you'll see the hillside spiked with sotol, a plant the Apaches used for many purposes, including weaponry. The bamboolike sotol stalk is light, flexible, tall, and straight—no wonder the Apaches made lances of it.

At 1.25 miles you pass flowing Apache Spring, the site of several battles between soldiers and Apaches. The tiny spring still trickles out clear water, in a quiet little rock alcove. You'll see some velvet ash trees, with their gray furrowed bark and rounded crowns. If you have a filtered water bottle, this spring is a good spot to take a drink and fill the bottle for the trip back, just in case the Fort Bowie ranger station is closed.

After you pass Apache Spring you'll enter a wavy, open grassland, with the Fort Bowie ruins and ranger station perched above you. The original fort (circa 1862) lies south of the trail past the spring, while the larger, second fort (started in 1868) lies to the east, ahead of you at trail's end. You'll pass remnants of other military buildings as you trek up to the main fort site: an artillery storehouse, officers' headquarters, and powder magazine. Finally, after 1.5 miles of hiking, you'll come to the ranger station (elevation 5,000 feet) and turn right to wander into the main fort ruins.

The once-proud ramparts have been timeworn into rounded humps that look more like adobe sculptures than fort walls. Each section of the ruins has its own story sign: Why it was constructed, and what events happened there. As you stare out across the grasslands you can see why this spot was chosen for the fort: It commands an all-points view of the surrounding valley, including any settlers or Apaches who may have approached. If the adjoining ranger station is open, stop off there and study the Fort Bowie exhibits inside.

Fort Bowie ruins to trailhead. 1.5 miles, (3.1 total miles) 600-foot elevation gain, moderately difficult.

After you have finished your tour of the ruins and studied the ranger station exhibits, walk behind the east end of the station to follow the Overlook Ridge Trail sign. As the name implies, this trail climbs up a ridge behind the fort to overlook Fort Bowie and the surrounding countryside. The bird's-eye views are worth the moderate ascent you must make to top the ridge. As you head up this trail you'll find more signs and stories about the history of conflict between the cavalry and Apaches who fought to control

this area. Looking down at the trail you have just completed, you can imagine Cochise and his warriors lying in wait up here on the ridge, waiting to ambush the cavalry soldiers who paused at Apache Spring. Which is exactly what he did, in one famous skirmish known as the Battle of Apache Pass.

A short distance up the trail you top the ridge (5,200 feet elevation) to savor views of Fort Bowie, the flat sweep of southeastern Arizona, and the Chiricahua and Peloncillo mountain ranges to the southeast. This dry trail has some enormous Palmer agaves next to it. This is the largest native agave in the United States, with its 18-foot stalks jutting up from the succulent leaves at its base. You'll also find plenty of ocotillos, bear grass, and sotols.

About halfway along the trail, the geology changes from granite to wavy gray limestone, with an accompanying switch from an ocotillo to a bear grass landscape. The fault between the granite and limestone strata here created Apache Spring, that historic magnet for life and death in the West.

As you switchback down the high point of the trail you can see the trace route of the old Butterfield Stage, wending its way through Siphon Canyon below you. On this trail segment, you can take a break at one of the bench seats conveniently placed along the trail, giving this wildlands pathway a parklike touch.

At 0.8 mile. the trail switchbacks down to the floor of Siphon Canyon, where you cross the old stage road at 4,770 feet. After trekking another 0.25 mile, you turn right to rejoin the Fort Bowie Trail and complete the last 0.5 mile to your car, safely back from the land of Cochise and Geronimo.

Camping

There is no camping in or near the Fort Bowie area. The nearest campgrounds are at the 24-site Bonita Canyon Campground in the Chiricahua National Monument, 8 miles south of the Apache Pass turnoff on AZ 186 (see Echo Canyon Loop, Hike 1).

For more information, call the Fort Bowie visitors center at 520-847-2500, or visit the official Fort Bowie web site at www.nps.gov/fobo.

Tucson and Nogales Areas–
Sky Islands Country

4

Atascosa Lookout Trail: Following the Abbey Road

Location: 60 miles south of Tucson near Nogales, Mexico in the Atascosa Mountains of the Coronado National Forest.

Total distance: 4.8 miles

Hiking time: 3.5 hours

Total elevation gain: 1530 feet

Difficulty: Difficult

Best months: October through April

Auto accessibility: Good overall, with a bumpy ride the last 5 miles.

Maps: USGS Ruby

Rules: Horses permitted. Dogs must be on leash. No bikes or mechanized vehicles.

Comments: Follow this panoramic trail up to a historic lookout that was once occupied by a famous writer. Pack plenty of water; you won't find any on the way up this short but steep trek. Keep an eye out for rattlesnakes.

"May 22, 1968, Atascosa Lookout. A golden eagle floated by under the kitchen window this morning as I poured myself a cup of coffee."

–Edward Abbey, *Confessions of a Barbarian*

I stood inside the tiny lookout cabin at the end of the remote Atascosa Lookout Trail, standing next to a Bronze Age potbellied stove and a rusty spring cot that might have escaped from a 1950s prison. Someone had actually lived up here, perched on this windy mount near the Mexico border, alone with his or her 360-degree views of the rough-hewn Sonoran countryside. What type of person would embrace such solitary magnificence?

And then I saw a photocopy of a book chapter, carefully affixed to the wall by the cabin's rickety writing desk. It was an excerpt from one of Edward Abbey's classic works, *Confessions of a Barbarian*, detailing his stay here at the lookout in May 1968. Abbey, best known for his cult classics *Desert Solitaire* and *The Monkeywrench Gang*, was one of the twentieth century's seminal outdoor writers, an avid environmentalist and desert loner who uncompromisingly opposed all threats to his beloved Southwest wild lands.

Working as a seasonal forest lookout, Abbey had stayed here at Atascosa and at the Grand Canyon's North Rim, recording his thoughts in a journal that he used in several of his books and that was posthumously edited to become *Confessions of a Barbarian*.

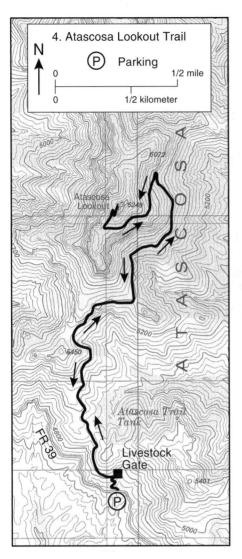

4. Atascosa Lookout Trail

N

(P) Parking

0   1/2 mile

0   1/2 kilometer

5000

6072

Atascosa
Lookout   6249

5200

5200

5450

5200

Atascosa Trail
Tank

FR 39

4800

Livestock
Gate

5401

(P)

5000

The Atascosa (Spanish for "marshy") Mountains are named after a marshy spring in the area, but this volcano-born mountain range is anything but a swampy flatland. Sprawling along the Mexico border near Nogales, the Atascosa countryside has sunny, open grasslands that underline its rolling hills and upthrust buttes. This solitary terrain is corralled by a half dozen small mountain ranges: the Pajaritos, Tumacacoris, Sierritas, Luis Mountains, Baboquivaris, and Las Guijas Mountains. The numerous mountains and canyons create a "corduroy" countryside around the Atascosa Trail: As you peer down from the lookout, the land below seems to ripple with waves of sepia peaks and ridges flowing into buff-colored canyons. Hiking up to the overlook, you have a rare opportunity for a far-reaching study of the craggy desert terrain of two nations, from Tucson down through Nogales, all the way to—on a very clear day—a glimpse of the gleaming Sea of Cortez. If you want a lot of scenery for a little rigorous hiking, look for the Lookout Trail.

Getting There

From Tucson, go 55 miles south on I-19, turning off at exit 12, Pena Blanca/Ruby Road. Then go west on AZ 289 (Ruby Nogales Road), an attractive and well-paved road populated with farms, canyons, and live oaks. After 9 miles you will pass a Pena Blanca Recreation Area sign, then turn left at mile marker 10 to start along Forest Road 39. Bounce along this canyon-bordered road for 4 miles until you pass a horse corral and junction with FR 39A, continuing another 0.8 mile farther on FR 39. On your right, you'll see a narrow trailhead sign with 100 on it, and on your left is a broad dirt parking area. Park your car and walk past the trailhead sign to begin the hike.

In his journal, he mentions the wonders he sees from his secluded vantage point at the Atascosa Lookout, describing the rocky crags and golden grassy hillsides he savors from his "island in the sky" (Confessions of a Barbarian). Once you journey up the Atascosa Lookout Trail, following Abbey's road to the top, you'll discover the primitive beauty of the desert landscape that Abbey so jealously guarded in his life and works.

Stunning vistas await hikers on the Atascosa Lookout Trail.

The Trail

Trailhead to 1-mile sign, 1 mile, 690-foot elevation gain, difficult.

From the trailhead (elevation 4,720 feet), you start to switchback up a dirt trail paved with pinkish rocks and lined with dryland cactus, ocotillo, and agave. The trail shows off the many valleys and hills near the Mexico border, with the Pajarita Mountains swelling up behind you. With no forest to occlude your view, the route offers open views all the way up to the top, so you won't be waiting long for vistas to appear. Some trail segments are rocky and steep, how-ever—I was glad I brought my walking stick and ankle-supporting boots!

After 0.25 mile, you open a livestock gate, and the path becomes a ridge trail with expansive Mexico valley views behind as you face out toward Arizona and Tucson's Santa Rita Mountains to the north-

east. On this portion of the trail you'll see small groves of manzanitas and juniper trees, part of Atascosa's pygmy forest habi-tat. As you pass the gate, you'll see a yel-low-green butte looming high above you in the distance. If you squint up at the top, you'll see the white dot of an overlook tower on the summit, your final destination.

As you pass a desiccated wooden sign that indicates you are at the 0.5-mile mark, the trail steepens a bit, but now you can see more mountains and valleys from your ele-vated perspective. This trail segment ex-hibits many of the desert plants that make the Sonoran landscape so colorful: the prickly pear cactus, with its Mickey Mouse leaf ears; the blue-green leaves of the Mexican blue oak; and the sinuous red trunks of the Arizona madrone. As you hike this area, see if you can find any of the rare golden beehive cacti *(Coryphantha recur-*

vata) that grace only the Atascosas and Tumacacoris. The beehive is a half-foot-tall, cantaloupe-shaped cactus with a crown of golden needles. Its delicate spines look crocheted onto the cactus, so tightly do they wrap around it.

Near the 0.75-mile point you'll come to a junction with a false trail leading to your left. Stay to the right and continue up to a small brown sign indicating that you are at the 1-mile point (5,410 feet in elevation). The views have changed from impressive to spectacular, as you can see more mountain ranges marching into the distance around you.

1-mile sign to Atascosa Lookout, 1.4 miles (2.4 miles total), 830-foot elevation gain, moderately difficult.

From the 1-mile point the trail continues to climb steadily. More oaks and piñon pines make their appearance as you continue past the 1.5-mile marker (elevation 5,570 feet) to reach the 2-mile mark. As you near the 2-mile point, a number of soft, silver-needled pines appear, looking like desert Christmas trees.

Just past the 2-mile mark, you come to a rock wall looming 100 feet above you as you curve left on the switchback and continue up for the final 0.5 mile to the top, with the now-prominent lookout tower waiting patiently above you. The surrounding butte rock has become bright white as you stairstep up the last 0.25 mile, passing a primitive campsite, to arrive at the Atascosa overlook tower (elevation 6,250 feet).

It's easy to understand why the Forest Service would build a fire overlook here—the cabin oversees everything in southern Arizona. Built in the early 1930s, the 14-foot-square lookout has two old spring bunk beds, several modern backpacker chairs, and an iron stove and desk. It also has a cistern fed by runoff from the roof, a practical but rarely used water-saving device.

From the overlook you can see 6,422-foot Atascosa Peak rising immediately in front of you to the north, with Pena Blanca Lake to the east of it. Nogales and the rest of Mexico sweep out to the south of you, with Arizona's popular Sycamore Canyon (see Nearby Trails) beneath you to the southeast. This is a good spot to take out a map and play "what mountain range is that?" because so many surround you.

Atascosa Lookout to trailhead, 2.4 miles (4.8 total miles), 1,530-foot elevation gain, moderately difficult.

Return the way you came, enjoying the constant downhill trail grade. On my way down the last 0.5 mile of the trail, a golden eagle floated beneath me on the ridge hillside, reminiscent of Edward Abbey's words some 35 years ago. Perhaps Abbey sent the eagle as a gift from up above, where he now acts as a lookout for planet earth.

Camping

The Camp Rock Campground is located at the junction of AZ 289 and FR 39, near the Pena Blanca Recreation Area sign. The 15-site campground, located in Pena Blanca Canyon, adjoins an attractive little fishing lake by the same name. The shady campground has picnic areas, rest rooms, drinking water, and a boat ramp. Fee is $10 per night. Backpackers can find several campsites at and near the end of the trail.

Nearby Trails

One of the reasons the inspiring Atascosa Lookout Trail receives so few visitors is that so many hikers flock to the neighboring 10.5-mile (round trip) Sycamore Canyon Trail. The trails are two different breeds of cat. Where the Atascosa Trail rises above the countryside, the Sycamore trail rambles through a lowland canyon. The Atascosa is dry and sunny; the Sycamore Canyon Trail follows a tree-shrouded stream. It's the perfect terrain counterpoint to the Atascosa Trail.

Special thanks are due to the Green Valley Hiking Club, for helping to restore the Atascosa Lookout cabin.

For more information, contact the Nogales Ranger District at 303 Old Tucson Road, Nogales, AZ 85621. Telephone 520-281-2296.

5

Juan Bautista de Anza National Historic Trail: A Hike with a Mission

Location: 45 miles south of Tucson on I-19, in the towns of Tumacacori and Tubac.

Total distance: 9.0 miles (4.5-mile shuttle hike)

Hiking time: 3.5 hours

Total elevation gain: 70 feet

Difficulty: Easy

Best months: October through April

Auto accessibility: Excellent, right off the Tumacacori exit on I-19.

Maps: USGS Tubac. Free trail map at the Tumacacori National Historic Park near the trailhead.

Rules: Pets on leash. Horses permitted. No camping. No bikes. $3 fee to enter either Tubac or Tumacacori historic sites, but no fee to hike the trail.

Comments: Step back into history as you stroll along a 1700s trail that goes all the way to San Francisco! Summer floods can wash out the wooden bridges that cross this small river, and it can be dangerous to ford it then. Check the river conditions before you set out.

Amy had just returned from a horseback ride up the Anza Trail to Tubac Presidio State Park. As she and her daughter loaded their amber mares into their apple-green horse trailer, they waxed enthusiastic about the Anza Trail, one of their riding favorites: "I feel like I'm on a vacation from Tucson, when I come here, it looks so different . . . all the cottonwoods and greenery!" For Amy, a Tucson trail regular, the Tumacacori-Tubac Trail was a beautiful anomaly: a riverside trail in the middle of the Sonora desert.

Certainly, the Anza Trail is one of southern Arizona's most unique routes. How many trails anywhere start in a national park with an 1800s Spanish mission and a finish at a state park with a 1700s Spanish presidio (fort)? On this hike you will follow a part of the historic route journeyed by Juan Bautista de Anza, who set out from Culiacan, Mexico on a 1,200-mile journey to found the first European colony in San Francisco. Leading his party of 240 people (including 155 women and children) across a searing desert landscape, he needed to follow water whenever possible. Thus, this section of the Anza Trail borders the Santa Cruz River. For almost its entire length, it's a verdant riparian stroll filled with trees and birds.

For a walk back into history, pack a lunch and venture out onto the friendly de Anza Trail, a hike with a mission—and a fort to boot!

Getting There

From Tucson, drive 45 miles south on I-19 toward Nogales, and turn left at exit 29,

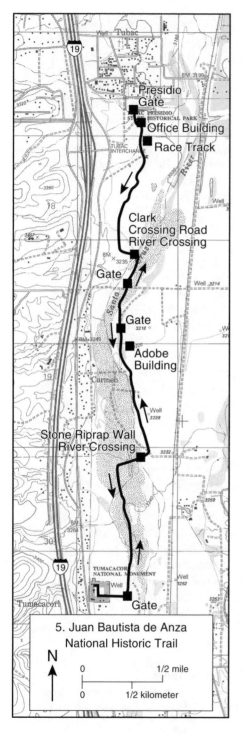

Tumacacori. From the exit, make a left to drive 0.25 mile and make another left to drive 0.8 mile to the trailhead in a parking lot across the road from the Tumacacori Post Office. The trailhead is some 200 yards past the Tumacacori National Historic Park.

To start at the north end of the trail and hike 4.5 miles down to Tumacacori, turn off I-19 at Exit 34, Tubac, and start from the north end of this trail next to the Tubac Presidio State Historic Park. Many hikers leave one car at the Tubac Presidio State Park and the other at the Tumacacori National Historic Park, making the trek a 4.5-mile shuttle hike.

The Trail

Tumacacori trailhead to Tubac Presidio State Park, 4.5 miles, 70-foot elevation loss, easy.

The trail starts at 3,330 feet and changes little in elevation. The route is lined with scores of white plastic trail markers, most within sight of one another, so follow the white posts and you won't get lost.

You start by walking through a sparsely vegetated field for 0.25 mile to make a left at a signed junction for the trail and the Santa Cruz River. Hiking past the junction, you'll see the lush riverside vegetation appear alongside you, 60-foot cottonwoods backed by many broad and rounded Mexican elder trees. You'll also find a number of bosques (small forests) of 20-foot velvet mesquite scattered along the way, showing off their yellow-green, frondlike leaves. In spring and summer the route is decorated with Indian paintbrush and a variety of daisies, adding their reds and yellows to the foliage display.

After 1.25 miles you walk through a gate and come up to the first river bridge, walking over its twin planks to bear left and continue along the trail. On your right you'll see the Santa Rita Mountains following you on

On the De Anza Trail

your way north to Tucson, topped with the snow-streaked peaks of Mts. Wrightson and Hopkins. As if to remind you that civilization is not far away, I-19 highway noises drift in from open spots between the thick walls of trees.

At the 1.5-mile benchmark, you cross a second twin-planked bridge over the river. Here the slow-moving water is blanketed with tiny green water plants, and the riverbanks are collared with a delicate lacework of ferns—it's as pacific and verdant as a Deep South stream. Most of the area's 300 bird species like to perch in the cottonwoods by the river's edge, and here you might look for spike-headed kingfishers and green-backed herons. With some luck you may spot a vivid vermilion flycatcher or the parti-colored, elegant trogon—a magnificent-looking bird. Although I didn't spot either one on my March trek here, I did sight a large gray hawk and a glossy purple phainopepla, as well as scores of tiny wrens and warblers. This hike is Birdland at its best: Walk quietly, wait patiently, and you'll be well rewarded.

Just beyond the 2-mile mark, you'll pass an abandoned adobe building as you tramp along a dry wash next to a fence. Finally, at 3.25 miles, you come to the third bridge crossing over this sandy-bottomed river, to follow some power lines that march through the low-lying velvet mesquite and cane cholla. The highway sounds become a bit more prominent here, but there are still a number of birds to distract you from the sporadic drone of tractor trailers passing in the distance.

The trail turns left and then right to move along the backs of some houses to a gate and parking lot that signal the 4.1-mile point of the trail at 3,260 feet. From here you can walk another 0.4 mile to the front of the Tubac Presidio State Park, Arizona's first state park. The Presidio is a replica of the original 1752 Spanish fort, and it features some intriguing displays of eighteenth-century life in this outpost. After visiting the park

Cane cholla

and stopping off at the water fountain, re-trace your steps south along the Anza Trail, unless you have left another car here to make a shuttle hike.

Tubac Presidio State Park to trailhead, 4.5 miles (9.0 total miles), 70-foot elevation gain, easy.

Your hike back to the trailhead should be easy and uneventful, as long as you follow the white plastic road markers along the way. One word of warning, though: The final bridge crossing, near trail's end, is hidden from view on your way back. You may miss the bridge and continue on a branch road that joins the trail here, looking for the third bridge. To avoid this problem, just remember to look for the bridge when you come to the river after crossing the second bridge.

Nearby Trails

There are no other trails connecting to the Anza Trail, but there are plenty right off the highway on your way to the park. Take exit 69 (Continental) to drive to the Madera Canyon Recreation Area, a local paradise for birding and hiking. (See Florida Canyon Trail, hike 6). The Tucson Sierra Club chapter maintains an excellent web site for several Madera Canyon hikes at www.arizona.sierraclub.org/trail_guide.

Camping

There is no camping near the trail, but there's a campground farther south, near pretty little Pena Blanca Lake (see Atascosa Lookout Trail, hike 4). Take exit 12 off I-19, and drive 9 miles along Ruby Nogales Road (AZ 289) to the recreation area. You'll see the White Rock Campground (15 sites) near the lake.

For more information, contact Tuma-cacori National Historic Park at 520-398-2341, and Tubac Presidio State Historic Park at 520-398-2252. The historic journey along the Anza Trail is described at www.nps.gov/juba/anzatrai.htm.

6

Florida Canyon Trail: Solitary Spectacle

Location: Mount Wrightson Wilderness, 30 miles south of Tucson, in the Santa Rita Mountains.

Total distance: 9.0 miles

Hiking time: 5 hours, 15 minutes

Total elevation gain: 3,580 feet

Difficulty: Strenuous

Best months: May through October

Auto accessibility: Good. The well-maintained road is easy to follow to the trailhead.

Maps: USGS Mount Wrightson. A free Madera Canyon hiking trails map is available at local ranger stations.

Rules: Dogs on leash and horses permitted. No mountain bikes.

Comments: Canyon views abound in this panoramic "backdoor" entrance to the Mount Wrightson Wilderness. A favorite trail for Tucsonians who hike with their dogs. The wildflowers explode into bloom after a spring rainfall.

Where were all the hikers? I had heard that the Mount Wrightson Wilderness could be a trekker freeway on sunny December weekends, with the trailhead parking lots filled to capacity. But there I was, jaunting back down the spectacular Florida Canyon Trail, with all of Arizona spread out before me, and I had yet to meet anyone. Was I misinformed? Read on...

It's true that the Mount Wrightson Wilderness has some of Tucson's most popular trail venues, filled with trekkers who seek out the wilderness's 7,000-foot overlooks and awesome canyon scenery. Yet, as I later discovered, the accessible Florida Canyon Trail is relatively unattended by the wilderness's weekend hiking hordes. That's because this is one strenuous route, a 3,600-foot, switchbacking climb to a network of wonder-view trails at the Florida Saddle. That said, those who take on this trail are rewarded with sweeping, statewide views and an amazing bounty of seasonal wildflowers, as they hike through everything from sun-baked cactus savannahs to cool and moist subalpine forests. The Florida Canyon Trail is not for the faint of heart (or foot), but its solitude and varied beauty make it one of southern Arizona's best climbs.

The 25,260-acre Mount Wrightson Wilderness lies in the heart of the Santa Rita Mountains between Tucson and Nogales, Mexico. The wilderness features the "sky island" of 9,453-foot Mount Wrightson, the highest point in the region. This impressive pinnacle vaults some 7,000 feet above the surrounding valley floor, and is accessed by several scenic, mile-high trails that ramble up to its top. Sprinkled with springs and laced with stream-carved canyons, the wilderness offers a bounty of sights and sounds from its varied habitats: the songs of 200 bird species, the shady and cool environs of tall Douglas firs, and a pastiche of vivid cactus blooms and wildflowers. Climbing through one of the main wilderness canyons, the Florida (Flo-REE-dah, Spanish for "flowered") Canyon Trail features all these elements, without the crowds often found on the other wilderness trails.

Getting There

From Tucson, drive 40 miles south on I-19 and turn off at exit 63 (Continental). Head east for 7 miles along FS 62, turning right to continue on FS 62A, a wide and flat dirt road, for 3.5 miles to the Florida Work Center parking lot and the Florida Canyon trailhead.

The Trail

Trailhead to campsites, 2.1 miles, 2,060-foot elevation gain, strenuous.

From the trailhead (4,340 feet elevation), you start out on a rocky but straight route through a sunny grassland decorated with ocotillo, prickly pear, and barrel cacti, with a chorus of small birds piping in the neighboring oaks and junipers. If you are hiking here in spring or early summer, look for some of the dozen butterfly species that grace this trail section, including a variety of eye-catching swallowtails and blues.

After you pass through an entry gate at 0.3 mile, you begin to climb more steeply as you start up the side of tree-lined Florida Canyon on your right. As you hike, don't forget to take some of the "side walks" that branch right on this part of the trail: These

are short paths that lead over to the canyon's edge. From the edge you'll gain the best views of Florida Canyon plummeting 500 feet below you, and you'll also savor wide-open views of the neighboring mountains: the Santa Ritas immediately around you, the Rincon Mountains to the right (east) in the distance, and the Catalina Mountains north of Tucson. Stopping to appreciate the scenery will also allow you to catch your breath!

At 0.7 mile you'll pass a dry stock tank as the trailside life zone becomes dominated by piñon pines and alligator juniper. At 1.3 miles you'll pass by a water-filled concrete stock tank, an opportunity to load your filtered water bottle, if you can get past the idea that cattle or horses may have drunk from it. Depending upon the season, the trailside stream may also be flowing, providing you with an alternative water source.

As you chug up the trail, the 180-degree views behind and beside you have become even more spectacular, until you dip into a wildflower-filled opening fed by trickling Robinson Spring. Here you may find monkey flowers, columbines, and lupines scattered about. You will also find shade for some solitary and scenic backcountry camping.

Campsites to saddle, 2.4 miles, (4.5 total miles), 1,520-foot elevation gain, difficult.

Once past the campsites, the trail continues through dense stands of oaks and, in damp areas, sycamores. Some of the sycamores support tangles of wild grapevines, which attract raccoons and their high-tailed cousin, the coatimundi. Farther on, the path initiates a series of long, steep switchbacks among some surprisingly large firs and pines, some more than 5 feet thick. The trail will open up in spots here for peek-a-

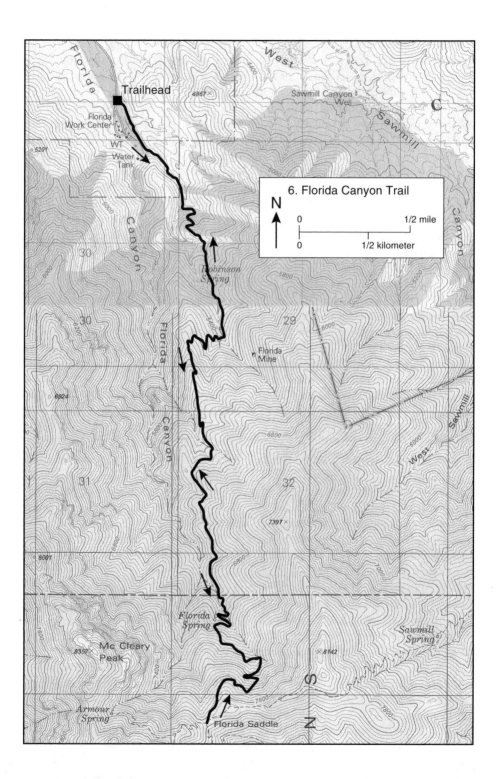

Florida

West

Sawmill Canyon
Well

C

Trailhead

Florida
Work Center

WT

4861 ×

5400

Water
Tank

5201

5000

5000

Canyon

30

5800

6000

Robinson
Spring

6. Florida Canyon Trail

N

0   1/2 mile

0   1/2 kilometer

5400

30

6924

6000

Florida
Canyon

6000

Florida
Mine

29

6000

5800

6600

West

Sawmill

6000

31

6000

32

7397 ×

6800

7000

8001

6800

Florida
Spring

McCleary
Peak

7600

8357

8142 ×

Sawmill
Spring

S

7800

Armour
Spring

7800

7800

N

Florida Saddle

Florida Canyon

boo views of southern Arizona laid out beneath you, with the region's mountain ranges marching off in all directions. After switchbacking up the trail, you'll see several more campsites off the trail to the right. This a good place to pitch camp and unload some gear as you continue up to your destination, the Florida Saddle (elevation 7,920 feet), located at the terminus of the last, long switchback. Surrounded by columns of massive ponderosa pines and Douglas firs, the shady saddle has a directional sign pointing you to other connecting trails. From here you can set out along other wilderness routes, or return the way you came.

Saddle to trailhead, 4.5 miles (9.0 total miles), 3,580-foot elevation loss, moderately difficult.

As the old saying goes, "it's downhill all the way" on your return. Keep an eye out for some of the steeper inclines, however, because they have loose dirt and rocks that can turn your trailside into a trail slide.

Nearby Trails

From the Florida Saddle, many hikers like to continue up to the top of Mount Wrightson via the well-known Crest Trail. This 3.2-mile hike (elevation gain 1,840 feet) has spectacular mountain and valley views almost every step of the way–it's one of the most scenic trail sections in the state. For those seeking a shorter jaunt, follow the sign from the Florida Saddle over to Armour Spring, a 0.7-mile hike that ends at a tiny spring trickling out of a cliff. From the spring you can follow an unmarked trail up to 8,367-foot McCleary Peak for Olympian views of the surrounding countryside.

Madera Canyon Recreation Area is the main Mount Wrightson Wilderness entry point, and the one that attracts the most visitors, especially the birders who migrate to this world-class birding site from March through September. From the Roundup parking lot (sometimes filled on weekends) you can access a network of attractive trails. If you want company on your journey into the wilderness, this is the place to go. The Tucson chapter of the Sierra Club maintains an excellent website for several Madera Canyon hikes at www.arizona .sierraclub.org/trail_guide.

Camping

There is a handful of backcountry sites along the last half of the Florida Canyon Trail, and several near the beginning. The Bog Springs Campground is the only campground near the Mount Wrightson Wilderness. The campground has 13 sites that accommodate vehicles up to 22 feet (no RV hookups), with drinking water and toilets nearby. Pets on leash are allowed, but no pack animals. The campground is shady and has its own scenic trail, the 5-mile, moderately difficult Bog Springs Trail. The campsites can fill up fast in prime time, however, so get there early in the day. Fee is $10 per night.

For more information, contact the Nogales Ranger District at 303 Old Tucson Road, Nogales, AZ 85621. Telephone 520-281-2296.

7

Brown Mountain: From Mountain to Museum

Location: West Tucson, in Saguaro National Park West, near the Arizona–Sonora Desert Museum.

Total distance: 4.8 miles (2.4-mile shuttle hike)

Hiking time: 2.75 hours

Total elevation gain: 1,215 feet

Difficulty: Moderately difficult

Best months: October through April

Auto accessibility: Excellent

Maps: USGS Brown Mountain

Rules: Dogs on leash, mountain biking permitted.

Comments: A short Tucson day hike that is very accessible and scenic. You can easily walk from your campsite to the trailhead and over to the museum.

When was the last time you took a backcountry trail to a world-class museum? Hike the Brown Mountain Trail and you'll ramble across three low-lying crests to pop down to the famous Arizona–Sonora Desert Museum, once voted by American museum directors as the museum they would most like to visit on a vacation. On this suburban hike you will enjoy studying a wide variety of cactus-country plants on your way up to 360-degree mountain and valley views, all within a short drive of the Tucson city limits.

Brown Mountain, which is actually a series of three hills, is named after one of the founders of the Tucson Mountain Park system, established in 1929. This rugged park adjoins the Saguaro National Park's western section, and together they comprise a four-season playground blessed with peaks, canyons, valleys, and saguaro forests. With the Arizona Sonora Desert Museum and the Old Tucson Wild West town within its confines, the Tucson Mountain Park offers diversions for everyone, from casual strollers to backcountry hikers. The Brown Mountain Trail is one of the park's most popular treks, a moderately rigorous mountain hike that ends at the desert museum picnic grounds. The path is a wonderful introduction to desert hiking and to the multifarious Sonora desert landscape.

Getting There

From Tucson, head south on I-10 to exit 257 (Speedway Boulevard), and head west on Speedway for 5 miles until it becomes Gates Pass Road. Continue another 5 miles on

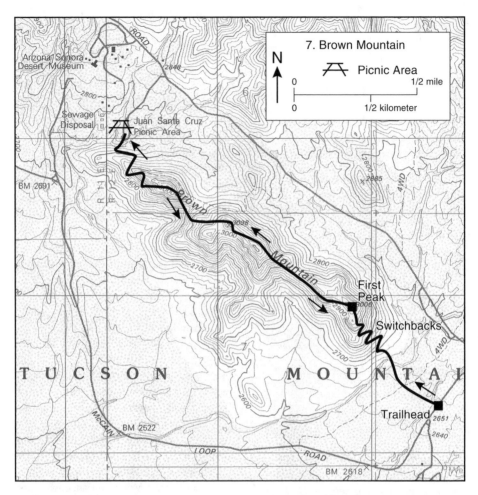

Gates Pass Road until it dead-ends at Kinney Road. Make a right onto Kinney Road, and drive 0.5 mile to McCain Loop Road, then make a left and go 0.4 mile to the Gilbert Ray Campground entrance. The Brown Mountain trailhead, marked by a short wood and stone sign next to a paved parking area, is directly opposite the campground.

The Trail

Brown Mountain trailhead to First Peak, 1.2 miles, 375-foot total elevation gain, easy with a few moderately difficult spots.

Starting from the trailhead at 2,650 feet, you maneuver along a relatively flat path that shows off some of the area's 50 cactus species: teddy bear cholla, saguaro, fishhook cactus, and Engelmann's hedgehog. The well-marked trail has several signs directing you to Brown Mountain and to branch trails such as the 0.7-mile Cougar Trail. After 0.5 mile along this gravelly trail you'll cross a shallow wash and begin the climb up to Brown Mountain via a series of gentle switchbacks.

From a distance, the Brown Mountain area looks like a naked pile of sepia rock. Hike up to the mountaintop, however, and your closer views will reveal a banquet of colors, shapes, and sounds from the

Saguaro cactus

Sonora flora and fauna. This trail segment could have been called the Rosy Rock Trail, given all the pinkish-red rhyolite rocks all along it. At sunrise you can see the rocks glow with a soft pastel light, vividly contrasted with the green spectrum of surrounding palo verde, ocotillo, mesquite, and creosote—it's a vibrant morning light show.

As you climb up the trail, the larger saguaros begin to appear at trailside, along with the many chirping and squawking birds that live in these 30-foot cacti. Among the saguaros you're likely to spot some flitting black-dappled gilded flickers and red-capped Gila woodpeckers, and hear the high-pitched chi-chi of the Lucy's warbler. Anyone who thinks a desert is a featureless wasteland should take a morning stroll on the Brown Mountain Trail.

At 1.1 miles you reach the first crest of the Brown Mountain Trail (elevation 3,025 feet). Now you can see a saguaro-studded valley sprawling below you, with Kitts' and Baboquivari Peaks topping the western skyline. To your right (northeast) the craggy Tucson Mountains run beside you, directly above tourist artery Kinney Road. Stop and enjoy this view, but don't use all your film— the views are more expansive from your next destination, the second peak.

First Peak to museum picnic ground,1.2 miles (2.4 total miles), 275-foot total elevation gain, easy.

Following the trail straight ahead, you dip to 2,940 feet before climbing up to the main peak of Brown Mountain (elevation 3,130 feet) at the 1.6-mile point of your journey.

The first peak's 270-degree views become 360-degree mountain vistas on the second peak, with distant studies of the Superstition Mountains west toward Phoenix, the Santa Ritas to the southeast, and the Rincons and Catalinas to the east.

From the second peak you'll gradually descend to move along for 0.25 mile to the flank of a third and smaller peak, then switchback down a steep trail section to the Juan Santa Cruz picnic ground (elevation 2,650 feet). From the picnic ground you can hike over to the museum for refreshments and a tour of one of the best museums in the world, then hike back the way you came. Many hikers leave a second car near the picnic grounds and use the Brown Mountain Trail as a 2.4-mile "eye-opener" hike to start their day of museum exploring and scenic drives. Nice work if you can get it!

Nearby Trails

Opposite the Arizona–Sonora Desert Museum lies a trail that rivals the Brown Mountain route for scenery, the King Canyon Trail. This 4.6-mile round trip to the Sweetwater Trail junction has springs, desert animals such as javelinas, awesome canyon and mountain views, and even a picnic ground en route. One *Arizona Highways* writer referred to the King Canyon Trail as "...among the most delightful hikes in the Tucson area."

Camping

The Gilbert Ray Campground is a short walk from the Brown Mountain trailhead, and it's the perfect place to camp for a sunrise hike to the mountain and the museum. This popular campground has water, electricity, and modern rest rooms, with 130 sites for RVs ($12) and tents ($7). Camping is on a first-come, first-served basis. Peak season is November through April.

For more information, Pima County has posted a free list of Tucson area hiking trails, complete with locator maps, at www .co.pima.az.us/pksrec/home2/home2.html.

8

Douglas Spring Loop: Waterfall Wander

Location: Saguaro National Park East, 2 miles east of Tucson on Speedway Boulevard.

Total distance: 7.2-mile loop

Hiking time: 4.5 hours

Total elevation gain: 1,110 feet

Difficulty: Moderately difficult

Best months: October through March

Auto accessibility: Excellent

Maps: USGS Tanque Verde Peak, Mica Mountain. A detailed map of the Douglas Spring trail system is available free at the national park visitors center on Freeman Road.

Rules: Permit required for backcountry camping at Douglas Spring. No dogs on trails. Horses permitted on some trails. Bikes permitted on 8-mile paved loop drive, but not on Douglas Spring Trail.

Comments: With springs, tanks, and a waterfall, this watery trail showcases unspoiled wilderness overlooks and stately saguaro forests, all within a few miles of the Tucson city limits. There are lots of trail junctions on your route, so pay attention to the trail signs.

"We'll have a hundred people through here by noon." A Saguaro National Park staff assistant, sitting in the comfort of a trailhead ramada, was loading me with information about the trails at the Douglas Spring trailhead. After several squadrons of hikers and runners passed as I palavered with him, I had no reason to doubt his estimate.

The Douglas Spring trail system sprawls along the outskirts of Tucson, so it's easy to see why it would be filled with weekend wanderers. That said, I took the Carrillo Loop trail on a peak-usage Saturday and encountered few people until the last part of my journey near Douglas Spring, and I thoroughly enjoyed my well-watered ramble through the saguaro scenery. The majority of hikers take the well-known Douglas Spring section making this the trail for seekers of solitude.

The eastern section of Saguaro National Park was created to preserve the stands of saguaro that grace Tucson's eastern city limits. These tall, graceful cacti fill the low-lying portions of the park, eventually giving way to a high-country plant community of pine, scrub oak, and smaller cacti near the foothills of the Rincon Mountains. With almost 130 miles of interconnected trails in this national park, it's a desert hiker's paradise. The trail loop described here cobbles together five different trails to give hikers maximum distance and scenery on their journey through the lovely environs of Saguaro National Park.

Getting There

Drive east on I-10 to the eastern edge of Tucson, taking exit 279 (Colossal Cave)

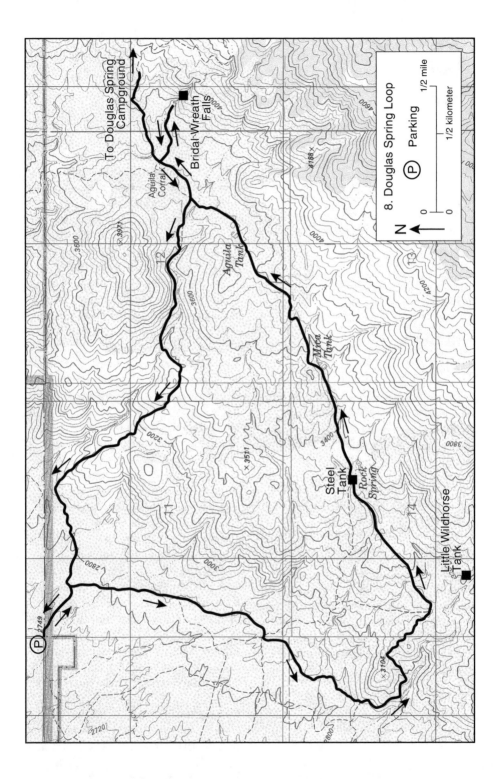

To Douglas Spring Campground

Bridal Wreath Falls

Aguila Corral

12

Aguila Tank

Mica Tank

13

Steel Tank

Rock Spring

11

14

Little Wildhorse Tank

8. Douglas Spring Loop

Ⓟ Parking

N ◄

0   1/2 kilometer

0   1/2 mile

2749

2720?

2800

3000

3200

3400

3600

4000

3400

3800

4400

4600

× 4188

× 3551

× 3104

north. Drive north on Colossal Cave Road for 6 miles to its junction with Old Spanish Trail Road, making a left onto Old Spanish Trail. Cruise another 10 miles through the attractive desert suburbs until you pass the Saguaro National Park entrance, and make a right immediately past it onto Freeman Road. Drive 3.5 miles on Freeman Road, and make a right onto Speedway Boulevard, then go another 3.5 miles until the road dead-ends at the Douglas Spring trailhead.

The Trail

Douglas Spring trailhead to Wild Horse trailhead, 1.6 miles, 110-foot elevation gain, easy.

Walk past the trailhead sign (elevation 2,770 feet) to stroll 0.2 mile to the small black sign that designates the start of the Garwood Trail. Turning right, you take this well-marked dirt trail to tour a panoply of cacti: yellow-budded cane cholla, bristly fishhook cacti, the purplish Engelmann's prickly pear, and, of course, the graceful saguaro. On the way you'll also find a number of birds perching near their holes in the saguaros, embellishing the cactus garden's visual beauty with their songs: purple martins, Lucy's warblers, cactus wrens, and western kingbirds. Looking up to your left, you'll see the Rincon Mountains cresting along beside you as you gently ascend into the desert, leaving the trailhead crowds behind.

After 1 mile, you arrive at a sign for the Bajada Vista Trail on your right. Continue straight on the Garwood Trail for another 0.6 mile, undulating through several washes and giant saguaro stands, to arrive at the Carrillo Trail junction (2,880 feet elevation). Turn left at the junction to start up the Carrillo Trail. Note that there are two left branches at the junction. The one that has wooden posts around it and a STOCK

PROHIBITED sign is the wrong trail—it takes you 0.5 mile over to the lovely natural granite formation of shady Little Wildhorse Tank. Take this side trip if you have time; otherwise you continue on the Carrillo Trail.

Carrillo Trail to Douglas Spring Trail junction, 2.8 miles (4.4 total miles), 1000-foot overall elevation gain, moderately difficult.

As you trek up the Carrillo Trail, you'll wonder why they didn't call it the "Teddy Bear Trail" for the teddy bear cholla that pepper the landscape. After 0.5 mile the trail tops at 3,120 feet among some green-skinned palo verde trees. From here you can see the Rincon Mountains. From this point you switchback up to the Three Tanks Trail to an enormous steel water tank about 1.3 miles from the Carrillo Trail junction. At the junction you will leave the Carrillo Trail and continue on the Three Tanks Trail, climbing up from the dry sandy wash to head northeast. (If you find yourself hiking along a flat, sandy wash, you are on the wrong trail.)

The Three Tanks Trail (Douglas Spring East on the trail sign here) gradually climbs up past a natural water tank and through a narrow grassland. The trail crests at 3,800 feet, revealing the entire Tucson Valley, the Santa Catalinas, Santa Ritas, and other mountains in the distant east. I met a hiking couple there who told me: "We take this trail because it's so peaceful," as they sat on the side of a tree-shaded hill, studying the Rincon countryside with their binoculars.

On this trail segment you'll likely see red-headed woodpeckers and various butterflies flitting around. Shrub oaks and ocotillo have replaced the saguaro, as the trail rolls up and down the low-lying hills over to the Douglas Spring Trail junction (elevation 3,700 feet), 1.3 miles from where you started on the Three Tanks Trail.

The Rincon Mountains, seen from the Douglas Spring Loop

Douglas Spring Trail Junction to trail-head parking lot, 2.8 miles (7.2 total miles), 980-foot elevation loss, moderately difficult.

From the Douglas Spring junction, turn right and head to Bridal Wreath Falls (elevation 3,750 feet), an easy 0.5-mile jaunt over to a water stream trickling some 60 feet down a granite ledge to the bouldered bottom of a wash. This cataract isn't a gusher, but any waterfall in a desert is a wonder to behold.

Returning to the Douglas Spring–Three Tanks Trail junction, you now continue down the Douglas Spring Trail. The path is downhill all the way for the next mile, but it's a bit difficult to hike because you have to step down several steep trail sections. (Those with knee problems might want to start this trail loop by going up the Douglas Spring Trail and then looping down to the Carrillo Trail.) The Douglas Spring Trail is extremely popular with Tucsonians, so expect company. After seeing only a few people for the first 6 miles of the hike, I trooped down the Douglas Spring Trail with a party of 30 schoolchildren who were visiting Bridal Wreath Falls.

As you climb down the Douglas Spring Trail, you'll have expansive views of the Tucson cityscape spread out below you, all the way west toward Phoenix. You'll also spot several small canyons and rock formations interspersed among the saguaros that dot the land below you. At 0.8 mile the trail levels out into an easy stroll through mesquite, saguaro, and dark purple cholla as you return to the Douglas Spring parking lot and trailhead.

Nearby Trails

The Douglas Spring trailhead area is veined with a score of short to medium-length trails, so you can easily build your own trail length and features. Stop off at the Saguaro National Park visitors center on you way to the Douglas Spring trailhead, pick up their free map of the trails, and ask the helpful attendants about what trail is best for your interests; for example, which is the longest trail, which has the most spectacular cacti, and so on.

Camping

The Douglas Springs Campground is perfect for those who want a relatively short (5.6 miles) hike to a backpackers' campground. It has three sites and a chemical toilet, but spring or stream water may be available only after rainy periods. There is a $6 fee per night.

For more information, contact the Saguaro National Park visitors center, 3693 South Old Spanish Trail, Tucson, AZ 85730-5601. Telephone 520-733-5153, or visit the Saguaro National Park web site at www.nps.gov/sagu/index.htm.

9

Romero Pools:
Taking a Dip in the Desert

Location: Pusch Ridge Wilderness in the Catalina Mountains of the Coronado National Forest, 15 miles north of Tucson.

Total distance: 5.6 miles

Hiking time: 4 hours

Total elevation gain: 1,070 feet

Difficulty: Difficult

Best months: October through March

Auto accessibility: Excellent, paved road all the way to the trailhead.

Maps: USGS Oro Valley, USFS Coronado National Forest

Rules: Pets allowed only on the first mile to the wilderness boundary. Not recommended for horses. No bikes. Park entrance fee $6.

Comments: Climb up the Romero Canyon Trail, enjoying mountain and valley vistas on the way, to splash in the waterfall-fed Romero Pools. Pack at least a half gallon of water if you hike in warm weather. High-top boots are a must for the rocky terrain on the upper trail portions. The pools are at their best after a rain, but the rocks around them are often slippery.

The Pusch Ridge Wilderness has an amazing diversity of habitats, owing to the 7,000-foot difference in elevation from the desert lowlands to the top of Mount Lemmon. At lower levels near the Romero Canyon trailhead, you'll find the saguaros and palo verdes of the Sonora desert, while the 8,000-foot reaches have enough subalpine aspens and firs to resemble a Colorado forest. Just as intriguing as the varied flora is the dramatic wilderness rockscape. The Catalinas rocket thousands of feet from their desert bases, their saw-toothed granite and gneiss summits eroded into fantastical shapes, including some of the best granite hoodoos (bizarre rock pillars) this side of Utah.

One of the best entry routes into the Pusch Wilderness is via the popular Romero Canyon Trail, a 7-mile hike that ends in the heart of these mountainous wild lands. Many hikers on the Romero Trail, however, venture no farther than that high desert oasis of sculptured rock dipping pools known as the Romero Pools. Some come here to sunbathe on the rock shelves around the pools, others to refresh themselves before venturing farther into the wilderness. Either way, the Romero Pools route is one of the most memorable trails in southern Arizona, one that attracts many repeat visitors.

Getting There

From downtown Tucson, drive north on Oracle Road (AZ 77) 12.5 miles until you come to the sign for Catalina State Park.

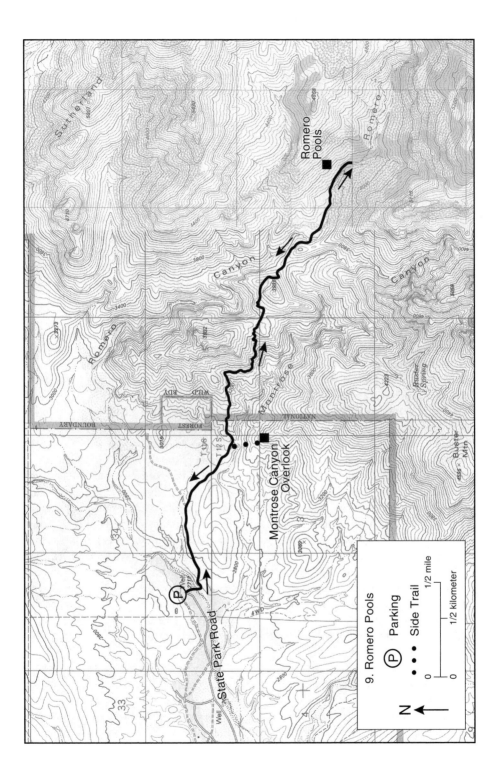

9. Romero Pools

Ⓟ Parking

••• Side Trail

N

1/2 mile
1/2 kilometer
0
0

Romero Pools

Sutherland

Romero

Canyon

Canyon

Montrose Canyon
Overlook

Buster
Spring

Buster
Mtn

State Park Road

Well

BOUNDARY

FOREST

WILD BDY

NATIONAL

Turn right and drive 0.25 mile to the state park entrance and pay the $6 daily fee. Then drive 1.5 miles to the large paved parking lot, with rest rooms next to the trailhead.

The Trail

Trailhead to Montrose Canyon junction, 0.9 mile, 190-foot elevation gain, easy.

After you walk behind the large trailhead sign (elevation 2,750 feet), bear right at a trail junction for the Romero Canyon Trail. The wide dirt trail pulls you through a classic Sonoran desert fauna mix of prickly pear and fishhook cactus, white desert globe mallow, and tall saguaro. This trail segment is easy to hike; the path is soft underfoot and heads straight to the mountains. To your right runs the block-fault skywall of Pusch Ridge, as jagged as the spine of a stegosaurus. To the northeast you can see the dramatic outlines of Mount Lemmon (9,157 feet) and Cathedral Rock (7,952 feet), two wilderness landmarks.

At 0.5 mile, you pass a trail junction for the Canyon Loop and the Romero Canyon Trail, continuing right on the Romero route. You'll arrive at another signed junction, this one for Romero and Montrose Canyons, at 0.9 mile (2,940 feet elevation). Before you continue up the Romero Trail, turn right and walk the 100 feet over to the Montrose Canyon overlook, which is benchmarked by a bench. Looking down into the canyon, you'll see doughty Montrose Creek boiling down over its boulder-strewn desert path, as splashingly rambunctious as a high mountain stream. After enjoying the view, return to the junction and bear left to follow the Romero Canyon Trail.

Montrose Canyon junction to Romero Pools overlook, 1.9 miles (2.8 total miles), 880-foot elevation gain, difficult.

From the Montrose Overlook point you climb steeply up this now-rocky trail via some long, looping switchbacks. The trail slopes are covered with blocky gneiss boulders, a metamorphic rock that covers the granite heart of the Catalinas. This rocky region is a bighorn sheep management area, and in cooler weather you might spot a few cliff-hugging sheep up above you.

At 1.1 miles, you pass a wilderness sign that signals your entrance into the Pusch Ridge Wilderness. (No dogs are allowed beyond this point.) As you ascend the rocky trail you'll see several short side trails to your right; they lead to some photo-op overlooks of Montrose Canyon's streaming audiovisuals. As you climb, the views of the granite-faced Santa Catalinas become more dramatic, with the deep, shadowed cut of Montrose Canyon far below you. In spring you'll also notice handfuls of gold, orange, blue, and white wildflowers, vivid against their boulder backdrops. Your journey to the pools will have lots of scenery from this point on.

At 2.3 miles and 3,610 feet you'll top a high ridge. Walk over to the left edge of the ridge, and there below you is the streaming staircase of the Romero Pools. Continuing along the trail, you circle left around the high ridge in front of you, to top off at 3,720 feet. You'll hike along the ridge through some tall oak trees, and then drop down some 100 feet to encounter the stream that feeds the Romero Pools on your left (2.8 miles, 3,620 feet elevation). The topmost Romero Pool is next to you, one of several boulder-shrouded rock basins. To reach the lower pools, hike across the top pool to follow a short trail on your left down to the lower regions.

In years gone by, the pools were sometimes deep enough to dive into. But the Romero Pools are presently reinventing themselves. The 2003 forest fires in the Catalina Mountains brought an avalanche of

Fabulous views greet hikers on the Romero Canyon Trail.

silt to fill the old pool basins. As a result, new pools are forming themselves even as you read this, and what they will look like is anyone's guess. The main waterfall still streams down its 30-foot rock shelf, however, and it's still possible to dangle your feet in the cool stream that waterfalls its way into the newly reconfigured basins. And the pools still hoard a wealth of butterflies and wildflowers among the junipers and cattails that thrive along the pools' swampy grass edges, an amazing contrast to the austere Sonoran landscape only a few feet beyond these water bowls. In other words, the pools are still a sight to see.

Romero Pools overlook to trailhead, 2.8 miles (5.6 total miles), 970-foot elevation loss, moderately difficult.

The return trip shows you lots of valley and mountain landscape. As you switchback down the trail, you can enjoy the sweep of the Oro Valley below you, its plain broken by the humps of the Tortolita Mountains to the northwest. Less than an hour and a half from the pools, you'll be back at the trailhead parking lot, finishing one of Arizona's most unique day hikes.

Nearby Trails

The 7-mile Romero Canyon Trail connects to a wide variety of other trails. The Canyon Loop Trail is at the first junction with the Romero Canyon Trail, 0.5 mile from your start. The Loop route is a moderately difficult, 2.2-mile ramble across the desert countryside back to the Romero trailhead. If you continue along the Romero Canyon Trail past the Romero Pools, you'll climb steeply up to some spectacular vistas of the Santa Catalinas and accompanying canyons. You can also access the famed Sabino Canyon from the end of the Romero

Canyon route, or hike to the top of Mount Lemmon via its own trail.

Camping

About 0.4 mile before the pools, near the first high-point overlook, you'll find a wide, flat area shaded by four or five oak trees that makes a fine backcountry camping spot. Other spots are near the pools and farther along the Romero Trail from the pools. There are no campgrounds in the park.

For more information, contact the Catalina State Park office at 520-628-5798. The Sierra Club's Tucson chapter maintains a web site with a trail description and photos at www.arizona.sierraclub.org/trail_guide/hike23.htm.

10

Aravaipa Canyon:
The Journey Is the Destination

Location: Aravaipa Wilderness, 70 miles north of Tucson, near Mammoth.

Distance: 24 miles (12-mile shuttle hike)

Hiking time: 16 hours

Total elevation gain: 370 feet

Difficulty: Moderately difficult terrain, strenuous distance

Best months: March through May and September through November

Auto accessibility: Good to the west end trailhead, fair to the east end trailhead.

Maps: USGS Brandenburg Mountain, Booger Canyon, Holy Joe Peak, Oak Grove Canyon

Rules: No pets. Horses have a stock limit of five. No bikes. Hikers need a wilderness trail permit; call 928-348-4400, or use the reservations website at www.az .blm.gov/rec/aravaipa.htm.

Comments: One of Arizona's most magnificent wilderness trails can be enjoyed by anyone, with the right preparation, attention, and attitude. Monsoon season starts in mid-July and runs through August, when there is the greatest danger of flash floods in the canyon. High-top boots and a walking stick are necessities.

"This place is a whole 'nother education."

–University of Arizona graduate student, camped out near the pictographs at Painted Cave Canyon in Aravaipa.

I love Aravaipa Canyon. There are countless wonders along the Aravaipa Trail, with calendar-worthy scenery almost every step of the way. Hiking this trail is a cultural experience, like touring a combination zoo, botanical garden, arboretum, Native American art museum, and geology exhibit. And I would encourage you to explore Aravaipa's nether regions at least once in your lifetime. That said, you should know what to expect if you plan to explore the 11-mile wilderness corridor that is Aravaipa Canyon.

1. Expect to get wet. Whether you hike the entire distance or only a couple of miles, you will have to cross the stream many times. Some hikers take off their boots before wading in; others hike in river sandals, risking a turned ankle on the pebbly creek bottoms. I just wade right in at the first stream crossing, get my feet wet, and keep going—with sandals packed for camping or lollygagging. In many spots the best route through the canyon is right through the slow-moving stream, which can be more than 4 feet deep. So don't get cold feet about having wet feet. But don't get in over your head, either.

2. Don't expect a well-marked trail. As one group of Aravaipa hikers jokingly remarked to me: "You mean there's a trail here?" You'll always hike near the river, but the path will veer from one side to the other,

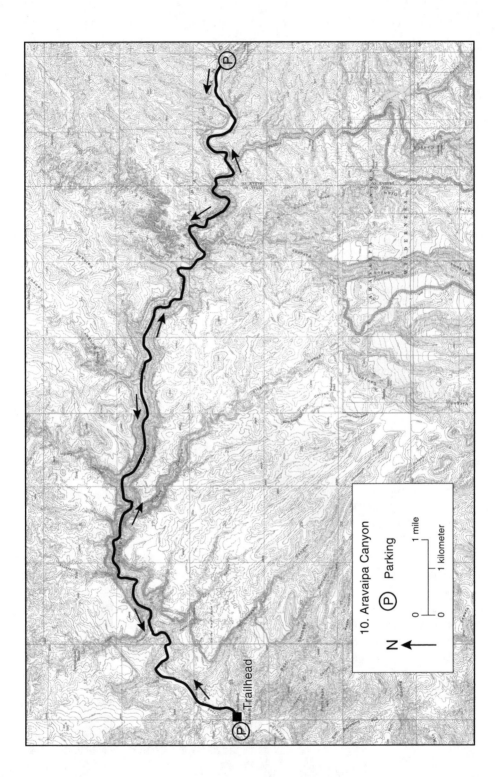

10. Aravaipa Canyon

Ⓟ Parking

N ←

1 mile

1 kilometer

0

0

Trailhead

crossing the stream and sometimes running right through the middle. If you find yourself bushwhacking, look to the opposite bank for an easier route.

3. Expect to hike slowly. You'll be searching both banks for the next trail segment and goggling at all the eye candy around you: 1000-foot parapets, tree-sized saguaro, and bighorn sheep. So expect to go about 1 to 1.5 miles an hour. In Aravaipa, many of us don't try to finish the entire route; we hike until we are full, letting the journey be our destination.

4. Expect to respect the wilderness. The hiking route is so flat and easy to follow that you'd think you were on a walk in the park. But flash floods can occur, rattlesnakes and scorpions love the Aravaipa, too, and Aravaipa's many wild side canyons should be explored only if you have a working cell phone or someone with you. The last time I was up the creek I saw a note from the Pinal County Search and Rescue Team, urging a lost hiker to use the flares they left as a signal for them to find him. Prepare for the trek as you would any wilderness adventure (see Introduction).

All that being said, I hasten to remind you that this is one of my favorite hikes in America, one to which I will often return, as I believe you will if you are willing to meet expectations.

Getting There

From Tucson, drive 30 miles north on AZ 77 (Oracle Road), turn right at Oracle Junction, and drive 20 miles along AZ 77 to Mammoth. From Mammoth, head north 10 miles on AZ 77 and turn right at the sign for Aravaipa College (past mile marker 125), onto Aravaipa Road. Drive 9.2 miles to the Brandenburg ranger station and campground. Then bounce down another 3 miles to the trailhead at 2,690 feet elevation.

The Trail

Brandenburg (west) trailhead to Horse Camp, 4.8 miles, 120-foot elevation gain, moderately difficult.

You start out by climbing up a short trail segment and descending to a bouldered wash near the river. At riverside, the desert habitat changes to a lusher riparian one of 5-foot-thick cottonwoods flanked by tall saguaros, with an understory of thick grass next to desert-loving catclaw acacia—it's a curiously mixed habitat. As you hike into the canyon, you'll be surrounded by sycamores, alders, cottonwoods, and willows. The route is as jungly as a southern Arizona trail can be.

You'll soon come to the first of many stream crossings. From here on, the wilderness experience begins, because you'll have to scout out your own path, crossing the stream back and forth and sometimes just wading right through it if the water is not too high. Near 1.5 miles, you'll pass a water flow tower standing in the right side of the creek.

At the 2.0-mile point (elevation 2,660 feet), you'll enter what I consider the canyon proper, as the roseate walls now rise hundreds of feet above you, and flocks of bamboo-jointed horsetails appear. You'll see a wide, level campsite on your left, the first of many idyllic bivouacs along the way. The spectacle of 1,000-foot canyon walls looming directly in front of you will draw you farther into the canyon, luring you with their promise of scenic wonders to come. At 2.25 miles you'll have your first of several deep wading adventures, entering a narrow chute with waist-high water. Step carefully as you shuffle across its smooth stony bottom, so you can detect any drop-offs in the streambed.

From here you'll alternately hike the sides of the creek and wade through its middle (which I enjoyed), now surrounded

The creek in Aravaipa Canyon

by neck-craning canyons of dark red porphyry rock. Your slow hiking pace should enable you to sight more of the wildlife that abounds around you, so keep your eyes open. Look straight up and you may see bald eagles or peregrine falcons gliding along. Stare at the high pinnacles and you may spot nature's original rock climbers, bighorn sheep. Study the trees right above you and you may spy Bell's vireos, yellow warblers, or others of the 150 bird species here. Look around at ground level and you can often spot coatimundi, javelinas, even elk; all are there to imbibe Aravaipa's cool waters. And under your feet may swim some of the seven species of native fish that make the creek one of Arizona's special fish preserves. If you're not a "good-looking" hiker, you'll miss half the fun of this trek.

After trekking to the 4.5-mile point, you'll pass Virgus Canyon on your right (south) side, and then popular Horse Camp Canyon on the left (north) at the 4.8-mile point of this wading-pool journey (elevation 2,810 feet). Many hikers pitch camp at one of the shaded and level spots with fire pits here. Scramble past the Horse Camp Canyon's gateway boulders to soak in the water-fed rock pools, photograph its minifalls, or risk a climb to the rear canyon caves. This is a spot to which many trekkers often return, on a pilgrimage to worship Aravaipa's remote and unique magnificence. As you enjoy the canyon scenery, keep your eye out for some of the Ara-vipers: rattlesnakes sunbathe on its boulders.

Many visitors make this the end point of their Aravaipa journey, content to return home after a serene night or two. Others, however, venture farther on to Booger Canyon or the eastern trailhead.

Horse Camp to Klondyke (East) trailhead, 7.2 miles (12.0 total miles), 250-foot elevation gain, moderately difficult.

On this trail segment you'll again find yourself hiking through the creek, walled in by spectacular, 1,200-foot orange and red canyon cliffs. Look up onto the serrated rock walls and you'll see 40-foot saguaro perched on their ledges, their arms outspread as if they were preparing to cliff-dive into the deep pools alongside you.

In this section, Booger Canyon (elevation 2,880 feet) should be one of your hiking destinations, reached at the 6.3-mile point. There are several scenic and level camping spots around the canyon entrance, which is a handy base camp for venturing farther upstream to explore Virgus or Hell Hole Canyon. Hell Hole Canyon (at the 8.4-mile point) on the north has a natural arch that you can see if you scramble into the canyon for a short distance—most hikers go right past the arch because they can't see it from the trail. Virgus Canyon requires some serious bouldering to enter, but those who go to the trouble often have it to themselves.

As you pass the Hell Hole Canyon section you'll notice the canyon walls becoming more cream- and brown-colored, departing from the more red and gray walls behind you. The steep walls shorten as you finally arrive at the eastern trailhead (3,060 feet elevation) next to a parking lot and rest rooms. If you have had the patience to make the 4.5-hour drive from the western trailhead to the eastern one for a shuttle hike, this is where you will pick up your second vehicle for the return trip. Otherwise you will turn around at this point to experience Aravaipa's wonders again on your return trip.

Nearby Trails
Aravaipa's branch canyons offer some of the best scenery in the state, and are worth the mile or so hike into them. Horse Camp Canyon has over a mile of solitary adventuring for you. Turkey Creek Canyon, near the east end, is a narrow, 3-mile canyon with a lush riparian environment to go with its excellent camping spots and a 500-year-old Sabado Native American dwelling.

Camping
Primitive camping sites abound throughout the canyon, shady, level places right next to the creek. Both the west and east entrances have campgrounds, but the one on the west side is very small. Campground information is available on the web site at www.az.blm.gov/sfo/aravaipa/camping.htm.

For more information, contact the West Aravaipa Canyon Wilderness Brandenburg ranger station at 520-954-4333, or the East Aravaipa Canyon Wilderness Klondyke ranger station at 928-828-3380. The Bureau of Land Management's (BLM) web site, which features Aravaipa Trail details and reservation information, is at www.az.blm.gov/rec/aravaipa.htm.

Phoenix Area—
Urban and Suburban Wilderness

11

Barnhardt:
What Can You Say?

Location: Mazatzal Wilderness, in the Tonto National Forest, 70 miles north of Phoenix and 13 miles south of Payson.

Total distance: 12 miles (17-mile loop possible)

Hiking time: 7 hours

Total elevation gain: 1,810 feet

Difficulty: Difficult

Best months: March through November (But hike early in the day in summer.)

Auto accessibility: Very good. The last 4.7 miles of forest road are bumpy but passable by passenger cars.

Maps: USGS Mazatzal Peak. A Mazatzal Wilderness trail map is available at the Mesa and Scottsdale ranger stations for $7.

Rules: Pets on leash permitted; not recommended for horses. No bikes or motorized vehicles.

Comments: This stunning wilderness gateway is a favorite of Phoenicians and Paysonians alike, from day hikers to backpackers. Spring thaws line the trails with artistic little waterfalls, and the trees' fall colors decorate the upper trail segments.

OK, say you live in Phoenix and you have an East Coast visitor from, say, Connecticut. After you bring your visitor back from the airport, she says she could never live in a place as barren and featureless as the desert. So, you go into the next room and bring her a color chart and say to her: "Pick three colors, any colors, and I'll find them for you in the desert." And let's say she does. Then you take her up on the Barnhardt Trail to find those colors. Whatever shades she picked, chances are you will find them along Barnhardt, with its full palette of wildflowers, cactus blooms, parti-colored birds, and painted rocks. And when you do find them, what would she say then? Oh, did I neglect to say that the trail also has the jaw-dropping scenery of plummeting canyons and skyscraping peaks? As the premier route in the 250,000-acre Mazatzal Wilderness, the Barnhardt Trail is one of the state's best hikes, 'nuff said.

Getting There

From Phoenix, head north up AZ 87 for 65 miles past mile marker 239, and make a left at the sign for the Barnhardt Trail. Follow Forest Service 419, a rippled gravel road, for 4.7 miles straight toward the Mazatzal Mountains looming in front of you. If you are driving in the early morning (a must for summer hikes), you'll enjoy seeing the roadside wildlife scurrying about the piñons and cacti: quail, oar-eared jackrabbits, and maybe that most colorful of Mazatzal residents, the variegated western tanager. The

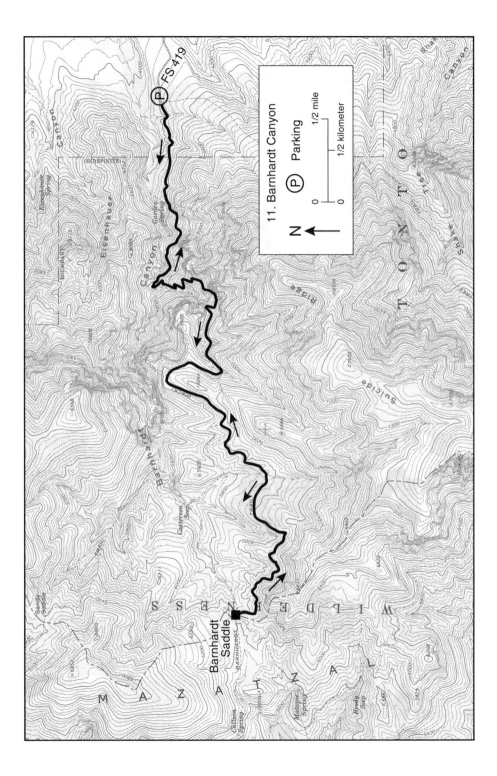

11. Barnhardt Canyon

Ⓟ Parking

N ←

1/2 mile
1/2 kilometer
0
0

FS 419

Barnhardt Saddle

View from the Barnhardt Trail

road ends at a wide parking lot, where the trailhead is next to a large brown wooden trail map (elevation 4,210 feet).

The Trail

This is a long day hike, but the route has a gradual slope for the most part, making it easier than many trails with this much elevation gain.

Trailhead to second unsigned trail junction, 1.2 miles, 640-foot elevation gain, moderately difficult.

The trail is quite rocky for the first 0.25 mile, then becomes a more foot-friendly dirt and rock path that gradually switchbacks up into the Mazatzal Mountains through precipitous Barnhardt Canyon. In spring and early summer, your head will be bobbing up and down to study the wildflowers below you and the mountainscapes above. Here you'll see a painter's palette of blooms: the lemon chiffon hues of the prickly pear cactus, the vivid orange of the globe mallow, deep purple lupines, and bright red claret cup cactus. And that's only a sample of the Mazatzal's shades and hues. The looming Mazatzal Mountains are an earth-colored rainbow, where wine-colored basalt mixes with rose, cream, and buff quartzite. As it will be for the rest of the hike, the scenery is truly captivating.

At 0.6 mile you pass the wilderness entry sign, and 0.1 mile later you come to an unsigned trail junction. The unsigned trail to the right descends toward the creek whispering below you, but you want to continue to your left unless you already need to fill your water bottle. (Bring at least a gallon per person—or per dog—when it's hot.) The trail continues to switchback up until you come to a second unsigned junction at 1.2 miles (4,850 feet). You've gained quite a bit of elevation already, but the gradual gradient has made it relatively

Prickly pear cactus

easy to conquer. Bear right at this junction to forge on up the trail.

Second unsigned trail junction to Sandy Saddle Trail junction, 3.5 miles (4.7 total miles), 1,110-foot elevation gain, difficult.

From the junction, the trail continues to wind up into Barnhardt Canyon, but some of the switchbacks become quite steep here, so you might want to stop occasionally for a scenery break. On some parts of the trail you will have an eagle's-eye view of the Rye Valley and the scattered mountains behind it, and on others you will see the rock castles and ramparts of the Mazatzal Mountains that you are approaching. Near the 2.6-mile point, about 50 feet from the trail, there is a seasonal (March to June) waterfall that gushes down some 20 feet from a microcanyon—it's worth the side trip to see it, if it's flowing.

The mixed-habitat trail environment of this trial segment has a number of gnarly alligator junipers and brushy piñons laced with a manzanita understory. Arizona sycamore and walnut trees appear alongside the seasonal streams and runoffs, adding to the plant potpourri. The trail also has some irritating bugs; pack along some repellent, because they are repellent! And keep an eye out for tarantulas and rattlesnakes; they're also part of the trailside show.

At the 4.7-mile point you'll come to the junction with the Sandy Saddle Trail (elevation 5,960 feet) and bear left to switch your way up to Barnhardt Saddle and the end of the trail.

Sandy Saddle Trail junction to trail's end, 1.3 miles (6.0 total miles), 60-foot elevation gain, easy.

The hike levels out after the trail junction, making your final 1.3 miles a relatively easy walk through ponderosa pines and manzanita, with Mazatzal Peak rising in front of you. Finally, at the 6-mile point of your jour-

---

ney, you come to the Barnhardt Saddle (elevation 6,020 feet) and a junction with the Davenport and Divide Trails. From the saddle you can see down into the vast sprawl of the Verde River Valley all the way over to Sonoma, as well as views down spectacular Barnhardt Canyon.

If you are camping out, you can go to your right for a mile to Chilson Spring, a water source with some fine camping spots. If you would like to complete a 17-mile loop back to your car, follow the Mazatzal Divide Trail here (see Nearby Trails) to the Y-Bar Trail. If you are just making a long day's hike of your journey, return the way you came.

Trail's end to trailhead, 6.0 miles (12.0 total miles), 1,810-foot elevation loss, moderately difficult.

For all the elevation loss on the way back, the gradual decline is easier on the knees than you might expect, and you can make good time on your return trip. Watch out that you don't take the wrong turn at the unsigned junction just before the wilderness sign, which is approximately 0.7 mile from the trailhead. If you are heading down sharply toward the creek, you have taken the wrong turn. (This is the voice of experience speaking!)

Nearby Trails

From the Barnhardt Saddle, follow the Mazatzal Divide Trail left (south) to join the Y-Bar Basin Trail for a 17-mile loop. Backpackers often hike 4 miles along the route for water and camping at Windsor Spring before completing the loop the next day.

Camping

There are several backcountry camping spots after the Sandy Saddle trail junction, about a mile before the end of the trail, with other good campsites scattered around dependable Chilson Spring, a mile's hike to the right from trail's end. The Ponderosa Campground, with over 100 units, is 2 miles north of Payson on AZ 87, about 14 miles from the AZ 87 turnoff onto the Barnhardt Trail. This trailer-friendly campground has showers and flush toilets. For the latest camping information, go to www.fs.fed.us/r3/tonto.

For more information, contact the Mesa Ranger District, 26 N. MacDonald, Room 120, PO Box 5800, Mesa, AZ 85211, telephone 480-610-3300; or the Payson Ranger District, 1009 E. Highway 260, Payson, AZ 85541, telephone 928-474-7900.

12

Boulder Canyon: Obvious Subtlety

Location: Superstition Wilderness in Tonto National Forest, 40 miles west of Phoenix near Mesa.

Total distance: 14.4 miles (12.2-mile shuttle hike)

Hiking time: 7 hours

Total elevation gain: 1710 feet

Difficulty: Moderately difficult

Best months: March through May and October through December

Auto accessibility: Excellent

Maps: USGS Beartooth Superstition Wilderness

Rules: Pets on leash permitted. Horses permitted. No mountain bikes.

Comments: With pinnacles, mountains, canyons, and a lake, there's a lot to see on this rocky ramble into the heart of the Superstition Wilderness. In summer, most day hikers turn around at the canyon bottom. This wide-open trail has little shade until you arrive at the canyon bottoms, so bring sunscreen and plenty of water.

"You have to get over the color green; you have to quit associating beauty with gardens and lawns: you have to get used to an inhuman scale."

—Wallace Stegner, "Thoughts in a Dry Land," from *Where the Bluebird Sings to the Lemonade Springs: Living and Writing in the West*

A rock is a rock—unless it's not. To the inattentive hiker, a trek through Boulder Canyon may be just a dry run through a pile of featureless stones. Those who attend to the rockscape with a studied eye, however, will find a smorgasbord of stony scenery to savor: shapes that range from knife-edge to ovoid; crumbly, spongy, or crystalline textures; and a palette of earth tones from rose to black. Eons of erosion have sculpted Boulder Canyon's volcanic rock and compacted ash (tuff) into the panoply of forms it boasts today. Much of this subtle beauty lies in the pinnacled walls that this ridgeline trail follows, but there's also the solitarily spectacular Weaver's Needle and Battleship Mountain, looming larger with each turn in the trail. So drive up to Phoenix's Canyon Lake and traipse along the Boulder Canyon Trail. With a little attention to detail, its subtle beauty will be obvious.

Getting There

From its intersection with I-10 in Phoenix, drive 34 miles east along US 60 to exit 196 (Idaho Road) to head for Canyon Lake. Head north up Idaho Road 1 mile to turn onto AZ 88 (Apache Trail Road). Drive winding Apache Road for 15 miles, passing mile marker 210, to turn left into the Canyon Lake Marina. Park in the marina lot (rest rooms are available) and walk across the highway to the beginning of the Boulder Canyon Trail (#103) opposite the marina entrance.

The Trail

Trailhead to Second Water Trail junction, 4.0 miles, 680-foot total elevation gain, moderately difficult.

From the trailhead (1,760 feet elevation) you'll start up a steady grade to the wilderness entry sign at 0.6 mile. The trailside vegetation of palo verde and cholla is characteristic of this arid land, but the water-filled lake gorges beneath you are not. They resemble fjords with their deep canyon walls surrounding clear blue waters. Ahead of you, the prominent pinnacle of Weaver's Needle beckons you to head farther into the canyon.

As you pass the 1-mile point along a high ridge, look behind you to see azure Canyon Lake sprawling below you (with the marina thankfully occluded). You'll shortly top off along the ridge at the 1.3-mile point (2,280 feet elevation), from which you can study a gallery of gigantic jagged pinnacles and buttes, with Weaver's Needle rising up to the south. From here you'll round a ridge and dip down to 2,210 feet before winding your way back up past some low-lying mountains. This trail segment is patched with teddy bear and cane cholla, but spring rains bring surprise sprinkles of lilac-colored lupines, sunflower-yellow brittlebush, and orange mariposa lilies. So far your hike has followed Apache Trail Road below you on your left, but that will soon change.

At 1.7 miles, you turn away from Apache Trail Road and venture into Boulder Canyon, passing a wall of chiseled rock columns high above you. Just before the 2-mile point you'll pass some jagged tan and red boulders so pocked and ragged that they look like titanic sea sponges. As you continue into the canyon, you'll pass by several colorful cliffs of wine and black lava rock, another new note in this trailside rock concert.

Now you can see the trail stretching out below you into Boulder Canyon, heading south to Weaver's Needle and the Peralta Trail. But the most dramatic sight here is massive Battleship Mountain in front of you on your left, guarding the entrance to La Barge Canyon and seasonal La Barge Creek. You'll pass several precipices on your right at the 2.6-mile point, worth the short side trip to peer into the canyon formations below you. From here your hike is a rubbly descent into the canyon bottom, flanked by the cloud-grabbing walls of Battleship Mountain, its sheer ramparts looking like the gateway to heaven.

At 2.9 miles the trail ceases its rubbly ways to level with you as you bottom out, crossing intermittent La Barge Creek at 1,780 feet elevation, and walk south along the wide sandy trail of tree-lined and shrubby Boulder Canyon. Here the low-lying canyon walls have a rose and buff tint, glowing brightly in the desert sunlight. Follow the rock cairns scattered along the trail—there are lots of side trails here, many leading to campsites.

At 4 miles you come to a signed trail junction (1,840 feet) for the Second Water Trail on your right, leading into a side canyon of black volcanic rock and Second Water Spring 0.3 mile down the trail. This junction is the turning-around point for many hikers, particularly in hot weather. But if you pursue the trail to its end, more sights await.

Second Water Trail junction to Boulder Trail terminus, 3.2 miles (7.2 total), 430-foot elevation gain, moderately difficult.

From the trail junction you'll hike through Boulder Canyon along a relatively level

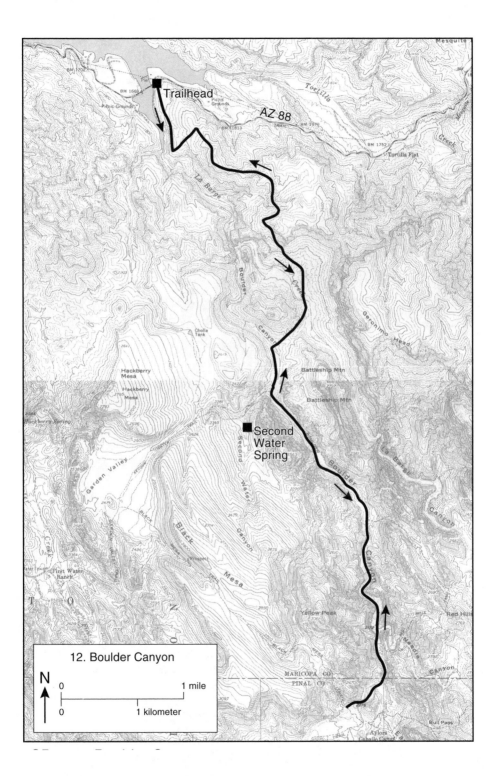

Trailhead

AZ 88

Second
Water
Spring

12. Boulder Canyon

N

| 0 | | 1 mile |
| 0 | | 1 kilometer |

Canyon Lake

route for the rest of the way. You'll see scores of pinnacles, canyon walls, and rock formations as you pass the junction for the Cavalry Trail at 1.5 miles and head past Yellow Peak on your left to finish at a multi-trail junction (2,270 feet elevation) at the 7.2-mile point. The junction leads to a number of trails, such as the Dutchman, Black Mesa, and Peralta Trails. This is the turning-around point to return to the trailhead.

Boulder Trail terminus to trailhead, 7.2 miles (14.4 total miles), 600-foot total elevation gain, moderately difficult.

The return trip is a relatively easy day hike, if you are hiking Boulder Canyon Trail as a two-day trip. If you are hiking it all in one day, especially during warm weather, you will likely find the return to be long and exhausting.

Nearby Trails

With all the connecting trails on this route, you can make any number of scenic, extended day hikes or overnight backpacking trips. One of the most scenic and popular shuttle hikes is a combination of the Boulder Canyon Trail and the moderately difficult Second Water Trail (#236), which takes you past Second Water Spring for water and through scenic Garden Valley on your way to the Second Water trailhead at Lost Dutchman State Park off AZ 88, which you pass on your way up AZ 88 to the Boulder Canyon Trailhead.

Camping

There are at least a half dozen level and soft campsites past the 3-mile point, along the canyon bottom. Lost Dutchman State Park has the nearest campground, with 35 sites. It's 5 miles north of Apache Junction on AZ 88. Campground information is at www.pr.state.az.us/parks/parkhtml/dutchman.html.

For more information, contact the Mesa Ranger District, 26 North MacDonald Street, Mesa, AZ 85201. Telephone 480-610-3300.

13

Peralta Trail: Weaving Up for a Needle in Your Eye

Location: Superstition Wilderness in Tonto National Forest, 40 miles west of Phoenix, near Mesa.

Total distance: 11.8 miles

Hiking time: 6.5 hours

Total elevation gain: 2,680 feet

Difficulty: Difficult

Best months: October through March

Auto accessibility: Good

Maps: USGS Weaver's Needle. A detailed Superstition Wilderness topographic map is available from Beartooth Publishing at Arizona bookstores and at www.maps4u.com.

Rules: Pets allowed on leash. Not recommended for horses. No mountain bikes. $4 entry fee.

Comments: The scenery never slackens on this bell-shaped trail into the heart of Phoenix's famous Superstition Wilderness. Expect weekend crowds on the trail segment to the saddle, but expect almost no one after that. High-top boots will save your ankles along this rocky trail. Pack a gallon of water per person for the entire route, half that if you turn around at Fremont Saddle.

Sometimes, the people you meet on a hike are as memorable as the scenery. Woody, a cross between John Wayne and John the Baptist, was just such a person. With bull-hide boots, weathered jeans, and a wide-brim hat, Woody could have stepped out of a Western movie set. So why was he sitting alone on a windswept mountain saddle in the rugged Superstition Wilderness, miles from any ranch on this hikers-only trail? Woody came up to hand out Bibles (new King James version) to the weekend throngs who climb the 1,300 feet up the Peralta Trail for an eyeful of 4,553-foot Weaver's Needle, the wilderness's signature rock composition among its thousand volcanic formations. Woody said he wanted to capitalize on the awe and reverence that The Needle provokes, distributing Bibles to channel observers' reverence for nature towards reverence for its Creator.

This cowboy Christian was right; the Peralta Trail's views are inspirational, regardless of your religious persuasion. But this hike is no one-trick pony: Weaver's Needle is only one of a host of scenic prospects along its 5.9-mile length. On this wilderness hike you'll see everything from hoodoos to buttes, from valley vistas to multi-mountain overviews. Small wonder it's one of the Southwest's most popular wilderness trails, a few miles from cities but a few light years from civilization. So take a hike up the Peralta Trail, and you'll get more than just an eyeful of magnificent Weaver's Needle. But be ready for some wilderness proselytizing among those heavenly views.

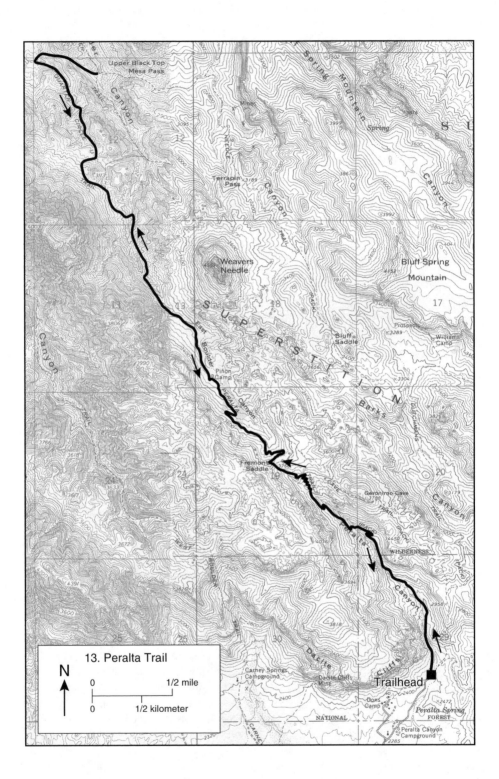

13. Peralta Trail

N

0   1/2 mile

0   1/2 kilometer

Weaver's Needle

Getting There

From its intersection with I-10 in Phoenix, drive 42 miles east along US 60 to mile marker 204. Make a left into the Peralta Trails subdivision, driving 7.5 miles along Peralta Trail Road (FS 77) to the wide parking lot next to the trailhead. Rest rooms are available here.

The Trail

Trailhead to Fremont Saddle, 2.3 miles, 1,350-foot elevation gain, difficult.

As you set out from the trailhead at 2,410 feet, you'll immediately start your climb up into the mouth of Peralta Canyon via its rocky but identifiable trail, flanked by mesquite and tall saguaros. Even at the outset there's plenty to see along this hike. Craggy volcanic parapets sweep up above you on your left, composed of tall rock chimneys. The varied formations should entertain you as you stairstep up the wide, pebbly path.

At 0.8 mile, you'll pass through a wash shaded with a thick canopy of brush and trees, a good spot for a break during hot weather. As you continue, you'll see more towers emerge on both sides of the trail, each with its own personality. With their smooth and angular faces, the volcanic columns on your right look like Easter Island statues. For textural contrast, look to your left and you'll see pinnacles as raggedly jagged as broken glass.

When you near the 1-mile point you'll see an enormous butte in front of you, its dark, mottled body belted with a horizontal layer of buff tuff, like mocha ice cream sandwiched between scoops of rocky road. From here the scenic rock concert continues, with the appearance of several balancing rocks near the 2-mile point, as you've climbed high enough to be almost eye to eye with the pinnacles that lorded above you at the start. The canyon walls narrow around you now, the better to see the basalt hoodoos and chimneys that flank the trail—it's easy to find lots of rock shapes here, and children of all ages can enjoy looking for them.

From the hoodoos you'll hike up several smooth and bare rock shelves to encounter a square-shaped pinnacle in front of you. It has a wide, white band running vertically through it, banded yet again by sherbet-orange rock. From here you'll negotiate several short switchbacks to finally arrive at Fremont Saddle (elevation 3,760 feet). Looking into Peralta Canyon, you can see why so many hikers make the trip up here; the thumb-shaped massif of Weaver's Needle rises 2,000 feet from the valley beneath it, reigning in solitary splendor, with a retinue of tiny spires around it. The needle is a volcanic plug, meaning it's formed of solidified lava that once filled the vent of the volcano cone that surrounded it, only to be left standing as a solitary spire when the softer cone eroded from around it. Today the Needle soars above the Boulder Canyon floor, its singular shape and size an Arizona landmark. Once your eyes and soul are filled, you can return to the trailhead (as most hikers do) or descend into the canyon via the rest of the Peralta Trail.

Fremont Saddle to Dutchman's Trail junction, 3.6 miles (5.9 total miles), 1,330-foot elevation loss, moderately difficult.

From the saddle you will switchback down toward Weaver's Needle. This trail segment is a bit less precipitous and rocky than your initial climb, making it easier and faster to hike. Don't forget that you have to hike back up the trail, however, so save some energy (and water!) for the return trip.

After you switchback down the saddle for 0.5 mile, you'll snake down into the canyon amid a host of agaves, prickly pear, cholla, and yucca—classic desert landscape. There are many rock structures to see here, with a number of tubular formations. The terrain is flatter around you, and you'll see a number of level campsites with fire rings past the 3-mile point of your hike. Near the 4-mile point you will be directly opposite Weaver's Needle high above you, while across from you is a butte so jaggedly eroded that it could be the front of Mordor Castle from *The Lord of the Rings*. The view here of Weaver's Needle vaulting above you is one that many hikers never venture down to see, but it's a wonderful photo-op. The saguaros have mostly disappeared here, replaced by brittlebush, jojoba, and piñon pine.

At 5.0 miles the high ridges of the canyon have sloped down into rounded hills around you, as you gradually descend to your turnaround point at 5.9 miles, the junction with Dutchman's Trail #104 (elevation 2,420 feet).

Dutchman's Trail junction to Peralta Trailhead, 5.9 miles, 1,340-foot elevation gain, difficult.

From the junction you head back up the Peralta Trail, a long, steady climb that mitigates the 1,300-foot elevation gain to Fremont Saddle. From the saddle your return to the trailhead offers the sight of multiple mountains and buttes marching off from you toward the south. You'll pick your way down the rocky trail to the trailhead, having gotten an eyeful of The Needle and its splendid companions.

Nearby Trails

The Peralta Trail has both shuttle and loop hike options for extended day hiking or overnighting. Many hikers use the Peralta Trail as part of an 11.2-mile shuttle hike, leaving from the First Water trailhead to end at the Peralta trailhead. From the end of the Peralta Trail, others head east along Lost Dutchman to return to their Peralta starting point via the solitary (and difficult-to-follow) Terrapin and Bluff Springs routes, a 12-mile loop hike. Either trek is best done as an overnighter.

Camping

The trail north of the saddle has a half dozen level campsites with fire rings, with several near the 4- and 5-mile points from the trailhead and near the trail junction. Piñon Camp, a wide, flat group camping spot, is at the 4-mile point when you draw opposite Weaver's Needle. The nearest campground is at Lost Dutchman State Park, with 35 sites, 5 miles north of Apache Junction on AZ 88. For campground information check the web site at www.pr.state.az.us/parks/parkhtml/dutchman.html.

For more information, contact the Mesa Ranger District, 26 North MacDonald Street, Mesa, AZ 85201. Telephone 480-610-3300.

14

Lookout Mountain: Neighborhood Watch

Location: Lookout Mountain Park in Phoenix

Total distance: 1.2 miles round trip

Hiking time: 45 minutes.

Total elevation gain: 500 feet

Difficulty: Moderately difficult

Best months: October through May

Auto accessibility: Excellent, with paved roads all the way.

Maps: USGS Midway, Sunnyside

Rules: Dogs allowed on leash. Horses permitted in park. No mountain bikes allowed on Lookout Mountain Trail, but permitted on other trails.

Comments: This is a short hike up to the scenic summit of one of Phoenix's "neighborhood mountains" near the heart of the city. Don't underestimate this short trail; it is steep and rocky in spots. Wear hiking boots, bring a walking stick, and tote at least a quart of water on warm days.

"What's this spot on the map?" I was studying my Phoenix map as I drove into the city at dawn, noticing a small square of green that indicated a city park. I thought I knew most of Phoenix's many fine mountain and city parks, but this one had eluded me. So, taking a quick turn off I-17, I wandered over to this unnamed (on the map) spot of green. One turn off Greenway Boulevard and another off 16th Street, and I soon entered the completely empty parking lot of Lookout Mountain Park, with its namesake mountaintop looming in front of me.

I wandered up the first trail that inclined upward, and within a half hour I was treated to 360-degree views from the top of my own private mountain, alone and far from the madding crowds that grace most of the parks in the Phoenix Mountain Preserve. As dawn silhouetted the Superstition Mountains to the east, I watched Phoenix's hills and suburbs slowly come to light, the shadows withdrawing westward like a receding black tide. Later, as I picked my way down the rocky trail, I encountered many of the park's neighborhood residents, making their peak pilgrimage to watch the sun rise. I met Paul, a Wisconsin expatriate who exclaimed: "I've been hiking this trail for two years and it's the only one I've taken here, I like it so much." With such intriguing views so handily available, it's easy to see why anyone, neighbor or visitor alike, would regularly look out from Lookout Mountain.

Getting There

From I-17 in Phoenix, turn onto exit 211, Greenway Boulevard, and head east for 4.5

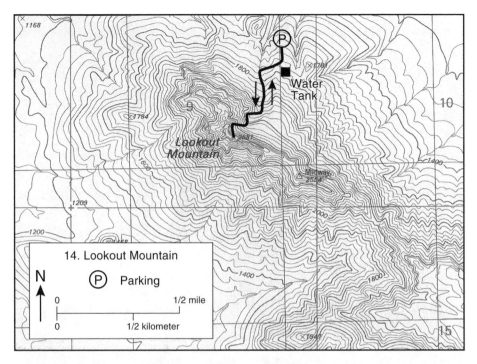

miles. On the way, you will pass 16th Street after a mile and continue east to pass the junction of 7th Street and Greenway, to come to another 16th Street. Turn right onto 16th Street and drive 0.2 mile to dead-end at the park and trailhead (1,540 feet elevation).

The Trail

Trailhead to Lookout Mountain Summit, 0.6 mile, 500-foot elevation gain, moderately difficult.

You'll start up the rubbly but open Lookout Mountain Trail #150, to veer left at the second trail junction, where you can already see the cityscape of northern Phoenix stretched out below you. At the third trail junction (0.2 mile), you hike left up a moderately steep section. Here the trail terrain is dotted with palo verde trees, their wispy branches drifting like green smoke over the barren boulder fields. In winter or spring you might find this Spartan landscape surprisingly fragrant with the blooming mistletoe

that hangs on the palo verdes and the tiny violet flower bursts of the desert lavender around them. As you hike, you'll cross a number of unsigned trail junctions. Just remember to bear left and seek the route that heads up toward the summit that is clearly above you.

At 0.4 mile you'll see a sign indicating that Trail 150 is to the right, as you stairstep up a steep slope of volcanic rocks. From this trail junction, you can study the suburban croplands of cloned houses below you, each breed flourishing in its own identifiable square. Another 0.1 mile brings you to another trail junction, this one directing you to the right to loop around to the top of the summit along another rocky staircase. In this trail section you'll see the southern portion of the Phoenix megalopolis, including its Stonehenge of downtown skyscrapers. The view of all this urban "splendor" somehow makes this friendly little trail seem all the wilder, and more precious.

Lookout Mountain

Soon you arrive at the summit (2,040 feet), marked with a small, castle-shaped turret and a 150 sign. At the summit you have a fine, 360-degree view encompassing the Phoenix area, the Superstition Mountains, and neighboring Squaw Peak. Right beneath you, a host of low-lying desert mountains roll up into the edges of the suburbs, sepia waves breaking upon a tract-house shore.

Studying Lookout Mountain Park beneath you, you can see that the mountain lowlands are stitched with all manner of trails near your route. Different locals use different trails: dog walkers often take the lowest paths, trail runners run the loops, and others follow the trail you just completed to the top, trekking it as a weekly ritual. The summit is a good spot to plot any extra hiking you may want to do on your return trip, because you can see where every trail route goes.

Lookout Mountain summit to trailhead, 0.6 mile (1.2 total miles), 500-foot elevation loss, moderately difficult.

As you loop down from the summit, you'll pass a colorful patch of lichen clinging to the craggy boulders here, a mixture of old gold, bright green, and pasty white. This summit area is often visited by white-speck-led rock wrens, tiny sirens that pierce the air with their high-pitched trills. There are several trail branches leading down from here. To find your original route, look for the prominent trail signpost below you, the one you passed on your way up. Take a few switchbacks down, while saying hello to the park neighbors hiking past you, and you're back at the trailhead, ready for the rest of the day.

Nearby Trails

A half dozen well-trodden but unsigned trails in the area, branching off from the Mountain Overlook trailhead, allow you to add miles to your trip without getting lost. The only other signed trail in the park, the Lookout Mountain Circumference Trail (#308), is a pleasant, 2.6-mile loop around the park edge. The circumference trail connects to the summit trail, for an engaging, 3.8-mile day hike.

Camping

There is no camping available in or near this small urban park.

For more information, contact Phoenix Parks and Recreation at 602-262-6861. The parks website is at www.ci.phoenix.az.us/parks.

15

Alta-Bajada Loop: Getting High on the Desert

Location: South Mountain Park Preserve in south Phoenix

Distance: 8.1 miles round trip

Hiking time: 4 hours

Total elevation gain: 1,250 feet

Difficulty: Moderately difficult overall, with one difficult portion.

Best months: October through March

Auto accessibility: Excellent, paved road all the way.

Maps: USGS Laveen

Rules: Pets on leash permitted. Horses and mountain bikes permitted on Bajada Trail, but not recommended on Alta Trail.

Comments: Some of Phoenix's best overviews await you on this trail's high mountain ridges, set in the one of the largest city parks in the world. The Alta Trail has a 1-mile section with nearly 1,000 feet of elevation gain, but it's easy the rest of the way. Many locals hike the Bajada or Alta in the morning, to see the saw-toothed Sierra Estrella Range light up before them.

"I heard you can take another trail back from here to the start, but I don't know anyone who's done it." After a hiker I met on the Alta Trail told me that, I knew I had to find out if I could make a loop trail (my favorite) out of the spectacular and popular Alta route. And I'm happy to report that you can use the Bajada and National Trails as a return route from your high-country hike up the Alta Trail, to traverse the highs and lows of this rugged desert landscape, all along a well-marked trail with lots of classic desert scenery.

Getting There

Central Avenue heads directly into the main entrance to the 16,000-acre South Mountain Park; it's a 6-mile drive from the city center. From the park entrance gate you'll drive 5.8 miles along San Juan Road, passing the park visitors center in the first 0.5 mile, to dead-end at the San Juan trailhead. The Alta Trail begins on your left at 1,540 feet elevation, behind a large trail sign for the Alta and National Trails.

The Trail

Alta trailhead to Bajada trailhead, 4.3 miles, 1,030-foot total elevation gain, difficult.

Behind the trail sign, take the trail fork that immediately begins to go up the side of the mountain, not the unsigned far left fork that immediately descends. You start your 1,000-foot ascent via a series of long, looping switchbacks along the high mountain ridges of the Ma Ha Tuak Range, part of the Salt River Mountains. The trail is a bit rocky

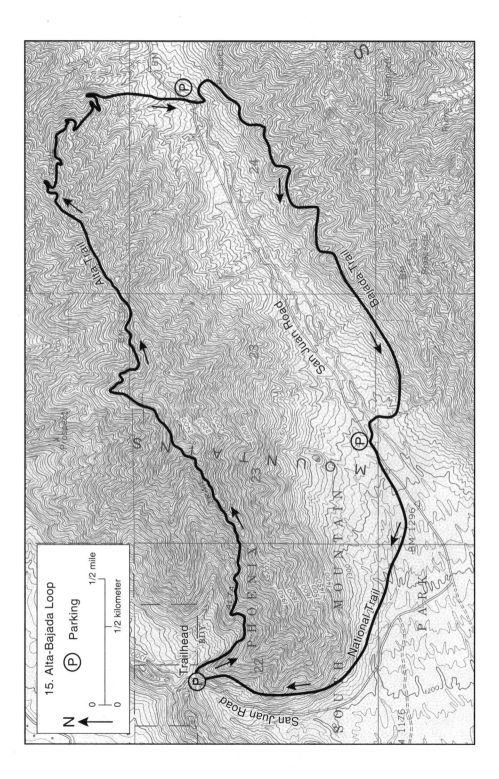

15. Alta-Bajada Loop

P Parking

N

0   1/2 kilometer
0   1/2 mile

Trailhead

Alta Trail

Bajada Trail

San Juan Road

San Juan Road

National Trail

SOUTH MOUNTAIN PARK

PHOENIX MOUNTAINS

but is clearly identifiable; you can see almost your entire route up the ridgeline.

At 0.4 mile you'll pass signpost #11 at 1,620 feet, to continue your nonstop ascent to the mountaintops. The trail terrain has scattered creosote bushes and wispy palo verde trees, its sparse vegetation a testament to the region's aridity. After you pass the #10 signpost at the 0.6-mile point (1,820 feet), there is a false trail that veers to the left to the edge of the canyon, but you continue to switchback up to your right. The landscape is so open that you can see your vehicle parked below you, along with promising glimpses of the soon-to-be-revealed cityscape of Phoenix.

As you wind up on the trail, you'll see bunches of barrel cactus and teddy bear cholla providing some local color to the rock block flocks around you. The barrel cacti have cranberry needles that contrast with the black basalt boulders from which many of them spring, and the fuzzy-looking cholla glow golden in the morning sunlight—they're both fun to see. The views from here are, to use contemporary parlance, "awesome." You can see the Sierra Estrella in all its jagged glory right across the valley beneath you, including Butterfly Mountain and Montezuma Peak. But the views improve as you top out along a high mountain ridge past signpost #8 (2,470 feet). Here you can study the entire urban sweep of the burgeoning Phoenix Valley, all the way over to the Bradshaw and Superstition mountain ranges.

Looking around from this vantage point, it is as though you are in your own personal time machine. Want to see what burgeoning Phoenix will look like in the future? Look below and to the left and you can see the remaining open spaces that the suburbs are explosively invading. Wonder how the terrain looked before it became so "civilized?"

Glance to your right and you can see the uncluttered terrain of the South Mountains and the park preserve directly below you, looking much the same as it did millennia ago. It's a fascinating, albeit unsettling comparative study of man's capability to denature nature.

From signpost #8 you'll start winding down the trail. Now you'll roll up and down a number of shallow depressions, adding another 100 feet of elevation gain to your initial climb to signpost #8. Finally, near the 2,370-foot elevation point at signpost #6, you begin a steeper descent from the Alta Trail to the Bajada trailhead. You'll eventually pass signpost #1 and cross San Juan Road to come to the Bajada trailhead and parking area at 1,570 feet.

Bajada trailhead to Alta trailhead, 3.8 miles (8.1 total miles), 220-foot elevation gain, easy.

To start the Bajada Trail, you stroll down the gulch to the left of the trailhead sign, and pass its first metal signpost. "Bajada" means "slope" or "skirt" in Spanish, and both terms suit a trail that skirts the lower slopes of the Gila Mountains. The Bajada Trail is an easy walk through the open desert countryside, where you ramble across several washes lined with large palo verde trees accompanied by saguaro, ocotillo, and teddy bear cholla. In winter you'll often be treated to bouquets of pale blue lupines or sun-gold poppies—the flowers alone are worth the trip.

The Bajada Trail is easy to follow. It's almost impossible to get lost because you follow San Juan Road below you on your right, and the pool-table terrain has no obstructions to seeing the road. You'll cruise quickly along, a change from the rock 'n roll ramble along the Alta Trail. Don't become too relaxed, however—you have to step carefully along several rocky depressions. And

The Sierra Estrellas from the top of the Alta Trail

prepare to be startled by coveys of Gambel's quail bursting out in front of you.

As you hike past Bajada signpost #9 (1,320 feet) at the 2.2-mile point, you can see a small ramada on your right; it's near the National Trail that you will soon join. Another 0.2 mile and you come to a junction with the National Trail, where you turn right to immediately cross San Juan Road and pass by the short trail leading to the ramada and parking lot at the end of the Bajada Trail. Now you are on the last part of the 14.5-mile National Trail, a pleasant 1.4-mile segment that takes you back to your starting point.

From the National Trail junction you gradually wind around the Alta mountaintops you recently hiked up, to circle back along the San Juan Road to your trailhead. All in all, this is one of Phoenix's best desert day hikes, if—like me—you don't mind looking down on urban encroachment.

Nearby Trails

The 14.5-mile National Trail is a rigorous all-day hike across the backbone of South Mountain Park, with plenty of views and scenery along the way. You can connect to most park trails from here for mountaintop and canyon explorations. The National Trail is best done east to west as a shuttle hike. A detailed trail description can be found at www.azcentral.com/travel/hiking/trails/nationaltrail03.html.

Camping

There is no camping in the park or near its entrance.

For more information, contact the City of Phoenix Parks and Recreation Department, 10919 S. Central Avenue, Phoenix, AZ. 85040. Telephone 602-534-6324. Or check the web site at www.ci.phoenix.az.us/parks/hikesoth.html.

16

Waterfall Canyon and Black Rock Loop: Glyph Gallery

Location: White Tank Mountain Preserve, 25 miles west of Phoenix.

Distance: 3.1 miles round trip

Hiking time: 3 hours

Total elevation gain: 210 feet

Difficulty: Moderately difficult

Best months: October through March

Auto accessibility: Excellent, paved road all the way.

Maps: USGS White Tank Mountains.

Rules: Pets on leash permitted.

Comments: This is an easy desert day hike to a seasonal waterfall and a score of ancient rock petroglyphs. The waterfall may be at its best after recent rains. You'll meet all sorts of folks along the Waterfall Trail, but you may not see anyone on most of the Black Rock Loop. Allow extra time for glyph gazing.

Cliff divers in the desert? Did my ears deceive me? I'd overheard an attendant at the White Tank Mountains office recounting his recent visit to Waterfall Canyon, where he spied several teens jumping 20 feet off the canyon walls into the 8-foot-deep tank at the bottom of the waterfall. The tank, a hollow depression in the rock, had completely filled after some 2 inches of autumn rain had soaked these gneiss and granite mountains, and several suicidal teens were exploiting its rare depths. The tank is filled by this 29,000-acre park's central attraction, a 180-foot seasonal waterfall that plunges down a white granite cliff. When fed by recent rains, this amazing waterfall springs to life like the phoenix the city was named after, gushing in the middle of a cactus forest. Who says deserts are flat and dry?

Catching a glimpse of the waterfall would be reason enough to trip up the 1.8-mile (round-trip) route into the cool confines of Waterfall Canyon. But this trail is not a one-hit wonder. Along the way you'll find 1,000-year-old Hohokam Native American petroglyphs, and some of the craggiest faces this side of Clint Eastwood. When you add in a branch hike along the scenic and informative Black Rock Trail, you've got a hike that shows off more desert features than you'll find anywhere: lovely cactus and cholla landscapes, precipitous craggy pinnacles, ancient Indian rock art, and the waterfall. All this is an easily accessible 3-hour hike just west of Phoenix. It's a fine early morning or late afternoon day hike.

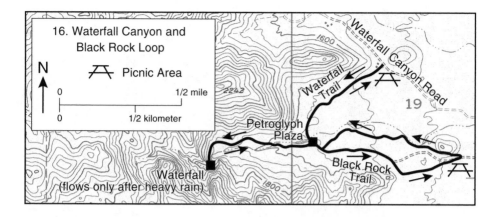

16. Waterfall Canyon and Black Rock Loop

N

Picnic Area

0 — 1/2 mile
0 — 1/2 kilometer

Waterfall Canyon Road

Waterfall Trail

Petroglyph Plaza

19

Black Rock Trail

Waterfall (flows only after heavy rain)

Getting There

From the center of Phoenix, drive 20 miles west on I-10 to exit 124, turning right onto Cotton Lane Road (AZ 303), to go north for 7.2 miles to Olive Road. Turn left onto Olive Road and drive 4.5 miles to the pay station ($5 fee) at White Tank Mountain Park. Then drive 2 miles to turn left onto Waterfall Canyon Road and drive another 0.5 mile to the wide parking area that surrounds the trailhead and picnic areas.

The Trail

Trailhead to Waterfall Canyon, 0.9 miles, 170-foot elevation gain, moderately difficult.

Starting from the well-signed trailhead (elevation 1,530 feet) you'll walk along a wide, barrier-free trail section so well groomed that you'll think you're in somebody's backyard. The trail wends gently through a classic desert landscape of buckeye cholla, teddy bear cholla, palo verde, barrel cactus, and tall saguaro. You have only to look behind you to see Phoenix spread out before you to the east, an impressive city view from this primitive landscape.

After 0.5 mile you'll pass a small ramada with three stone benches and a circular side

trail that leads to several petroglyphs. This is Petroglyph Plaza. From here you'll find the trail a bit rockier and steeper, but its elevation gain is still gentle. Anyone who wants a break can stop at one of the stone benches conveniently scattered along the trail.

As you move farther up the trail you enter Waterfall Canyon, its blocky granite and gneiss sides so sharp-edged they look like gigantic crystals. At 0.1 mile from trail's end you'll pass an old steel water tank on your right, with more petroglyphs decorating the nearby rocks. After scrambling over some granite blocks and under some mesquite tree branches, you arrive at the waterfall (1,700 feet elevation), which is fronted by a large boulder. Directly behind the boulder is the brownish-green water of the tank, which is fed by the waterfall. The 180-foot waterfall is on the right-hand side of the tank, tumbling and crashing over the jagged canyon side to finally splash into the pool. Even when the falls have temporarily disappeared, their path is marked by a black trace on the rock face.

Waterfall Canyon to Black Rock Picnic Area, 1.1 miles (2.0 total miles), 210-foot elevation loss, easy.

From the waterfall you return 0.5 mile to

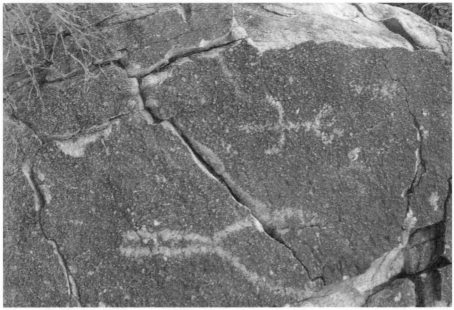
An ancient Hohokam glyph

Petroglyph Plaza, there to enter the unmarked Black Rock Trail on the right (1,660 feet). There are several false trails here, but you can tell you are on the right track because your trail is lined with rocks and has a rock bench visible below you from where you turned. After walking 0.1 mile, you come to a sign for the Black Rock Trail–Long Loop section (1,570 feet). Turn right to start along the loop. Here you'll walk along a pancake-flat path through wide fields of squat teddy bear cholla and hedgehog cactus, counterpointed by tall, stately saguaro. If you keep your eyes peeled, you'll spot the bright orange blooms of the globe mallows that dot the trailside.

You won't meet many hikers in this section, the better to spot some of the local wildlife. You might spy red-tailed hawks gliding around the mountain ridges on your right, or you might glimpse a group of pig-headed javelinas (peccaries) humping across the cholla and saguaro. After 0.5 mile along Long Loop you'll pass a trail junction with the Long Loop to continue along the Short Loop Trail to the Black Rock Picnic Area next to Waterfall Canyon Road (1,490 feet). Rest rooms are available here.

Black Rock Picnic Area to Waterfall Canyon trailhead, 1.1 miles (3.1 total miles), 40-foot elevation gain, easy.

From the picnic ground, you resume your counterclockwise path along the loop you've been hiking, taking the rest of the Short Loop Trail. Like the Short Loop section you just finished, this trail segment is groomed and flat, with nature signs explaining local flora and fauna. You continue along the Short Loop for another 0.2 mile from the picnic ground, passing a sign marker for nearby petroglyphs, and come to the trail junction for the Long Loop section (1,510 feet elevation). Walk behind the Long Loop sign and rejoin the Long Loop section of the Black Rock Trail. In 0.4 mile you'll come back to a signed junction for the Long Loop, and you make a right to continue along it, strolling 0.1 mile back to Petroglyph Plaza. From the Plaza it's an easy 0.4-mile jaunt back to your car.

Nearby Trails

The Waterfall Trail isn't the only spectacular hike in this park. The Ford Canyon Trail can be used for anything from a 9- to 16-mile (round-trip) exploration deep into the White Tank Mountains. On this quiet hike you'll find snow-white granite slabs and, after a rain, several dandy wading-size tanks as well as some wonderful mountain and canyon scenery. Joe Bartels has a detailed trail description on his excellent hiking web site, at www.hikearizona.com.

Camping

Backcountry camping is allowed at $5 a night. Make sure you notify the office when you enter the park. There is a family campground area near the Ironwood Trail in the park, accommodating everything from tents to RVs. The campground has rest rooms, showers, and drinking water and costs $10 a night.

For more information, contact White Tank Mountain Regional Park, 13025 N. White Tank Mountain Road, Waddell, AZ 85355. Telephone 623-935-2505. The web site at www.maricopa.gov/parks/white_tank includes a short video of the falls.

Camp Verde and Payson Areas—
Springs, Creeks, and Waterfalls

17

Bell Trail: Appeal for Everyone

Location: Wet Beaver Creek Wilderness in the Coconino National Forest, 98 miles northeast of Phoenix at Campe Verde.

Total distance: 6.6 miles (11 miles one way to Beaver Creek Trailhead)

Hiking time: 4 hours

Total elevation gain: 500 feet

Difficulty: Easy to the Weir Trail junction, moderately difficult after that.

Best months: March through October

Auto accessibility: Good. Some bumpy but negotiable spots near the trailhead.

Maps: USGS Casner Butte. A Forest Service trail summary and map are at www.fs.fed.us/r3/coconino/recreation/red_rock/bell-tr.shtml.

Rules: Pets on leash permitted. Horses and bikes permitted up to the Weir Trail junction.

Comments: Popular with trail runners, sunbathers, anglers, and backpackers, the multipurpose Bell Trail follows frenetic Wet Beaver Creek on its way through some butte-iful scenery, deep into the wilderness. This is one of the best summer trails in the central Arizona area, and you can refresh yourself in the water on hot summer days. Pick your spots for a dip during spring months with care, however, because the creek can be quite forceful after rains.

When it's a hot, sunny day in Phoenix or Sedona, where do folks go to relax? You'll see a lot of them tramping along the watery Bell Trail, a wilderness path whose trailhead areas are filled with weekend recreationists. Sunbathers willing to hike in 3 miles can recline on rosy streamside ledges that even a Mediterranean resort would envy, while swimmers and fishers can find prime spots all along the way. The Bell Trail is the only official trail into the Wet Beaver Creek Wilderness and, although the trail may be crowded at the outset, it becomes much more wild and solitary after crossing Wet Beaver Creek at the 3.3-mile trail point.

Getting There

From Phoenix, drive 95 miles north on US 17 and turn off at exit 298 (Oak Creek/Sedona). Go east 0.5 mile on AZ 179, and then go left to Forest Road 618 for 1.5 miles, and make a left at the forest ranger station sign and proceed 0.5 mile on FR 656 to the Bell Trail parking lot.

The Trail

Trailhead to Apache Maid Trail junction, 1.8 miles, 220-foot elevation gain, easy.

From the trailhead at 3,900 feet, you roll along a 6-foot-wide bench trail with Wet Beaver Creek gushing along below you on your right. In spring and summer you'll find a rainbow trove of wildflowers here: orange, violet, white, and yellow. As you walk, note that there are two contrasting habitats here, one on each side of the trail. Up on your left is a desert hillside environment of

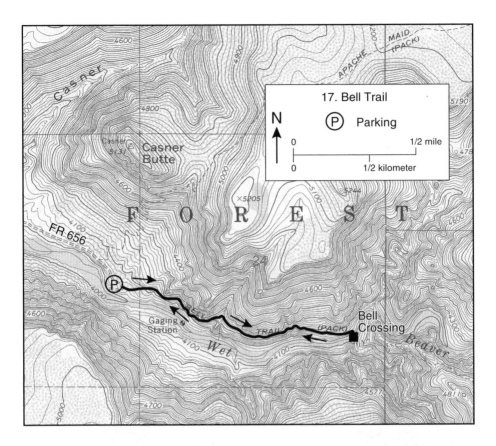

prickly pear cactus, piñon, and juniper, while on your right near the creek is a riparian environment lush with water-loving cottonwoods, sycamores, and grasses. The environmental contrast reaffirms water's power to engineer biomes by its presence—or absence. In the trail background on your left, you can enjoy the rosy red rocks of Casner Canyon and its buttes, with Longs Canyon stretching out on your right.

Trekking along, you'll see a number of side trails leading down to the creek. These are handy access trails for picking a primitive campsite or taking your dog for a dip, but look out for the poison ivy that proliferates here. The stream tends to be more placid after about a mile down the trail, with safer spots for waterside play. If you'd like to stay near the water, you can follow portions of a trace trail alongside the stream.

After 1.5 miles you come to a junction with the White Mesa Trail (4,060 feet elevation) and you bear to the right, continuing an easy stroll up the trail. At 1.8 miles you face a junction with the Apache Maid Trail (4,120 feet). You are now about 1.5 miles from Bell Crossing, your final destination.

Apache Maid Trail junction to Bell Crossing, 1.5 miles (3.3 total miles), 130-foot elevation gain, moderately difficult.

From the junction the trail becomes rougher, with several rocky spots, but it is still a relatively easy trek. At 2.1 miles you

Approaching Bell Crossing

come to a third junction, this one for the Bob Weir Trail, as you head left for Bell Crossing. At this point you enter the Wet Beaver Creek Wilderness (no bikes allowed beyond this point), and lose some of the crowds that may be on this route. Keep the Weir Trail in mind, however, because you might want to visit it on your way back (see Nearby Trails section).

From the Weir Trail junction the trail steepens, but your efforts are rewarded with bird's-eye views of Wet Beaver Creek crashing a hundred feet right below you, bulwarked by buttes in shades of rust red, sage green, and buff—it's a spectacular scene that unfolds beneath your very feet as you ascend. This trail segment is more like a mountainside ledge than a path, but it's wide enough to be safe. As you hike up this Andean pathway you'll stairstep through Upper Sonora Desert foliage dominated by large agave plants, yucca, spiny catclaw acacia, and Engelmann's prickly pear.

At 3.2 miles the trail descends from its high point of 4,250 feet to slope toward the creek, as you head through dry-country stands of cholla and junipers. As you near Bell Crossing you'll see a battered wooden sign indicating that Bell Crossing is just ahead and that Bell Rim is 1.5 miles farther. You'll also see an excellent backcountry camping site here, a flat spot with a sandstone ledge arching over the campsite like a stylized roof. Pass the campsite and continue down 0.1 mile to walk up to milky green Wet Beaver Creek (4,100 feet elevation) in front of you. This level, creekside spot is frequently visited by butterflies and birds, especially hummingbirds, so it's a good place to take a break and look around. It's a great picnic spot, too.

From the creek, if you turn to your left and scramble up the trail you'll find some wide, flat rock ledges hanging over jade-green pools of water, a primo sunbathing spot. There are several more sheltered campsites near the ledges, where you can pitch a tent for camping or for taking a shade break from sunbathing. These ledges mark the end of the 3.3-mile Bell Trail segment, but you can cross the creek here and head for Bell Rim, 1.5 miles farther on, or continue to trail's end, 11 miles from the trailhead. As for me, I was content to kick off my boots and soak in the warm March sun next to the creek.

Bell Crossing to trailhead, 3.3 miles (6.6 total miles), 150-foot elevation gain, moderately difficult.

After soaking up the creekside sun and scenery, return the way you came. On your return you'll see a number of beautiful canyon views that you turned your back on when you were hiking up the Bell Trail, so you'll have some pretty new perspectives on the scenery. If you've got the time and energy, make a left at the Weir Trail junction (see Nearby Trails section) and take this trail for more waterside fun.

Nearby Trails
The popular Weir Trail is right off the Bell Trail, and continues along the creek when the Bell Trail begins to climb above it. This 0.5-mile path is an easy jaunt along Wet Beaver Creek, and is blessed with a number of pools for fishing and swimming. It's very popular with the locals.

Camping
The best primitive campsites are near Bell Crossing at trail's end, but you can find spots alongside earlier stretches of the creek. The Beaver Creek Campground is just a few miles south of the trailhead on FS 618. It has 13 sites for tents and RVs at $8

a night. For more information, go to www .fs.fed.us/r3/coconino/recreation/red_rock/ beavercreek-camp.shtml.

For more information, contact the Red Rock Ranger District, P.O. Box 300, Sedona AZ 86339. Telephone 928-282-4119. Trail and campground information for the Bell Trail area is at www.fs.fed.us/r3/ coconino/recreation/red_rock/rec_ redrock.shtml.

18

West Clear Creek Trail: A Day at the Beach

Location: West Clear Creek Wilderness, near Camp Verde

Total distance: 15.0 miles (7.6-mile shuttle hike)

Hiking time: 9 hours

Total elevation gain: 2,200 feet

Difficulty: Difficult overall. Relatively flat over the first 5.5 miles, but steep and strenuous in the last 2 miles.

Best months: March through October

Auto accessibility: Fair. The last 5 miles are rutted and bumpy in spots.

Maps: USGS Walker Mountain, Buckhorn Mountain. A trail map and description are at www.fs.fed.us/r3/coconino/recreation/red_rock/west-clear-creek-tr.shtml.

Rules: Dogs on leash are allowed, but no horses. No bikes allowed in the wilderness trail sections. Red Rocks pass required ($5 a day, $15 a week).

Comments: This is a rigorous, all-day hike along a wilderness stream that rewards you with solitude and scenery. It's often safer to wade across the stream rather than rock-hop the slippery rocks: bring some sandals or aqua shoes. Check with the ranger station for creek water levels before you go, especially after thunderstorms or during the flash-flood season of July and August.

Wear a swimsuit in the desert? You bet, and bring your fishing pole, too! Rambling through the 15,300-acre West Clear Creek Wilderness, the West Clear Creek Trail amazes many first-time visitors with its profuse flowing waters and lush streamside flora. It's a place where cottonwoods, sycamores, and walnut flourish around trout-filled pools. Trek a few minutes away from its crystal waters, however, and you pass through piñon pines to find yourself in a Sonora Desert clime of catclaw and prickly pear cactus. These varied habitats are stretched along the feet of the canyon's varicolored walls of layered sandstone and limestone, so there are lots of scenic diversions along the Clear Creek Trail.

The trail's varied attractions lure a diversity of visitors. In the first mile or two, you're likely to see knots of swimmers jaunting along, lugging coolers. They're here to dip in the pools, sun on the sandy minibeaches along the trail, or shoot down some of the slick rock water slides. They're joined on the trail by anglers who ply Clear Creek's trout-filled waters. Move a couple of miles farther into the gorge, and you may find yourself all alone as you enter the gateway to the rugged West Clear Creek Wilderness, to undertake the trail's breath-taking ascent to the Mogollon Rim. For a hike that is, literally, a day at the beach, trek along the first 2 miles of this trail. For backcountry solitude and challenge, move past the third or fourth creek crossing. Either way, this is a hike you won't want to miss.

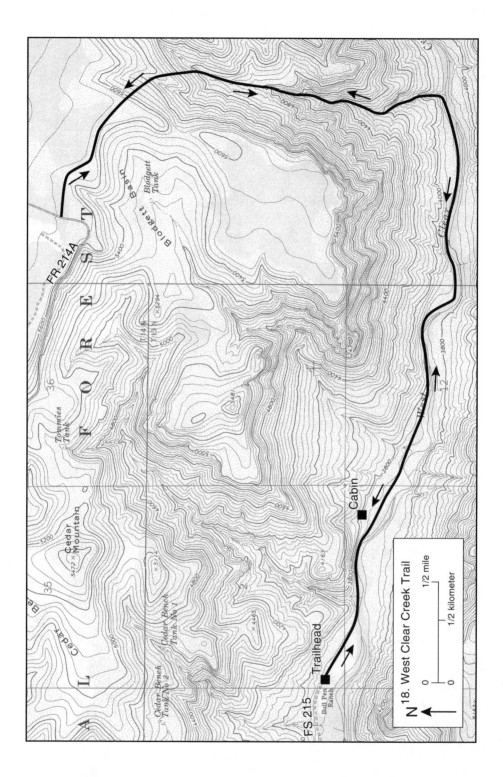

N 18. West Clear Creek Trail

Clear Creek

Getting There

From Phoenix, take I-17 north for 70 miles, and take exit 285 for General Crook Trail (AZ 260), heading east. Drive 6 miles east on General Crook Trail to mile marker 226, making a left onto FS 618, at a sign directing you to Beaver Creek. Drive 2.1 bumpy miles to make a right onto FS 215, next to a sign indicating that the Bull Pen Trail is ahead. Continue on FS 215 for 3 miles. You'll pass a rustic campground with a sign for the Blodgett Basin Trail on your left, and then you'll dead-end at a metal fence with an opening for the Clear Creek Trail. Sign in at the register and start along the trail (elevation 3,640 feet).

The Trail

Trailhead to fourth stream crossing, 4.7 miles, 340-foot elevation gain, moderately difficult.

From the trailhead, the wide earthen trail curves around some giant cottonwoods before it veers left up a rocky rise to a trail

marker. Go right at the marker to follow the Clear Creek Trail, which is now a flat old road. The creek boils along nearby on your right, with a backdrop of tall green and gray buttes on your right and low-lying, dusty rose buttes on your left. After 0.4 mile you pass a wide grassy field on your left with an old cabin that has prickly pear cactus growing out of the roof. This area is part of the old Bull Pen Ranch.

Just past the cabin, bear left along a fork in the trail to follow the creek—the right fork would take you down to the creek and some primitive campsites there. After a mile you come to your first stream crossing, where the creek is studded with dusty rose boulders among the junipers and sycamores. Here you'll rock-hop across the stream, or wade if the water is not too high. Once on the other side, you'll continue past a lovely small canyon on your left and enter the Clear Creek Wilderness, to come to a second stream crossing.

West Clear Creek Trail: A Day at the Beach

"Extraterrestrial" cactus

After you cross the creek again, you'll start along a red rock bench above the stream, gently climbing up the trail and away from the creek into a desert habitat of juniper, agave, and mesquite. Sycamores and oaks show up at various points along the trail, as you drop down near the stream. You'll also find several beaches and swimming holes along the way—and some healthy patches of poison ivy, too! In this rolling trail segment you'll alternately pass through riparian and desert habitats, between shade and sun, until at 2.2 miles you cross the stream for the third time. After wading or rock-hopping the stream, walk another 2.3 miles to complete the fourth stream crossing at 3,980 feet elevation.

Fourth stream crossing to trail's end, 2.8 miles (7.5 total miles), 1700-foot elevation gain, strenuous.

After the fourth creek crossing, the sunny trail is fairly level for most of the first mile, and then it turns left (north) to begin a series of steep switchbacks up to the Mogollon Rim, gaining some 1,700 feet in less than 2 miles—it's a gasser! Take your time on this trail segment, taking rest breaks to savor the sweep of the West Clear Creek Canyon gorge below you, and you'll make it to the top. As you near the end, the trail levels out and then you will see the West Clear Creek Trail sign at 5,680 feet. Congratulations!

Trail's end to trailhead, 7.5 miles (15.0 miles total), 1,900-foot elevation loss, moderately difficult.

The way back down is most downhill, but that doesn't mean it's all easy. Be careful of loose rock and dirt as you switchback down the first 2 miles from trail's end, or you'll skid down the trail. If you'd prefer to skip the descent, you can leave a car on FS 214A near trail's end for a 7.6-mile shuttle hike, or make a loop hike of the trip by hiking down the Blodgett Basin Trail. (See Nearby Trails section.)

Nearby Trails

If you would like to make the West Clear Creek hike a loop hike, and save a couple of hiking miles in the bargain, return along the Blodgett Basin Trail. From the end of the West Clear Creek Trail, hike along FS 214A for 1.3 miles to connect to FS 214 and proceed another mile to the Blodgett Basin Trailhead on your left. Along the trail you'll have some nice views of West Clear Creek Canyon as you switchback down some 1,700 feet to your start at the West Clear Creek trailhead.

Camping

There are primitive camping spots scattered between the first and fourth creek crossings along the trail, and the trailhead itself has a number of undeveloped pull-in spots near the creek. The nearest campground is the 18-site West Clear Creek Campground off FR 626 as you drive to the trailhead from Camp Verde. It's open all year. For more information visit the web site at www.fs.fed.us/r3/coconino/recreation/ red_rock/clear-creek-camp.shtml.

For more information, contact the Red Rock Ranger District, PO Box 300, Sedona, AZ 86339. Telephone: 928-282-4119.

19

Fossil Springs: Going Directly to the Source

Location: Fossil Springs Wilderness in the Coconino National Forest, 21 miles northeast of Payson.

Distance: 8.2 miles round trip (6.5-mile shuttle hike)

Hiking time: 4.5 hours

Total elevation gain: 1,280 feet on return

Difficulty: Difficult

Best months: March through May and September through November

Auto accessibility: Acceptable. The last mile of road is rutted in spots but manageable; the rest of the route is excellent.

Maps: USGS Strawberry

Rules: Pets on leash permitted. No horses or bikes. Avoid handling the poison hemlock in its designated area.

Comments: The path to this lush aquatic playground is on everyone's A-list of Arizona Hiking Trails. This is one of Arizona's best overnight hikes, a favorite of adults and children alike. Trek down to camp in one of the many shady and level sites near the wide spring-fed creek. Then hike back in the morning before it becomes too hot. One of the best fall color hikes in the region.

As one outdoors columnist put it: "If you don't like this place, you don't like being outdoors." Perhaps Barry Burkhart was gushing a bit, but that's appropriate when discussing one of the Southwest's largest gushers, Fossil Springs. A million gallons an hour! That's the water output of the Fossil Springs, constant through drought and monsoon, heat and freeze. A million gallons of room-temperature, diamond-clear, mineral-laden H_2O pours out into the desiccated Arizona landscape, nourishing a Nile-Valley oasis of ferns, cottonwoods, berry bushes, and other riparian plants rarely found in this desert clime.

Water-loving creatures of all types visit the travertine (calcite) pools here: javelinas, badgers, bald eagles, and ringtail cats. Chief among these spring creatures is the doughty *Trekkus aquarius* (water hiker), an Arizona mammal known to hike for miles (4.1 in this case) just to engage in its warm-weather rituals of diving, rolling, and generally cavorting in pools such as those in this ancient aquarium.

Fossil Springs is named for the thousands of fossilized sea creatures embedded in the walls of this 350-million-year-old seabed. Impressed with these geologic phenomena, King Woolsey, a Native American tracker, named this idyllic oasis in 1864. In 1916, a wooden flume was built to channel water to a Phoenix power plant, a function it performs to this day. In 1984 the area was designated as the 12,000-acre Fossil Springs Wilderness to preserve the spring from further development. Today Fossil Springs is a year-round destination for every-

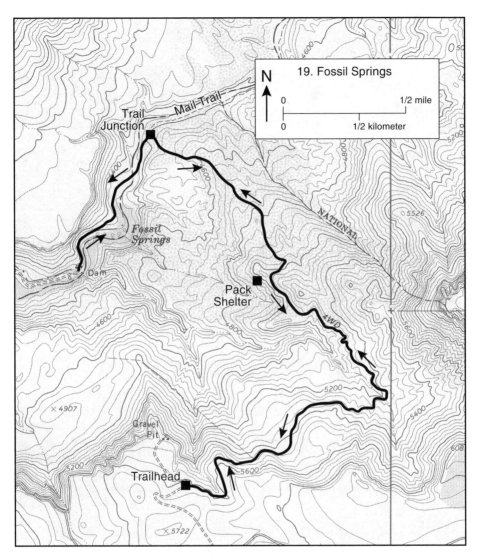

one from Boy Scouts to trail runners—and the aforementioned "trekkies." If you'd like to be a "trekkie," beam yourself down this scenic, canyon-view trail and dip your tail in its rejuvenating waters. You'll be glad you migrated here.

Getting There

From Payson, drive 17 miles north along AZ 87 to the town of Strawberry. Turn left onto Fossil Creek Road (FS 708) and bump along for 3.8 miles until you see the brown and tan Forest Service sign for Fossil Springs, turning right to go 0.4 mile to the spacious parking lot at the trailhead.

Note: There are two trails to Fossil Springs. Fossil Springs Trail #18, the one described here, is a more difficult, 4.1-mile hike to the springs with a trailhead that requires less driving time. The other path, the Flume Trail, is a moderately difficult, 4-mile hike that requires another 5 miles of driving.

Fossil Springs Creek

I've chosen the Fossil Springs Trail, since I usually seek the shortest driving distance between two points, and I've found this route to be quite scenic.

If you have two cars available, you can leave one at the end of the Flume trailhead and drive five miles back up FS 708 and start at the Fossil Springs trailhead, making a 6.5-mile hike from your start to the other car.

The Trail

Trailhead to Fossil Spring, 4.1 miles, 1,330-foot elevation loss, moderately difficult.

Setting out from the trailhead at 5,640 feet elevation, you head down a wide, winding dirt road lined with the alligator junipers and piñon pines that characterize much of northern Arizona's desert highlands. As you descend you can easily spot your destination, Fossil Creek, by following the green belt of cottonwoods and other trees that winds along the bushy streamside far below.

After hiking 0.6 mile down this wide road, you pass an overlook on your right and descend more steeply down the trail, with agaves and yuccas making their appearance in this habitat of pygmy forest and scrublands. At 2.1 miles, you pass an open campsite on your left (5,090 feet elevation), with a ramshackle pack shelter and a fire pit. From here the trail becomes a bit more rubbly, but it is still quite navigable if you pick your way carefully and wear ankle-supporting, high-top boots.

At 3.6 miles you come to a trail junction with the Fossil Springs and Mail Trails, making a left to continue on your route. From the trail junction you will drop down through a short field of TV-size boulders to climb back up onto a dirt road that now approaches the spring source. At 3.7 miles, you pass more campsites as you continue to the left at an unsigned trail junction. The trail now wends through a grassland habitat, with pale sandstone and limestone walls rising up around you, as you cross another small boulder field to find the spring-fed creek shimmering in front of you. You'll see a small spring gushing out next to the trail, by a large cottonwood. A turn to the left here takes you directly to the Fossil Springs source, a boulder-laden stream where the water threads out from a hundred small openings (4,310 feet elevation).

This is the end of the spring trail, but the best is yet to come if you venture farther along the Fossil Springs route. If you follow the creekside paths downstream, you'll be treated to a number of lovely watery scenes. Small curtains of water spill down from rocky shelves in the watercourse, feeding aquamarine pools deep enough to swim (which many hikers do). Campsites abound along both sides of the stream, which is heavily shaded with cottonwoods, alders, sycamores, and a dozen other tree species. Chubs and endangered topminnows swirl lazily in the pellucid waters, while many of the 100 species of birds twitter and chirp overhead. It's a scene that is almost tropical in its lushness. Small wonder that many come here to write, meditate, or contemplate. Its otherworldly clime stimulates otherworldly thoughts, and begs you to tarry before you return up to the desert.

If you hike farther along the stream, keep an eye out for fossils in the redwall limestone in and round the springs. The rock contains many tiny marine creatures that gave the spring its famous name. From the springs you might continue south along the Flume Trail for 0.4 mile to the Fossil Springs Dam. You might see several folks diving into the deep waters here, or perchance a nude sunbather. Whenever you decide to return, don't forget to fill up your filtered water bottle for the return trip up the dusty jeep road.

Fossil Springs to trailhead, 4.1 miles (8.2 total miles), 1,300-foot elevation gain, difficult.

The return trip is steep and can be hot in summer, which is the reason why many camp overnight and return in the morning. It's easy to beeline directly up to the trailhead as fast as you can go, but take the time to look behind you and savor the sweep of the canyon below you, perchance to stop at the shaded campsite near the 2-mile point on your return. Perhaps, like other hikers I've encountered here, you'll be planning your next visit as you finish up your first.

Nearby Trails

As you near Fossil Springs you'll pass a junction for the 3-mile (one-way) Mail Trail, a seldom-used, old mail route that follows Fossil Springs before it climbs some 1,000 feet up to some nice views of the Fossil Springs Wilderness canyons. Solitude seekers will like this trail.

Camping

Primitive camping spots are scattered all along the trail and creek, with the best spots available on weekdays. The nearest campground is at Kehl Spring, located off FS 300 near Baker Butte. The campground has 8 sites for tents and RVs up to 22 feet, with rest rooms and fire rings, but no water.

For more information, contact the Payson Ranger District, Tonto National Forest, at 928-474-7900. Camping and trail information is at www.fs.fed.us/r3/tonto.

20

Horton Creek: A Spring Trail for All Seasons

Location: North central Arizona, 15 miles east of Payson, in the Tonto National Forest.

Total distance: 6.8 miles

Hiking time: 4.5 hours

Total elevation gain: 1,020 feet

Difficulty: Moderately difficult.

Best months: March through May and September through December

Auto accessibility: Excellent

Maps: USGS Promontory Butte. A free Highline Trails Guide is available from the Payson Ranger Station.

Rules: Horses permitted. No bikes. Dogs must be on a leash.

Comments: An entertaining half-day riparian ramble up to a gushing spring. Don't believe the "easiest" rating that some guides give this route, and don't confuse this with the adjoining Horton Spring Trail.

"Oh, you'll want to go on the Horton Creek Trail, that's one of our best!" The ranger station attendant was quick to answer when I asked her about the best trails around Payson. Her ready response was a surprise to me: The Payson area has so many trails that I thought she might waffle on her reply. Then she added her reasons for choosing Horton Creek: The trail is very pretty, easy to follow, not too strenuous, and it follows a sizable, spring-fed stream.

After that glowing recommendation, I had to check out the Horton Creek Trail. I'm happy to say that it lived up to its advance billing. Hike this trail, and you can visit a dozen minifalls on your way up to its streaming hillside spring, and choose from a number of shady camping spots near tree-shrouded Horton Creek. In addition to having some of the best backcountry campsites in the state, the route is also one of central Arizona's best fall color hikes, an *Arizona Highways* Hike of the Month in 1999. Set in a climate that is rarely too cold or too hot, the Horton Creek Trail is a spring trail for all seasons.

The main challenge to hiking Horton Creek Trail (#285) is to figure out which trail segment you should choose. Horton Creek actually has two trails that run more or less parallel to one another: an old wagon road now used as a horse and hiker trail, and a trace trail that follows a shallow ridge alongside the creek. So, Horton Creek hikers may ask themselves, "Should I stay on the road or should I take the creekside trail?" For the best journey to the spring, the answer is to take both routes. You can hike the dirt and rock road, which is the easiest route to follow, all the way up to the spring, or push your way along the scenic but elusive trace trail that follows the creek. I opted for the combination route, following several visible side tracks off the road to trek nearer the creek. Taking the creekside trail allows you to enjoy more of the tumbling little falls that grace this pellucid stream. If you don't mind a little trail-finding, make the effort to go streamside and return to the main wagon trail when the going gets tough.

Getting There

The drive to the Horton Creek Trailhead is easy to follow and easy on the eyes. From Payson, drive 17 miles east on AZ 260, passing through piñon pine hills and countryside villages, to the brown sign pointing to the Tonto Creek Village and Fish Hatchery. Turn left here onto FS 289 and go 1 mile to the Tonto Creek Campground, where you turn left into the spacious parking lot next to Horton Creek.

The Trail

Tonto Creek parking lot to Old Wagon Road. .8 mile, 60-foot elevation gain, easy.

From the picnic ground parking lot (5,420 feet elevation), you'll cross FS 289 and move past the trailhead sign to start your trek to the spring. Following this foot-friendly dirt trail, you'll wend through several small grass fields to follow the creek, whose rippling surface is shadow-dappled by the tall sycamores that arch gracefully over both banks.

Finally, you'll cross a dry creekbed and go up to meet the old wagon road portion of the Horton Creek Trail (5,480 feet elevation). At this point you can follow the road left, or bear right and venture down the trace trail along the creek bank. I chose the road's wide-open path for this next trail segment.

Old Wagon Road to switchback, 2.1

miles (2.9 total miles), 810-foot elevation gain, moderately difficult.

As you hike up the rocky road, you'll pass stands of manzanita, oak, and cedar with water-loving maples in the upper trail segments. On this route you'll see several short side trails that venture back toward the stream. If you take these byways you'll go to the woodsy, sun-laced creek and watch it tumbling down wide rock shelves and over mossy boulders, attended by bouncing dipper birds. The side trails are well worth the tangential trip to the creek and back to the wagon road, or you can also stick with the creekside trail most of the way up to the spring, but you'd better be willing to climb over some fallen trees and boulders as you search for the path. But the trail-finding can be part of your hiking adventure, and there's little danger of becoming lost because the road will be on your left and the creek on your right, as it flows back to your starting point at FS 289.

If you return to the road to continue your hike, you'll clamber across several boulder-strewn trail segments until the trail turns sharply left to initiate a series of switchbacks beginning at 6,290 feet elevation. From the left turn junction, you can continue on the road up the switchbacks to the spring, or follow the narrow dirt trail that is directly in front of you.

Switchback to spring, 0.5 mile (3.4 total miles), 150-foot elevation loss, difficult.

The switchback trail section is very steep and rocky, but it's also the shortest trail segment of the hike. After the first switchback left, you'll turn right to see the endless wall of the Mogollon Rim looming above you, an awe-inspiring sight. Following the switchback, you'll push up the road until you see a gate and fence on your right at the end of the trail (elevation 6,440 feet). Go through the gate to quickly descend to your final

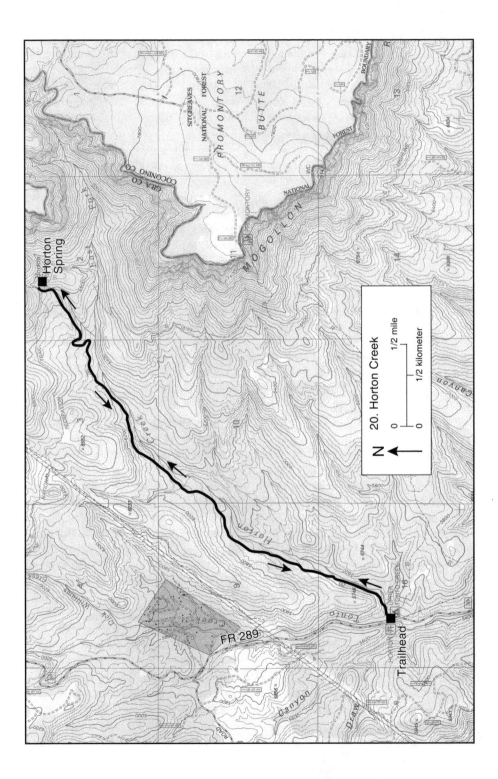

20. Horton Creek

N

0 — 1/2 mile
0 — 1/2 kilometer

Horton Spring

Trailhead

FR 289

Stemless primrose

destination, Horton Spring. Horton Spring gushes out of the hillside above you, cascading down a mossy rock wall to pool among the wildflowers at its feet. It's a picture-perfect water scene reminiscent of those in Ozarks or Smokies. Take a photo and send it to friends who think Arizona is all cactus and desert!

For an alternate route to Horton Spring from the switchback, veer off the road at the beginning of the switchback and go straight along the trace trail that leaves the road to follow the creek to the spring. This is an attractive route that is an easier hike than the road up to the spring. There are also several primo campsites along this trail section, wide and flat grounds among shady pines, with fire rings and log seats. Camp here and you can be lulled to sleep by the gentle susurrus of Horton Creek—does it get any better than that?

Spring to trailhead, 3.4 miles (6.8 total miles), 150-foot elevation gain, moderately difficult.

Your return trip has a slightly difficult, 150-foot climb back up to the switchback, but from there you'll pretty much coast down to the trailhead and parking lot, finishing one of the Rim Country's best day hikes.

Nearby Trails

If you continue up Horton Creek Trail above the spring you will soon connect to the famous Highline Trail (see Hike 21), which follows the base of the Mogollon Rim for some 51 miles. Arizona travelers have used this trail since the 1800s, and it's chock-full of spectacular views of the Mogollon Rim. You can also go right (east) along the Highline Trail from Horton Spring for 3 miles to join the Derrick Trail (#33), which loops back 2.5 miles to the Tonto Creek Campground where you started your hike.

For more information, contact the Payson Ranger District, Tonto National Forest, at 928-474-7900.

21

Highline Trail: A Wonder Wander

Location: Tonto National Forest near Payson.

Distance: 51 miles one way

Hiking time: 4 to 6 days

Total elevation gain: 2,900 feet

Difficulty: Difficult overall, sections range from moderately difficult to difficult.

Best months: March through May and September through November

Auto accessibility: Excellent at both the Pine Creek and 260 trailheads.

Maps: USGS Pine, Gila County, Buckhead Mesa, Kehi Ridge, Dane Canyon, Diamond Point, Promontory Butte, Knoll Lake, Woods Canyon. Free Highline Trails Guide map available at Payson Ranger Station.

Rules: Horses, dogs, and bikes permitted. No motorized vehicles.

Comments: Backpacker heaven lies along this 50-mile stretch of springs, streams, canyons, and Mogollon Rim spectacles. This National Recreation Trail has four auto access points between the route's beginning and the end, making it easy to subdivide the hike or meet someone along the way. Sturdy hiking boots, a water bag, and a filtered water bottle are must-haves on this rocky road across many water sources.

"Not all who wander are lost." A truck at the end of the Highline Trail boasted this bumper sticker. This quote from J.R.R. Tolkien's *The Lord of the Rings* epitomizes the spirit of many who venture onto the Highline Trail. This is a trail for days of wandering, where you can roam among the forest and chaparral habitats of the wild lands beneath Arizona's version of the Great Wall, the 200-mile Mogollon Rim that stretches from Sedona to New Mexico.

The Highline Trail follows a high ridgeline that plays beneath the Rim, passing by the many creeks and springs that flow from its thousand-foot palisades. Even though the route covers 50 miles of rugged backcountry, its elevation gains are generally modest. Nineteenth-century settlers originally used the route to move among local towns and ranches. The trail is now the site of the Zane Grey Ultramarathon, so named because this "frontier highway" was an inspiration to "the man who made the West famous," pulp novelist Zane Grey (1872-1939).

With negotiable elevation gains, awe-inspiring scenery, and numerous water sources, the trail makes for an enjoyable day hike if you take just one segment, or a weeklong venture if you hike it all. Either way, it's a wonder of a wander!

Getting There

From downtown Payson, take AZ 87 north for 14 miles to the roadside sign for the Pine Trailhead, making a right into the large open parking lot at the Pine Trailhead (5,390 feet elevation).

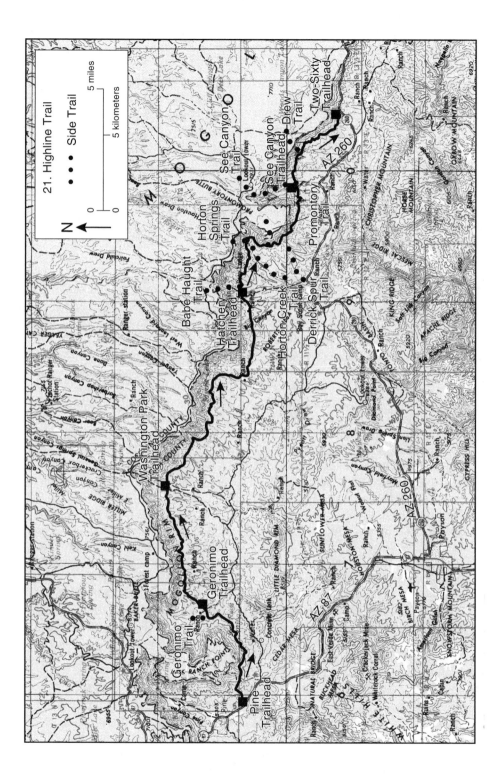

21. Highline Trail

Highline Trail
Side Trail

N

0   5 miles
0   5 kilometers

The Trail

Pine trailhead to Geronimo trailhead, 7.7 miles, 810-foot elevation gain, moderately difficult.

This trail segment is dominated by ponderosa pine and scrub oak forests, but you'll also see some stands of the elusive smoothbark cypress over the first few miles of trail. After hiking a mile to the Pine Canyon trail junction, you'll gradually climb up a ridge as you skirt the massive Baker Butte, sweeping above you. The Highline Trail has all manner of markers on it: metal diamonds, ribbons, and rock cairns, making it easier to follow than many shorter trails. In addition to magnificent Rim views along this segment, you'll also enjoy the craggy skyline of the Mazatzal Mountains off to the southwest near Phoenix. After topping off at the 2.6-mile point, you'll walk down to Red Rock Spring at the 3.5-mile point, just past the junction with the Red Rock trailhead. From the spring, you will gradually climb up to Pine Spring at the 5.6-mile point. From Pine Spring, the trail climbs near the 6,200-foot point before dropping some 450 feet to cross Webber Creek at 7.6 miles, to end at Camp Geronimo and the Geronimo trailhead (5,750 feet elevation). Make reservations if you plan to bivouac at Camp Geronimo; it's a popular spot, especially in hunting season.

Geronimo trailhead to Washington Park trailhead, 9.5 miles (17.2 total miles), 400-foot elevation gain, moderately difficult.

This trail segment does not have as many all-year water sources as the preceding one, so make sure you refill your water carriers at each creek or spring. After hiking 1.75 miles from Geronimo Camp, you'll come to Bear Spring for your first water break. From the spring, you'll roll up and down the trail for the next 7 miles, crossing Chase Creek (elevation 6,150 feet) near the 7.5-mile point to head into some shady spruce and pine forests. You'll likely encounter a number of snags (fallen trees) to scramble over, a recurrent feature of the entire trail. Near the 9-mile point of your hike you'll pass an old road with some overhead power lines, as you continue straight ahead down to the Washington Park trailhead (elevation 6,050 feet), where you'll find some good campsites near the East Verde River.

Washington Park trailhead to Hatchery trailhead, 16 miles (33.2 total miles), 420-foot overall elevation gain, difficult.

This trail segment makes for a long day hike, and it has several dips in elevation that add to the challenge of what is otherwise a moderately difficult trail segment, with several short elevation losses and gains. Along the way you'll pass the old site of Zane Grey's cabin. Grey immortalized—some would say invented—the romanticized image of the Old West with his many novels, the most famous of which is *Riders of the Purple Sage* (1912). The forest is regenerating here from the 1990 Dude Fire, allowing more open sunlight and Rim views than you'll see a decade from now. The recovering areas are where you'll likely spot elk and deer. If you want to make a two-day hike of this long segment, there are a dozen off-trail camping spots here, most of them near one of the four creeks you will cross. Ellison Creek (elevation 6,250 feet) is a handy spot for camping on a two-day jaunt.

As you finish the last several miles of this segment you'll have some particularly nice views of the Rim. After some nine hours of hiking you'll leave the burn area near the 15.5 mile point to end at paved FS 289 and Tonto Creek (elevation 6,170 feet), near the fish hatchery at the end of the road.

Hatchery trailhead to See Canyon trailhead, 10.7 miles (43.9 total miles), 610-foot elevation gain, moderately difficult.

The Mogollon Rim

From the trailhead (elevation 6,170 feet), you set out along one of the most scenic trail sections of this route. You'll move through several meadows along the trail to pass under a power line. Don't take the power line road; look for the trail markers here! You will meet up with Horton Creek and Horton Spring (see Nearby Trails section) at the 3.5-mile point at 6,780 feet elevation. Some of the Mogollon Rim views here are awesome. The wall vaults high above you, stretching into the distance in either direction. From the spring, you'll climb up a steep section to descend around the sweep of Promontory Butte above you, to finally meet up with the Derrick Spur Trail some 3 miles past Horton Spring. You are now at the 6.5-mile portion of this trail segment, and are at your last reliable water source for this part of the trail. From here you savor more Rim panoramas as you hike through 3 miles of fairly open terrain dotted with agave and yucca, to enter See Canyon and sharply descend 500 feet over the final mile to the See Canyon trailhead (elevation 6,180 feet) off FS 284, also called See Canyon Road.

See Canyon trailhead to 260 trailhead, 6.1 miles (51 total miles), 660-foot elevation gain, difficult.

Christopher Creek near the See Canyon trailhead is the last reliable water source on this relatively short trail segment, so load up. Setting out from the trailhead, you climb more than 600 feet up out of the canyon to top off near a gate after 0.8 mile. From here you start on an easy, rolling stretch of trail that lasts to the finish. At 2.1 miles you come to the junction with the Drew Trail as you bear right to continue on the Highline route. The trail undulates over the next 4 miles through pine and spruce stands that obscure any sweeping Rim views, until the sunny terrain changes to an alligator juniper and piñon pine life zone. Finally, you pop out on top of the 260 trailhead parking lot at trail's end (elevation 6,840 feet). There are several camping spots, complete with fire rings, if you choose to camp out.

Nearby Trails

The Highline Trail has a score of trails that branch from its main route, some of which lead to springs, others to canyons, and still others up to the Mogollon Rim. The Horton Creek Trail (see Hike 20) boasts a gushing spring and some excellent backcountry campsites. The panoramic Babe Haught Trail, adjoining the Highline Trail near the Hatchery trailhead, climbs all the way up to the Rim. Both are accessible by car from Fish Hatchery Road (FS 289) along Tonto Creek.

Camping

Backcountry sites lie all along the trail, especially near the creeks. Camp Geronimo is a popular off-trail spot that can also be accessed by car. Reservations must be made with the Payson Ranger District.

For more information, contact the Payson Ranger District, Tonto National Forest, at 928-474-7900. Camping and trail information is available at www.fs.fed.us/r3/tonto.

Prescott and Sedona Areas–
Granite Mountains and Red Rock Canyons

22

Thumb Butte Loop: Hands-Down Spectacular

Location: Prescott National Forest in Prescott, Arizona

Total distance: 2 miles

Hiking time: 1 hour, 15 minutes

Total elevation gain: 650 feet

Difficulty: Moderately difficult

Best months: March through November

Auto accessibility: Excellent

Maps: USGS Iron Springs

Rules: Pets on leash. No horses, bikes, or motorized vehicles. $2 entry fee.

Comments: Why is this the most popular hike in trail-laden Prescott? Come on up and find out! This underrated, 2-mile trail has 10 miles' worth of overlooks. The left (east) side of the loop trail is wheelchair accessible, albeit steep–hike clockwise to use it. Sunset lights up the butte for some magnificent photos.

If you were in downtown Prescott and asked a local where Thumb Butte was located, she would likely walk you outside and point to it. This tall, rosy red rock singularity rises so high from the Prescott Forest that it sticks out like, well, a sore thumb. Thumb Butte's easy accessibility is one reason that the trail draws hundreds of hikers each month, but its panoramic overlooks have to be the main attraction. Those willing to trek the mile to Groom Creek Vista will enjoy wide-ranging views of several valleys and mountain ranges, as well as the Prescott suburbs, all within a 1-hour round-trip hike.

Getting There

From the intersection of AZ 69 and Gurley Road in downtown Prescott, drive 4.5 miles west along Gurley Road, which becomes Thumb Butte Road. You'll pass the entrance to the Prescott National Forest and within 0.2 mile pull into the spacious Thumb Butte parking area on your right. You can see Thumb Butte looming in front of you for the last miles of your drive, so it's difficult to lose your way.

The Trail

Trailhead to Spur Trail Overlook 1.1 miles, 650-foot elevation gain, moderately difficult.

From the Thumb Butte parking lot (5,730 feet), walk across AZ 69 to start up Trail #33, moving counterclockwise by heading to the right along the wide and well-marked trail. The trail snakes its way up through an

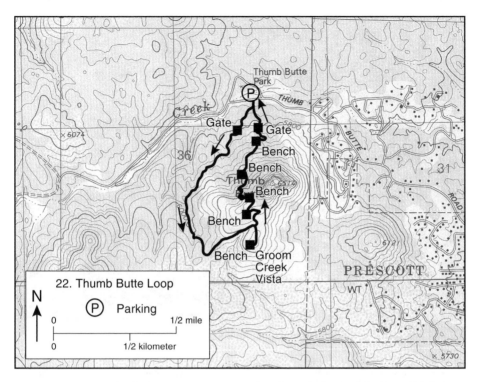

22. Thumb Butte Loop

open sunny forest of tall pines, squat manzanitas and gnarly scrub oaks. Within 0.5 mile, alligator junipers and prickly pear cactus join the trailside foliage show. Thumb Butte (elevation 6,514 feet) looms to your left like a miniature version of Wyoming's Devils Tower: tall, rectangular, solitary. You'll soon see the first of the many benches scattered along the trail, handy rest stops for this elevated walk. And you'll see several of the 13 trailside signs that enrich your knowledge of the butte's history and habitat.

At 0.6 mile you turn onto a paved (to prevent erosion) trail section, for your first of several glimpses of the wavy Bradshaw Mountains south of Prescott. From here, the shady and tall pine habitat changes to the sunnier environs of piñons, junipers, and century plants. The ridge trail soon shows off views of the Sierra Prieta ("dark mountains") Range on your right, basalt mountains that are shadowed with a thick juniper beard. Thumb Butte, so visible for much of your drive and hike to this point, has mysteriously disappeared, occluded by the ridgeline rocks and vegetation.

As you approach the 1-mile point of your hike, Thumb Butte suddenly reappears as you round a turn, more massive than ever. You will shortly arrive at a trail junction with a large alligator juniper at the 1-mile point (elevation 6,240 feet). The loop trail continues to the left, but you want to go straight ahead to jaunt up the 0.1-mile spur trail. You'll dead-end at Groom Creek Vista. The vista is a circular, rock-walled overlook (6,380 feet) filled with benches, likely because so many hikers come here to study the Cinerama views of the Prescott Valley. From here you can survey Flagstaff's Mount Humphreys and the rest of the San Francisco Peaks to your left, with the Black

Thumb Butte

Hills rolling to the right, toward Prescott. Directly opposite you is the humped, tree-covered Bradshaw Mountain, which encircles the Prescott suburbs directly below you. It's surprising that you have these 270-degree viewing prospects after such a short hike up. What a deal!

Spur Overlook to trailhead, 0.9 mile (2.0 total miles), 650-foot elevation loss, easy.

After savoring the diverse landscapes around you, you'll return 0.1 mile down the overlook to turn right and finish the rest of the loop trail. You'll negotiate several moderately steep switchbacks for 0.2 mile to arrive at another trail junction at 6,340 feet, next to a sign about the prehistoric Prescott Cultures. The loop trail, now paved, heads to the left. If you are in the mood for a little rock scrambling, however, the dirt trail to the right climbs some 60 feet over 0.1 mile to the base of Thumb Butte. It's not a route for weak knees or the weak-kneed, but it has some impressive

Prescott Valley and Bradshaw Mountain Range views. Rock climbers use the trail to climb the Butte.

As you head down the paved loop half, you'll notice that this side of the trail has a more dwelling-free view of the Prescott National Forest, a sharp contrast to the more urbanized surroundings of the other half of the trail. The trail descends steeply for 0.6 mile back to your start at the trailhead, along the paved and wheelchair-accessible portion of the trail. Now that you've finished your Thumb Butte trek, you can put your finger on why this tiny trail is so popular.

Nearby Trails

For a pleasant spring wildflower hike, you can't do much better than the 3-mile (round-trip) Pine Lakes Trail that starts from the Thumb Butte picnic area opposite Thumb Butte Trail. This moderately difficult hike rambles through a shady forest before following Willow Creek (look for wildflowers here) through a lush riparian habitat. You won't see any lakes unless your stroll past the end gate to the Pine Lakes subdivision, but it's still a very enjoyable hike.

Camping

The Thumb Butte–Copper Basin road loop has 20 dispersed camping sites along it, and the Thumb Butte parking area has a Granite Mountain group campground. The nearest regular campground is the Yavapai Campground in the Granite Mountain Wilderness, with 25 sites at $10 each. Toilets and water are available.

For more information, contact Prescott National Forest, 344 South Cortez Street, Prescott, AZ 86303. Telephone 928-443-8000 or check the web site at www .fs.fed.us/r3/prescott.

23

Granite Mountain Trail: Prospects Are Excellent

Location: Granite Mountain Wilderness in the Prescott National Forest near Prescott.

Total distance: 7.6 miles

Hiking time: 4.5 hours

Total elevation gain: 1,490 feet

Difficulty: Difficult

Best months: April through October

Auto accessibility: Excellent

Maps: USGS Iron Springs

Rules: Pets on leash. Horses permitted. No bikes in the wilderness trail section. There is a $2 entry fee. No rock climbing on top during peregrine falcon nesting season in winter and spring.

Comments: You can see lots of central and northern Arizona from this trail's many overlook points. This is one of the best summer hikes in the Prescott-Phoenix area, but it can be windy and cool along the Granite Mountain Saddle. High-top hiking boots and a walking stick will help you cope with several steep, rocky sections.

Granite Mountain is the high point, literally, of any hike in the Prescott area. This blocky, slab-sided singularity dominates the urban Granite Mountain Wilderness. Prescott hikers don't take this trail to reach the summit; that requires rock-climbing skills. Rather do they seek the excellent prospects of the valleys and mountains of northern and south-central Arizona, with views from Flagstaff to Phoenix.

Even if the trail didn't have its 360-degree overviews, the rock shapes, colors, and compositions here make it worthwhile journey. On this hike you'll find granite formations in pink, tan, and gray, shaped into blocks, shelves, cliffs, and spheres. And the jagged and dark lava rocks add further texture and color to the trail's intriguing rockscapes. As if the rocks and looks weren't enough, the elevation gain means you'll see three different habitats on your way up, traversing everything from agaves to aspens.

Getting There

From the junction of US 89 and AZ 69 in Prescott, go south on US 89A (Sheldon Road) for 1 mile, and turn right onto Montezuma Drive. Continue straight on Montezuma for 4.6 miles. Montezuma will become Whipple and then Iron Springs Road, and you will turn right onto Granite Basin Road (FR 374). Drive 3.8 miles on FR 374 to the Metate trailhead ($2 entry fee). The start of Granite Mountain Trail #261 (not be confused with Little Granite Mountain Trail) is across from the parking lot and rest rooms.

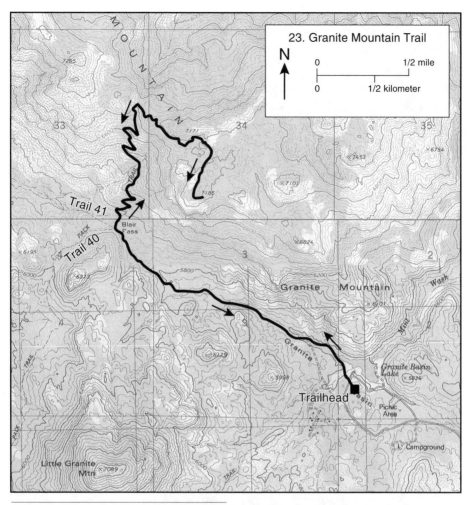

The Trail

Trailhead to Granite Mountain Saddle, 2.8 miles, 1,170 feet, difficult.

Starting out at 5,690 feet, you'll tramp along a wide sandy trail through a mixed habitat of 60-foot pines and alligator junipers. Even at the start, pale and massive Granite Mountain is clearly visible high above you on your right. You'll soon enter the wilderness and gain elevation through some thick stands of oaks, along with piñon and ponderosa pines.

At 0.8 mile the trail steepens markedly as you begin a series of switchbacks, trekking through several tumbles of boulders along the mountain's base. After a mile the tall pines have disappeared in favor of a chaparral habitat of manzanita and mountain mahogany, many of them ornamented with green-gold bunches of mistletoe. The blocky face of square Granite Mountain now dominates the skyline; there's no mistaking your destination ahead as you start up the side of it. From here on, keep your eyes open for peregrine falcons or kestrels—you may see one dive-bombing down from the mountaintop.

Near 1.8 miles, you come to a fenced junction with the Little Granite Mountain,

Granite Mountain

Clark Spring, Iron Spring Road, and White Rock Trails. From here you'll find that the trail is steeper but the views more grandiose. You can now see the smaller mountains around Granite Mountain; they are so boulder-covered they look like they are composed of gigantic marbles. Behind these rubbly hills are the skyscraper outlines of the distant Bradshaw and neighboring Sierra Prieta Ranges. You obviously don't have to wait until you get to trail's end for views.

In this trail section new plants and rocks appear, you'll see prickly pear and century plants show up along the arid, south-facing trailside. The boulders here have a lighter-colored mix of tan and ruddy red, shaded like Jonagold apples. Several large rock walls around you sport a large white stripe of granite through them, adding to the colorful variations of the granite, gneiss, and schist rocks.

After 2.8 miles (6,860 feet elevation) you arrive at the Granite Mountain Saddle. If you are not continuing on to Vista Point from here, take the 0.2-mile side trail that is behind the trail junction sign. This branch has hundred-mile views of the Verde Valley, with Mts. Wilson and Humphreys visible. If you are continuing to Vista Point you'll find these vistas and more, so you don't need the short branch route.

Granite Mountain Saddle to Vista Point, 1 mile (3.8 total miles), 320-foot elevation gain, moderately difficult.

From the saddle you'll continue on a trail section that cuts back and forth along the ridge to present you with alternating overviews of the Sedona and Prescott National Forests. From the junction, the route winds 1.1 miles up through some thick pines and gigantic alligator junipers. The squat, wind-sculpted pines and alligator junipers up here look like gigantic shrubs,

some 12 feet wide but less than 8 feet high. For contrast, some leeward pines are tall and wispy, with bowed branches and long delicate needles, like tropical trees.

When you are 0.75 mile from the saddle you'll pass a VISTA POINT 0.25 MILE sign, next to some massive rock slabs on your right. Now you'll wend along the edge of Granite Mountain above you, as you clamber along a windswept rock ridge piled with granite boulders with the salt-and-pepper texture of headstones, savoring wide views of the Prescott Valley. From here you'll push your way through brush and boulders to trail's end at Vista Point (7,180 feet), a spectacular overlook. Immediately below you lie Granite Basin Lake and Little Granite Mountain (7,089 feet). Behind them you can see the swell of mineral-rich Bradshaw Mountain—you are now at eye level with its 8,000-foot peaks. You'll also find several small aspens entrenched in the cliff and boulder sprawl here, an indicator of the cooler climes that summer hikers seek here.

Vista Point to trailhead, 3.8 miles (7.6 total miles), 1,490-foot elevation loss, moderately difficult.

Take your time coming down from the saddle; the trail has loose and rubbly rock in places. If you are still in the mood for a little hiking, consider taking one of the branch trails that you passed on your way up, such as the Little Granite Mountain route. (See Nearby Trails).

Nearby Trails

There's no shortage of trails around you, with some of the best at the 1.8-mile point of the Granite Mountain Trail. From here you can take the Little Granite Mountain Trail, with its fine views of Granite and Little Granite peaks. You can hike this trail for 2.7 miles and then connect with the 1.7-mile Clark Springs Trail, which will loop you back to Granite Basin Lake and your starting point for the Granite Mountain Trail.

Camping

You'll find several campsites along Granite Mountain Saddle, and several more on the trail from the saddle to Vista Point. As you drive FR 374 to the Granite Mountain trailhead you'll pass the Yavapai campground.

This site has 25 sites that take tents or vehicles up to 40 feet, along with 2 handicapped sites that have hookups. Toilets and water are available.

For more information, contact Prescott National Forest, 344 South Cortez Street, Prescott, Arizona 86303. Telephone 928-443-8000, or check the web site at www.fs.fed.us/r3/prescott.

24

Parsons Spring: A Prayer Answered

Location: Sycamore Canyon Wilderness in the Coconino and Prescott National Forests near Clarkdale, 80 miles north of Phoenix and 35 miles southwest of Sedona.

Total distance: 7.4 miles

Hiking time: 4.5 hours

Total elevation gain: 280 feet

Difficulty: Moderately difficult due to rock hopping and clambering.

Best months: March through December

Auto accessibility: Fair. The last 6 bumpy miles along a rutted road can be negotiated in an auto, but drive slowly.

Maps: USGS Sycamore Basin, Clarkdale SE

Rules: Horses permitted. Pets on leash. Camp only at the end of the trail near the spring.

Comments: This is a lovely and verdant trail that follows a spring-fed stream through multicolored Sycamore Canyon, a dryland oasis that is refreshing in the summer and colorful in the fall. Bring a pair of sandals or aqua shoes for creek crossings. Watch out for poison ivy.

The Parsons Spring Trail is another of Arizona's stereotype-buster routes. Endowed with a clear, spring-fed stream and lush trailside vegetation, this hike belies the preconception that the Phoenix region is all desert. If you are willing to rock-hop a half dozen times across its energetic creek, you'll enjoy trekking along a rolling trail shaded with tall sycamores and cottonwoods, flanked by canyon walls striped in an earth-color rainbow. For those hot-weather hikers seeking a trail oasis in the middle of the arid desert of Arizona's Central Highlands, the popular Parsons Springs trail is a prayer answered.

Getting There

From exit 287 on I-17, head east for 12.5 miles to the junction with US 89A, making a left to go 5 miles through Cottonwood toward Clarkdale. Immediately after you pass the Clarkdale city limits sign, you make a right at the brown Tuzigoot National Monument sign and go down 1 mile to make a left as soon as you pass over the Verde River, entering Sycamore Canyon Road. Drive 4.5 miles down Sycamore Canyon Road to pass a brown Forest Service sign, continuing another 6 bouncy, rocking miles on FS 131 to the Parsons Spring trailhead on your right. From the trailhead you can see the green ribbon of Parsons Spring flowing down below you.

The Trail

Trailhead to first stream crossing, 1.4 miles, 130-foot elevation loss, easy.

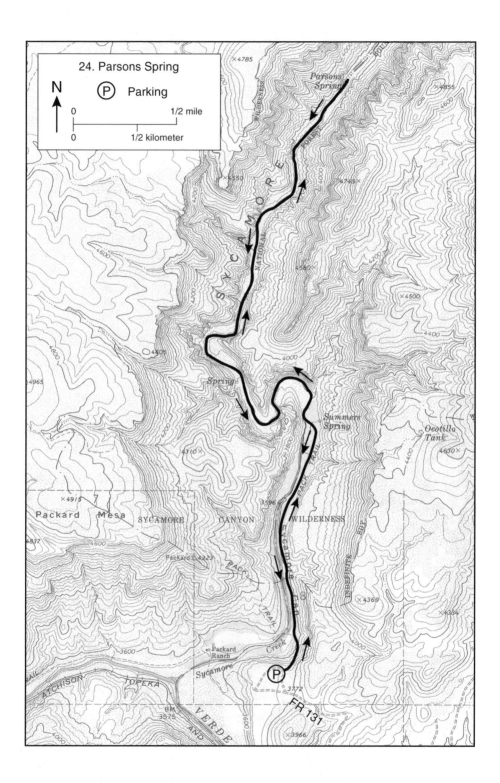

24. Parsons Spring

Ⓟ Parking

N

0   1/2 mile

0   1/2 kilometer

×4785

Parsons
Spring

×4855

×4600

×4745

×4550

×4200

×4000

×4500

×4200

×4400

×4600

4965

4800

×4905

4200

Spring

4000

4400

Summers
Spring

Ocotillo
Tank

×4630

×4310

4310

×4915

Packard   Mesa   SYCAMORE   CANYON   WILDERNESS

3596

4837

4600

Packard t. 4223

PACKARD

Sycamore Creek

×4369

×4384

4400

4000

3600

Packard
Ranch

Sycamore   Creek

Ⓟ

3772

ATCHISON   TOPEKA

VERDE   AND

BM
3575

FR 131

×3966

4000

A trailside pool

From the trailhead at 3,810 feet elevation, you descend 0.25 mile down the wide dirt and rock road to bottom out at a junction with the Packard and Parsons Trails, bearing right to continue along the level path. This trail section is covered with large shady cottonwoods, sycamores, maples, pines, and cypress. Many folks hike this segment just to picnic and play along the creek banks. I've seen entire school classes sprawled along the trailside.

As you hike into the canyon, pay attention to the walls that soar above you—they have an appealing variety of colors, textures, and shapes. Here the canyons rise some 10 stories above you, each side with its own colors and textures. The terra cotta sandstone bluffs on your left have a soft spongy texture, but the basalt and limestone ramparts on your right have a more craggy, brown, and coffee-colored appearance.

As if the water, canyons, and trees weren't enough scenic attractions, wildflow-ers regularly appear all along the trail. In spring and summer you'll find reddish woolly paintbrush, lavender Parry's penstemon, scarlet gilia, yellow columbine, and a rainbow host of accompanying blooms. There are berry bushes in these moist bottomlands too, a pleasant surprise in this arid region. You'll also be surprised to see small fields of grass and floating watercress lining the placid stream, another desert rarity. So, there's lots of ecological diversity to study on your way to the first stream crossing at 1.4 miles.

First stream crossing to third stream crossing, 1.4 miles (2.8 total miles), 60-foot elevation gain, easy.

If you look around the streambed at the first stream crossing (3,670 feet elevation), you'll spy two wire-covered rock cairns, one on each side of the stream. Scout around the cairns to pick your best spot to cross, making a decision to step across the rocks or wade right through the frequently shallow

Sycamore Creek. (You can check at the ranger station for water levels before you go.) After you cross the creek, proceed up the trail. You'll soon see a deep, placid green pool on your left; I've seen blue herons standing over it on a limestone ledge, likely looking for trout. This photogenic spot is perfect for taking a break from the hike.

Hiking past the pool, you'll spot prickly pear cactus and cholla on this drier trail section, along with the orange blooms of the desert globe mallow. The trail wanders along the creek bottom and veers left to roll alongside the canyon walls before it returns to the creek. The trail is but a trace outline here, so remember to mark your way in the sand or build a trailside cairn. About 0.2 mile from the first crossing, you will cross the water again. There are wire baskets of rocks on each side of the stream here, to guide your way.

Once across the stream, you'll enter an area with squarish boulders jutting among the trees on your right, as you walk over several wide flat ledges that hang directly over deep emerald pools of bell-clear water. This trail section could be called the "Trail of a Thousand Caves," for all the holes puncturing the sandstone and limestone parapets around you. From here you'll cross several more rock ledges over the spring, and see some small sections of columnar basalt on your right, a stack of tan and gray spires. In several places you'll actually walk under the rock walls sweeping a hundred feet above you, strolling under an arched rock roof.

After 2 miles, the clear water becomes so deep in some spots that you can't see the bottom, tempting you to take a dip. If you sneak up on them, you'll spy some keeper-size trout swimming near the banks here. You may also see swimmers and anglers visiting this section on weekends, because it's such an appealing spot. Keep an eye out for rattlesnakes and poison ivy as you hike along the rest of the trail. The lush Parsons Spring habitat is popular with all types of living things.

At the 2.8-mile point of the hike (3,730 feet), as you come down off the rocky shelves along the trail, you'll see cairns on each side of the stream, signaling your third stream crossing.

Third stream crossing to Parsons Spring, 0.9 mile (3.7 total miles), 80-foot elevation gain, moderately difficult.

Cross the stream and bear right past the cairn to continue along the trail. You'll soon come to another rock cairn for the fourth crossing. You'll also find several "unofficial" campsites along the way, but there is no camping permitted until you hit the end of the trail at the spring.

At 3.4 miles, you come to the fifth stream crossing, a jumble of pastel pink boulders that are scattered in and around Sycamore Creek. There are several more rock cairns here to guide you along, and some orange blazes on streamside trees. After you cross the stream, the trail becomes more rugged as you clamber over several spots littered with fallen rocks and trees—a good reason to wear ankle-supporting boots!

After 3.7 miles of hiking, you make your sixth stream crossing (3,810 feet) at the foot of Parsons Spring, which quietly seeps out of the canyon walls here to form a peaceful pool. From the spring you can bushwhack above it by crawling over the boulders that fill the streambed, but the seeping water soon ends and you're back in the drylands. Across from the spring you will see several level camping spots with campfire rings, the perfect place to pitch a tent for the night.

Parsons Spring to trailhead, 3.7 miles (7.4 total), 130-foot elevation gain, moderately difficult.

From the spring you backtrack the way you came, again crossing the stream a half dozen times. Don't forget to save some camera film for the return trip, the canyon walls will look dramatically different on the way back. Looking up into the wide expanse between canyon walls, I spotted a dark zone-tailed hawk, with its signature white tail patch, riding the air currents as it skirted the roseate parapets so far above me. What a sight, the perfect ending to a heavenly day on Parsons Trail.

Nearby Trails

As you descend to Parsons Spring from the trailhead you'll cross the junction with the Packard Mesa Trail (#66), a 5-mile entry into the Sycamore Canyon Wilderness. The solitary Packard Mesa Trail rambles across its namesake mesa for the most part before connecting to other trails within the Sycamore Canyon Wilderness. Check the trail description at www.fs.fed.us/r3/prescott /recreate/rec_trai_cv_pm66.htm.

Camping

There are a couple of primitive camping spots at the end of the trail at Parsons Spring. The Potato Patch Campground is some 15 miles east of Clarkdale (passing through the town of Jerome) on US Alt 89. The facility has 40 units, is open May through October, and has 40-foot trailer parking sites. Fees are $10 per night for tents and $15 for trailers. Check the web site at www.fs.fed.us/r3/prescott/recreate/ rec_camppp.htm.

For more information, contact the Verde Ranger District, PO Box 670, Camp Verde, AZ 86322. Telephone: 602-567-4121. A trail description can be found at www .fs.fed.us/r3/coconino/recreation/red_rock /parsons-tr.shtml. and a web search will bring up a score of others.

25

Boynton Canyon Trail: Vortex of Beauty

Location: Red Rocks–Secret Mountain Wilderness in Sedona

Total distance: 4.8 miles (add 0.4 mile for a round-trip visit to the energy vortex)

Hiking time: 3 hours

Total elevation gain: 710 feet

Difficulty: Easy overall, with some moderately difficult inclines at trail's end.

Best months: All year, but hike early in the summer.

Auto accessibility: Excellent. Any car can access the trailhead, and the drive is almost as scenic as the trail.

Maps: USGS Wilson Mountain, Loy Butte. An online trail map with hiking details can be found at www.fs.fed.us/r3/coconino /recreation/red_rock/rec_redrock.shtml.

Rules: Pets on leash, and horses permitted. Red Rocks pass required ($5 a day, $15 a week). No backcountry camping.

Comments: This is an easy trek into a New Age energy center that is also a stunningly beautiful canyon. Don't count on finding water; pack plenty of your own. And expect plenty of company, especially if you are hiking on a spring weekend.

"Thank God for this creation!"

—Author unknown. Comment written in the Boynton Canyon Trail register, March 27, 2003.

What is the most scenic trail in the Sedona area? That's like asking "What is the most beautiful Monet?" or "What is the best Picasso?" It's a difficult question to answer definitively, given the masterpieces from which to choose. To pick the loveliest trail in Sedona, however, the first place to start looking would be the Red Rocks–Secret Mountain Wilderness. The wilderness is a veritable gallery of landscape art: A score of different trails frame scenes of mile-wide canyons counterpointed with jade-green valleys, backdropped with a cerulean sky. Even though it's not difficult to find a trail that is a work of art, an argument can be made that the popular Boynton Canyon Trail is one of Sedona's best, if not the best, scenic trails, a favorite of hikers and photographers.

Hiking the Boynton route, you wind up along vibrantly colored butte and canyon walls that rise almost 1,000 feet above your head, and finish inside a roseate box canyon silvered with seasonal waterfalls. All this scenery is accentuated with songbirds, wildflowers, an occasional javelina, and lush vegetation. But the trail's most unique feature is its side trip to one of Sedona's premier "vortexes," energy centers where the earth's electromagnetic forces are concentrated. The Boynton Canyon Trail is more like a vortex of beauty, where all the ele-

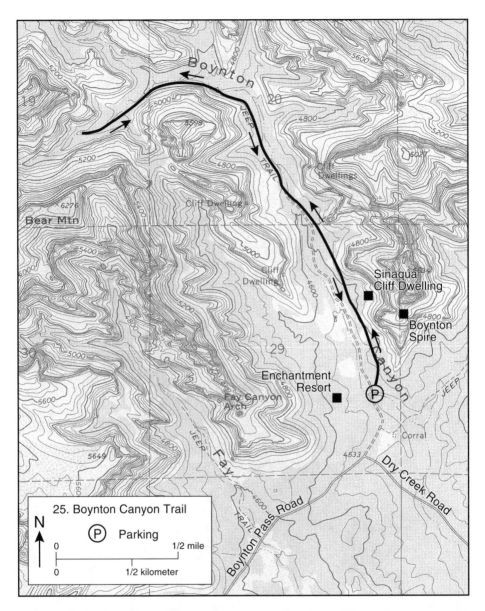

25. Boynton Canyon Trail

N

(P) Parking

0   1/2 mile

0   1/2 kilometer

ments of Sedona's outdoor allure converge in one spot, awaiting your enjoyment.

The Red Rocks–Secret Mountain Wilderness's canyons and pinnacles are strikingly layered with rocks from different geologic periods, forming an earth-color spectrum that varies from deep red to light cream to pale gray. If you see a wall or turret with a brick-red bottom and a light gray top, chances are it's a 300-million-year-old composition of a foundational layer of ancient ocean bottom (limestone), filled with middle sandstone layers from a succession of swamps and deserts, and topped off with a

Sandstone butte along Boyton Canyon Trail

basalt crown from more recent volcanic eruptions. So the erosion-sculpted rock you see is really a composition of rock strata that were added through millennia of dramatic climatic changes: This "desert" has been everything from a swamp to a volcano field.

Getting There

From the junction of US 89A and US 179 in downtown Sedona, head south on US 89A for 2.5 miles (toward Cottonwood) to make a right onto Dry Creek Road. Drive 2.7 miles along Dry Creek Road to its intersection with FS152C, going left for 1.5 miles, to make another right and proceed 0.1 mile to the Boynton Canyon trailhead on your right.

The Trail

Trailhead to trail's end, 2.4 miles, 730-foot elevation gain, easy.

The trail starts at 4,550 feet elevation, a wide, dusty red path that is easy to follow as you head toward the striated cream-and-rust canyon walls in front of you. You soon come to a junction for the vortex-centered Vista Trail, but for now you continue left along the Boynton Trail. In the first 0.25 mile of this sunny section you'll be treated to a variety of desert plants: low-lying manzanita, agave, yucca, and cedars. The colorful vegetation is a pleasant distraction from the mowing and construction sounds that often drift up to the trail from the nearby Enchantment Resort. You'll see Boynton Spire, a multicolored pinnacle, spiking up on your right, one of the trail's most-photographed landmarks.

After 0.25 mile of hiking, you'll face up to steep canyon walls above you as you continue to climb gradually up the trail. Here there are several Sinagua (from the Spanish for "sinagua," meaning "without water")

Native American ruins in the canyon walls around you. You'll see many scrub oaks and piñon pines along the trail, and in late spring and summer this shady trail segment is a welcome respite from the sun. Many lupines and other seasonal wildflowers will also be here, along with a lot of birds.

On my first Boynton Canyon Trail trip, I also spied two javelinas (collared peccaries) scrubbing around under the trees to my right. These bossy little pigs tried to run me off with a few fake charges before they gave up and returned to their rooting, not wanting to waste too much time on yet another tourist.

At 1.1 miles you'll come down the trail to a trail junction sign near the resort, bearing right to continue your entrance into Boynton Canyon. You'll start to see more Gambel's oaks and scaly-leafed Arizona cypress here, and some large ponderosa pines that add to the scenic variety. There are even some Douglas firs that manage to flourish here—this is certainly not a barren environment!

After 1.75 miles the canyon sides change from the brick red and rose of the limestone formations to pale gray basalt and cream-colored sandstone. The walls loom hundreds of feet above you, providing the shade that helps cultivate the trail's concentrations of trees and wildflowers. Near the 2-mile point, in a grassy and shady trail segment, you'll see several small, flat, open campsites for backcountry camping.

As you hike along you'll also spy several trailside clearings populated with small rock cairns. I always try to walk quietly here, because I've seen people meditating at these sites, their legs crossed in a half-lotus position. Maybe they come to draw upon the earth energies that reputedly converge here, or maybe because it's such a lovely and contemplative spot. Either way, it's one of the unique aspects of the Boynton Canyon Trail.

The last 0.25 mile is the most difficult part of the hike. You'll climb over several rock piles, stairstep up several hundred feet, and clamber up a large slant of bare rock at the foot of a canyon wall to arrive at trail's end (5,260 feet). You'll see a sign warning that proceeding any farther up the rock wall will damage the environment, so make this your end point. Now you are at the mouth of Boynton Canyon, it's tall rose-and-rust walls loom above you on three sides, with sweeping countryside views as you look back down the trail–what a scene! Move sideways to the right along the rock face you are standing upon, and you'll find some nice spaces to sit down and savor the flows and juts of the canyon surround, all of it illuminated by that special Boynton Canyon light.

Trail's end to trailhead, 2.4 miles (4.8 total miles), 710-foot elevation loss, easy.

The hike back down is easy and relatively quick, and you may catch yourself moving too fast to fully enjoy its beauty. Take time to study the canyon parapets; they have a different scenic perspective than what you saw on your way up–I hope you saved some film for them!

On your way back, consider taking the Vista Trail over for a vortex visit. (See Nearby Trails.) It's about 300 feet from the Boynton Canyon trailhead and is marked with a sign.

Nearby Trails
The Vista Trail is a short, 0.2-mile side trip off the Boynton Canyon Trail, and it's definitely worth the extra hiking. From the junction with the Boynton Canyon Trail, you head up the hill to follow the narrow trail around a small knoll surrounded by gnarled juniper trees. The knoll is supposedly the center of the vortex energies, so you might plunk down here, compose your mind, and see if you can feel the energy permeate you. Even if you don't feel anything, the scenery makes the trek worthwhile.

Camping
The nearest campgrounds are those lining US 89A north of Sedona, such as the Manzanita Campground. You will find more available camping space and solitude if you continue south on 89A near Cottonwood to Dead Horse Ranch State Park. This attractive park has a 6-mile stretch of the Verde River and full-service camping facilities for everyone from tent to RV campers. Go to www.pr.state.az.us/parks/parkhtml/dead horse.html for up-to-date information.

For more information, contact the Red Rock District, PO Box 300, Sedona, AZ 86336. Telephone: 928-282-4119. There's a useful trail description and map at www.fs.fed.us/r3/coconino/recreation/red_ rock/boyton-tr.shtml.

26

Brins Mesa Trail: Easy to Overlook

Location: Red Rocks–Secret Mountain Wilderness, 3 miles north of Sedona.

Total distance: 6.2 miles

Hiking time: 3.5 hours

Total elevation gain: 780 feet

Difficulty: Easy overall, with several moderately difficult inclines

Best months: All year, but hiking is best early in the summer.

Auto accessibility: Fair. The last 2.5 miles of bumpy forest road can be negotiated by cars that go slowly.

Maps: USGS Wilson Mountain

Rules: Red Rocks pass required ($5 a day, $15 a week). Dogs and horses permitted. No mountain bikes. Backcountry camping allowed 1 mile or more from trailhead.

Comments: Take a high-point tour of Sedona's best red rock scenery by walking to the top of Brins Mesa. This is an extremely popular trail, and justifiably so. The views on your way back are almost as stunning as the views on your way up! Don't count on finding trailside water except in spring months.

Many hikers like to delve deep into Sedona's Technicolor canyons, as you can do on the Boynton Canyon (Hike 25) or West Fork (Hike 29) trails. But how'd you like to be above all that? If so, take a sojourn on the Brins Mesa Trail. Sure, there are awe-inspiring Sedona trails that take you into canyon bottomlands, where the sheer rock walls rise up around you like a stone corridor into heaven. The elevated Brins Mesa Trail, however, opts to take you above it all, transporting you to eagle's-eye views of the sweeping grandeur that you see in many Old West movies, scenes where phalanxes of buttes and pinnacles march off to infinity. With a moderate gradient leading you up to the top, it's easy to overlook all of Sedona's arresting beauty on the Brins Mesa Trail.

Getting There
From the US 179 and US 89A intersection in downtown Sedona, drive south on US 89A for 2.5 miles to Dry Creek Road. Turn right onto Dry Creek Road and go north for 2 miles to a brown trail sign indicating that you should make a right to reach the Vultee Arch Trail. Turn right at the sign onto FS 152, passing a parks pass purchasing station on your right, to bounce 2.5 miles down a corduroy road to the spacious Brins Mesa parking lot on your right.

The Trail
Brins Mesa trailhead to Soldier Pass junction, 1.5 miles, 260-foot elevation gain, easy.

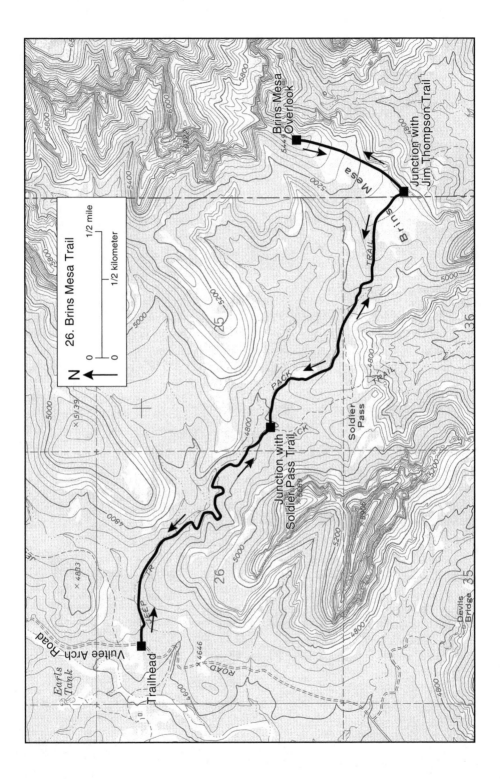

26. Brins Mesa Trail

N ←

| 0 | 1/2 mile |
| 0 | 1/2 kilometer |

Brins Mesa Overlook

Junction with Jim Thompson Trail

Brins Mesa

TRAIL

PACK

Junction with Soldier Pass Trail

Soldier Pass

TRAIL

JEEP TR

Vultee Arch Road

Trailhead

Earls Tank

Devils Bridge

Along the mesa top

Starting out at elevation 4,680 feet, you tramp up a red earth trail that is rocky in spots but generally easy on the feet. In spring you will cross a half dozen trickling streams and placid pools in the first mile, opportunities for (re)filling your filtered water bottles or giving your dog a cooling dip. You'll shortly pass through a wire gate to enter the Red Rocks–Secret Mountain Wilderness. And then the pageant begins.

Typical of the wilderness, this section is verdant with all types of Arizona's unique foliage. Alligator juniper and smoothbark Arizona cypress proliferate, each having its own reptilian characteristics. This unique cypress "molts" its bark like a snake shedding its skin, leaving a trunk so smooth that it looks as if it's been sanded. By contrast, the alligator junipers have thick, scaly bark like the back of an alligator, a texture incongruous with the tree's delicate, green-fingered leaves.

At 1.5 miles (elevation 4,940 feet) you arrive at a junction with the Soldier's Pass

Trail on your right, as you continue straight to head for Brins Mesa.

Soldier's Pass junction to Brins Mesa/Jim Thompson junction, 1 mile (2.5 total miles), 170- foot elevation gain, easy.

Along this trail segment a number of lovely blue-green agaves make their appearance at trailside, accompanied by groves of prickly pear cacti, as the trail gently curves its way to the top of the mesa. Make sure to stop and look behind you as you walk up this shady trail section—the views at your back are as impressive as the ones in front.

After 2 miles of hiking, the wilderness's striking canyons and towers emerge on either side of you, showing off their parti-colored layers of sandstone and siltstone. Cream-colored Shiprock and the smokestacks of Steamboat lie on your right. The views from here to trail's end will become increasingly spectacular, culminating with an awesome overlook point at the end of the trail. You'll also see several flat and open

Alligator juniper

areas near the top of the mesa that are fine for backcountry camping. At 2.5 miles you crest the mesa (5,110 feet elevation) and behold its unobstructed spectacle of varied rock formations.

Hiking along the mesa top, you'll catch the spicy scent of the its many piñon pines, a perfume wafted to you by the cooling breezes that swirl across this sunny tableland. You'll also hear the sweet, piercing songs of the many birds that hop among the pines here. This is a fine spot to sit down and enjoy the mesa's treats for the eyes, ears, and nose. Many hikers picnic here. On the right, you'll see a trail branch to the Jim Thompson Trail, but you'll continue left to follow a trace trail across the mesa to a wonderful viewpoint.

Brins Mesa/Jim Thompson junction to Brins Mesa Overlook, 0.6 mile (3.1 total miles), 350-foot elevation gain, moderately difficult.

The trace trail winds to the left (north) to follow the rim of the mesa, allowing you to tour the fantastic red rock scenery above and below you. It's like walking through a museum gallery of different landscapes; every trail bend and turn offers you a different scenic perspective. As you continue on this trace trail, take several of the short side trails that end at the edge of the mesa; each has its own extensive overlook. One favorite side trail is a path that leads over to a rock shaped like the prow of a ship: You can clamber up the prow and scan the countryside, from south of Sedona all the way over to Bell Rock in the Munds Mountain Wilderness—wow!

Continue along the trace trail as it ascends several wide rock ledges to culminate in an overlook at 5,460 feet, and you'll be glad you did. Here you've found a 360-degree spectacle of rocky ramparts, spires, and tree-covered valleys. It's one of the best vistas in the Red Rocks–Secret Mountain Wilderness. One New Jersey hiker, returning from this unnamed overlook, goggled at me and simply said, "Incredible." After you have finished your own goggling, retrace your steps down the trace trail to head back to the trailhead.

Brins Mesa Overlook to Brins Mesa trailhead, 3.1 miles (6.2 total miles), 780-foot elevation loss, easy.

The trail back down is an easy jaunt, with views of the eastern and southeastern portions of canyon country. After returning to the trailhead, your mind and camera filled with memorable snapshots, you'll be thankful you didn't overlook this trail of overlooks.

Nearby Trails

The Soldier Pass Trail is right (literally) off the Brins Mesa Trail, and it's a worthy side trip. This 1.5-mile (one-way) trek leads you over to several scenic spots, including the largest sinkhole in the area and the Seven Sacred Pools, a series of small rock basins that hold water even in the driest periods, a haven for the local wildlife.

Camping

You'll find backcountry camping sites as you near the top of the mesa, as well as at the top. The nearest spots are in the campgrounds that line US 89A north toward Flagstaff: Manzanita, Bootlegger, Cave Springs, and Pine Flat. For more details on these campgrounds, go to www.redrock country.org.

For more information, contact the Red Rock District, PO Box 300, Sedona, AZ 86336. Telephone 928-282-4119. There's a very useful trail description and map on the web site at www.fs.fed.us/r3/coco nino/recreation/red_rock/secret-canyon-tr.shtml.

27

Secret Canyon Trail: Become a Secret Admirer

Location: Red Rocks–Secret Mountain Wilderness in Sedona.

Total distance: 10 miles

Hiking time: 5.5 hours

Total elevation gain: 650 feet

Difficulty: Moderately difficult

Best months: All year

Auto accessibility: Fair. The last 3 miles are a jouncing ride down a rutted road, but the rest of the drive is excellent.

Maps: USGS Wilson Mountain. There's a trail summary and map on the Forest Service web site at www.fs.fed.us/r3/coconino/recreation/red_rock/rec_redrock.shtml.

Rules: Pets on leash and horses permitted. Red Rocks pass required ($5 a day, $15 a week). Backcountry camping must be a least 1 mile from the trailhead.

Comments: This summer-friendly trail features a Sedona landscape of chaparral, creeks, and colorful canyons. High-water periods create some arresting minifalls along the trail, but this also means you'll have to wade its seasonal streams. Bring wading sandals or shoes. Fall hikes are very colorful.

"I come back to this trail every year. It's just like visiting an old friend." Drew, a veteran Grand Canyon tour pilot, was telling me why he constantly returns to the Secret Canyon Trail. He might have added that it is like visiting a beautiful old friend, one that is easy to spend time with. Along with Boynton Canyon and the West Fork of Oak Creek (see Hikes 25 and 29, respectively), the Secret Canyon Trail has its supporters for the most scenic route in the trail-stitched Red Rocks–Secret Mountain Wilderness. This hike receives high marks not only for its Technicolor canyon scenery, but also for congeniality—it's relatively easy to access and to hike. With all these attractions, there's no secret why this is one of Arizona's best day hikes.

Getting There

From the junction of US 89A and US 179 in downtown Sedona, head south on US 89A for 2.5 miles (toward Cottonwood) to make a right onto Dry Creek Road. Drive 2 miles along Dry Creek Road, enjoying its stunning red rock scenery, to its intersection with FS 152, taking a right to drive 3.2 bouncy miles to the trailhead, where you'll see an old wooden Secret Canyon sign.

The Trail

Trailhead to David Miller Trail junction, 2 miles, 310-foot elevation gain, moderately difficult.

At elevation 4,690 feet, this trail starts through a lush selection of mixed vegetation. You'll see piñon pine and alligator

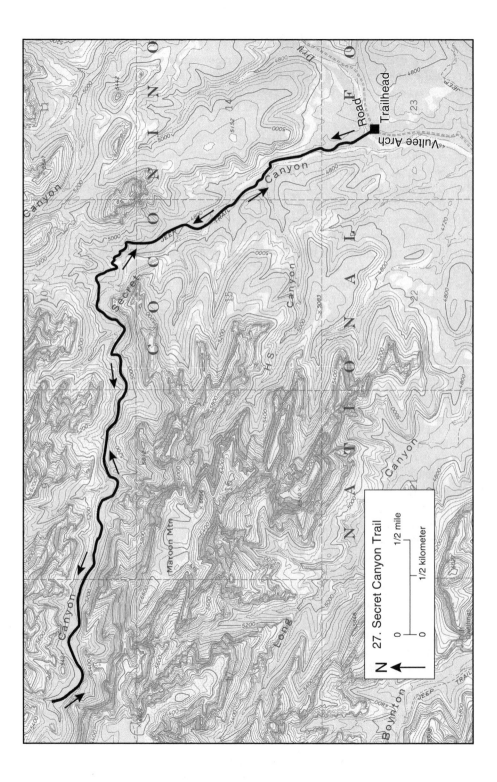

27. Secret Canyon Trail

N

0   1/2 mile

0   1/2 kilometer

juniper trees standing among an understory of chaparral and desert cactus habitats, with the ubiquitous manzanita as an ecological intermediary. The red earth path has a soft, crunchy texture that is perfect for hiking, yielding enough to ease your knees yet not so soft that it pulls at your feet. Hike here in cool weather, when the air is crisp and piñon-perfumed, and you'll feel as though you could go forever.

The canyon landscape unfolds before you as you crunch along. In the first mile, the roseate Secret Canyon walls sweep out before you in an open spectacle, but in a few miles these massifs will crowd around you like welcoming friends, sweeping over your head as you enter the canyon proper. A shape-shifting creek gurgles along this trail segment, morphing from emerald stream to silver chute to jade pool as you go along. By summer this carpet of water will be a mere thread and most of its pools a memory, but in spring it celebrates its fullness by serenading you with its cascading rhythms.

Along the trail you'll spy a variety of birds flitting among the trees and manzanitas, including the raucous red-cockaded woodpeckers that frequent these open spaces. Just 0.5 mile from the trailhead, agaves (century plants) show up along the path, adding their blue-green hues to the low-slung emerald landscape. After you make several (usually) shallow stream crossings you'll arrive at the junction with the HS 50 Trail at the 0.7-mile point.

You approach the mouth of the canyon at the end of your first mile. The trail steepens as you go up to meet the canyon walls that were waiting for you in the distance when you started. The stream now beats a calypso tattoo on the boulders that line its bottom. This is not a featureless dry gulch you are hiking into, but a verdant watery ascent with a comforting touch of humidity, a spicy pine fragrance, and an eye-filling landscape of red rock ramparts. It's a multisensory treat. After 2 miles of hiking you come to a junction (5,000-foot elevation) with the David Miller Trail on your right (See Nearby Trails).

David Miller Trail junction to trail's end, 3 miles (5.0 total miles) 340-foot elevation gain, moderately difficult.

Bear left from the David Miller Trail junction, continuing into Secret Canyon. The seasonal stream fights its way down several rocky channels here, creating small cascades and waterfalls for you to enjoy. Keep your eye out for poison ivy, by the way, because it's all by the way! Groves of manzanita trees now appear, their twisted oxblood trunks as thick as a python. I love looking at these contorted trees. Each has its own shape and shade, its own personality.

As you hike farther into the canyon, the trailside habitat will change to a shady zone of sycamores, box elders, maples, and oaks, all littering the trail with their leaves and cones. You'll repeatedly cross the stream over the next couple of miles, passing campsites under the shady trees. This trail segment is fun for some photography or rock watching, because the canyon turrets now soar hundreds of feet above your head and take all sorts of shapes: here a bird, there a person, another place a bear.

The canyon trail will narrow to a 50-foot gap as you clamber over a tumble of massive red sandstone slabs, looking as if someone had blown up a giant's sidewalk. Continuing on, you'll discover a small meadow with a stand of immense ponderosa pines that surrounds several more campsites.

Finally, at the 5-mile point, you come to a series of deep pools, where the stream cascades down in front of you over a 20-foot-wide, rocky ledge. You can continue for

Miles of Sedona canyons

miles past the pools and waterfall, but the trail becomes increasingly difficult to follow, so you might want to turn around here and enjoy a return hike that is almost as scenic as your hike into Secret Canyon.

Trail's end to trailhead, 5 miles (10.0 total miles), 650-foot elevation gain, moderately difficult.

As you return down the trail the valley floor spreads beneath you, revealing a panorama of Sedona's colorful canyons and pinnacles. After you complete this hike, I bet you'll become a Secret admirer, like the rest of us who have hiked it.

Nearby Trails

On your way to or from Secret Canyon, why not do a little exploring and take the short (1-mile) but strenuous David Miller Trail? Named in 1996 for a forest ranger who completely disappeared while hiking in the area, the route climbs up to a high plateau with jaw-dropping views. If you scramble farther along its trace trail you can connect to the Bear Sight Trail for a 6-mile loop hike back to the Secret Canyon trailhead. (The last stretch is along the forest road.)

Camping

There are all sorts of backcountry camping sites scattered along the trail. Several have stunning views and are just over a mile from the trailhead. The nearest campgrounds line US 89A north toward Flagstaff: Manzanita, Bootlegger, Cave Springs, and Pine Flat. For more details on these campgrounds, go to www.redrockcountry.org.

For more information, contact the Red Rock District, PO Box 300, Sedona, AZ 86336. Telephone: 928-282-4119.

28

Sterling Pass–Vultee Arch Trail: Capital Gains

Location: Red Rocks–Secret Mountain Wilderness, 7 miles north of Sedona on US 89A.

Total distance: 5 miles

Hiking time: 3.5 hours

Total elevation gain: 2,330 feet

Difficulty: Strenuous

Best months: March through October

Auto accessibility: Excellent. The trailhead adjoins US 89A, but it's tricky finding a place to park next to the road.

Maps: USGS Munds Park, Wilson Mountain

Rules: Pets on leash and horses permitted. Red Rocks pass required ($5 a day, $15 a week). Backcountry camping allowed 1 mile in from the trailhead.

Comments: If you can endure the elevation gain, this precipitous hike rewards you with solitude and spectacular scenery. Because it's shady most of the way and has a higher elevation than most area trails, this is one of Sedona's most comfortable summer hikes. Pack plenty of water, regardless.

Where have all the tourists gone? I had just driven out of a Sedona teeming with thousands of spring-break tourists who filled the roadside shops and trailheads, but here I was hiking up a nearby trail with no one in sight. Why wasn't the trailhead highway flanked with the rental cars of out-of-state visitors? Perhaps the Sterling Pass Trail is just a bit too far north of Sedona for some folks to drive, or perhaps it is the thousand-foot ascent to the pass that scares off casual day-trippers. Whatever the reason, hikers who want to be far from the madding crowd will like this scenic but challenging trail, a high-point "windowpane" into the spectacular backcountry scenery of the Red Rocks–Secret Mountain Wilderness. And don't let the breath-taking elevation gains stop you. After all: no gain, no pane!

Getting There

From downtown Sedona, drive 7 miles north on US 89A to the Manzanita Campground, located at milepost 389.5. About 300 feet away on the opposite side of the road, you'll notice a 3-foot-wide red dirt path snaking up from the highway. That path is the trailhead; you can see a small metal sign bearing the trail's name next to it. Park beside the highway, because there is no parking lot for this trail.

The Trail

Sterling Pass trailhead to Sterling Pass, 1.5 miles, 1,130-ft. elevation gain, strenuous.

As you start up the trailhead (elevation 4,860 feet) you begin an almost continual

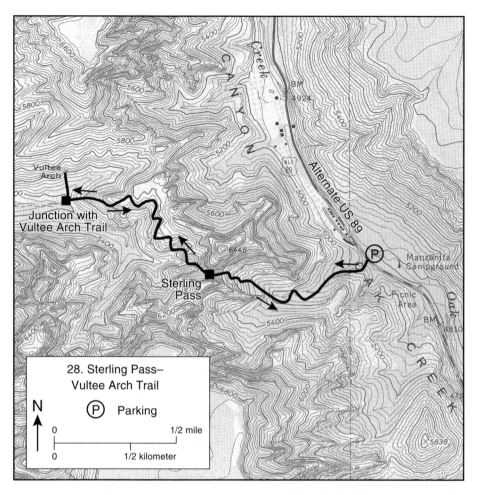

28. Sterling Pass–
Vultee Arch Trail

N

Ⓟ Parking

0   1/2 mile

0   1/2 kilometer

ascent that lasts for the next 1.5 miles, as you step up a series of rock shelf staircases to the pass. Fortunately, the trail is very shady, flanked by scaly-barked Gambel's oaks and alligator junipers at the outset, with tall pines appearing after the first 0.5 mile. As soon as you start hiking this route you'll spy vivid red sandstone walls and turrets on either side of you. One of my favorite rock shapes here is a junior version of New Mexico's Shiprock formation, which appears on your right after 0.5 mile up the trail. As you near the top after 1.25 miles, you'll also see a number of cream-colored Coconino sandstone pinnacles, indicating you've hiked up through some 20 million years of canyon geology.

Finally, at 5,990 feet, you top off at a wide slot between two rock monoliths. This is Sterling Pass. Some hikers stop here, content with their rigorous hike to the pass. But the next part of the trail leads to even more spectacular views, and it's an easy trip down, so we'll persevere onward!

Sterling Pass to Vultee Arch, 1 mile (2.5 total miles), 1,020-foot elevation loss, easy.

At Sterling Pass, take a minute to catch your breath and stare out at Oak Creek

Vultee Arch

Canyon below you. It's a pleasant vista, although the views on the way up were even better. Looking back the way you came (east), you can see over to the Mogollon Rim, so far is your perspective. Heading west from the pass, you embark on a 0.5-mile series of long switchbacks down a soft dirt path shaded with 80-foot ponderosa pines, until the trail levels out next to an energetic (in spring) creek at 4,870 feet.

Follow the creek west for 0.3 mile, trekking through a zone of white-barked Arizona sycamores, their hydra trunks branching in every direction. You'll cross the shallow stream several times before arriving at a steel sign that signals the junction of the Sterling Pass and Vultee Arch Trails. Take the right branch and you'll clamber about 0.25 mile and 180 feet in elevation up some red rock slopes to pause next to a metal commemorative plaque embedded in the slope (elevation 5,050 feet). From the slopes you can spy Vultee Arch on your left in the distance, looking like a highway bridge carved out of red and brown rock. You can bushwhack closer to the Arch, but most folks are content to stay here and study this magnificent rock formation, as well as the Technicolor canyon views to the west. It's one of Arizona's best sightseeing spots.

Vultee Arch terminus to Sterling Pass trailhead, 2.5 miles (5 total miles), 1,020-foot elevation gain, strenuous.

Return the way you came, making sure you are prepared for the 1,020-foot switchback up from the creek bottom to Sterling Pass. As you top the pass and descend, be careful picking your way down the steep trail, making sure you don't step on any of the loose rocks. (A hiking pole can be quite handy here.) As you emerge next to the road and head for your vehicle, you'll be a bit tired from all that climbing, but the long-term capital gains of pinnacled beauty and high-country solitude should have paid off your investment of effort.

Nearby Trails

The West Fork Trail (Hike 29) is 4 miles north of Sterling Pass Trail on US 89A. One of the most popular trails in Arizona, this 3-mile hike lets you stroll next to a lovely stream and lush riparian foliage as you savor the canyon walls that sweep above you on either side. Start early to beat the warm-weather crowds. The trailhead entrance is at milepost 384.5 on US 89A.

Camping

Once over the pass, you'll find several back-country camping spots on the downside of the trail and alongside the creek bottoms. For more formal camping, the 19-unit Manzanita Campground is only 300 feet from the Sterling Pass trailhead, but it's often full in peak season, and it does not accommodate trailers. If Manzanita is full or if you have an RV, try the 60-unit Pine Flat Campground a few miles further north on US 89A. Both facilities have drinking water and are open from May to September. Fee is $15 a night. For more details on these and other nearby campgrounds, go to the web site at www.fs.fed.us/r3/coconino /recreation/red_rock/rec_redrock.shtml

For more information, contact the Beaver Creek–Sedona Ranger District, 250 Brewer Road, Sedona, AZ 86336. Telephone 928-282-4119. There's a useful trail description and map at www.svinet2. fs.fed.us/r3/coconino/recreation/red_rock/ sterling-pass-tr.shtml.

29

West Fork Trail: Hiking with Red and Rocky

Location: Red Rocks–Secret Mountain Wilderness in Sedona

Total distance: 6.5 miles (14-mile shuttle hike)

Hiking time: 3.5 hours

Total elevation gain: 150 feet

Difficulty: Easy, with a few moderately difficult stream crossings.

Best months: April through October

Auto accessibility: Excellent, the trailhead is right off 89A between Sedona and Flagstaff.

Maps: USGS Wilson Mountain, Munds Mountain, Dutton Hill. You can find a trail summary and map at www.fs.fed.us/r3/co conino/recreation/red_rock/westfork.shtml.

Rules: Pets on leash and horses permitted. No bikes. Red Rocks pass required ($5 a day, $15 a week). There is a $5 parking fee. Backcountry camping must be at least 6 miles from the trailhead.

Comments: The most popular hike in Sedona's treasure chest of trails, West Fork Trail features the best attractions of Sedona's canyon country. This is a relatively comfortable summer trail, because most of the route is in a shady, moist canyon. Locals hike this trail in October, when the canyon is leafed of in gold and red.

The temperature is a crisp 60 degrees on this sunny day, typical of early spring weather in the Sedona area. I'm starting out on one of Arizona's best-loved canyon hikes, the West Fork Trail.

My constant companions on this journey are two handsome Oak Creek siblings, Red Canyon and Rocky Creek (a.k.a. the West Fork of Oak Creek Canyon and the West Fork of Oak Creek). Rocky Creek is a mercurial traveler. Along the way he constantly changes face from a tumbling emerald stream to a somnolent amber pool and back again. You have to keep your eye on him as you walk, because you never know what he'll do next. But then, that's why it's fun to follow him.

Red Canyon is almost as unpredictable as Rocky. He starts out stiff and upright, his red-orange sandstone cap glowing in the cloudless sky, standing hundreds of feet above me. But after I hike next to him for a mile he stoops protectively over me, allowing Rocky and me to travel in shade under his arched, mossy shoulders. Farther along the trail, Red stands back up and gives us some space, but his awesome presence is never far away. With Red and Rocky constantly switching their appearance, I'm entertained the entire trip along the West Fork Trail. Isn't it time you hiked with Red and Rocky? They certainly have lots to show you.

Getting There

From Flagstaff, go south on US 89A for 20 miles, passing mile marker 385. From the junction of US 89A and US 179 in downtown Sedona, head north on US 89A (Oak

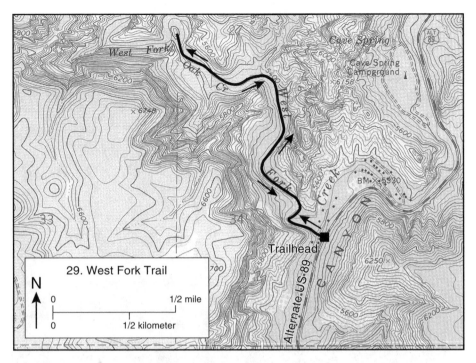

N

0   1/2 mile

0   1/2 kilometer

Creek Canyon Road) for 12 miles, just past mile marker 384. The West Fork parking lot is on the west side of 89A, but it fills early. If it's filled, drive 0.25 mile north to the Call O' the Canyon parking lot.

The Trail

Trailhead to trail's end, 3.25 miles, 160-foot elevation gain, easy with a few moderately difficult stream crossings.

Starting out at elevation 5,290 feet, the first trail mile whisks you away from civilization and into Oak Creek Canyon's precipitous walls of red Coconino and buff Kaibab sandstone, a gateway to the 44,000-acre Red Rock–Secret Mountain Wilderness. Stone mile markers are posted every 0.5 mile to help you along this twisty but level route.

In the first mile you pass an old homestead to gently climb through the pines and firs that line Oak Creek's feet, passing several wavy fields of ferns. If it's spring, the trees will be decorated with a palette of gaily colored songbirds. If it's summer you'll find one of the largest wildflower bounties in the Red Rocks Wilderness along the trail: yellow and crimson monkey flowers, ivory-white daturas, indigo larkspur, and golden columbine. And poison ivy, too, so be careful out there.

Over the second mile you may have to cross the creek a dozen times in rainy periods, but you can traverse the rocks and limbs that bridge this (usually) shallow stream to keep your feet dry. This is a good place for a walking stick and river sandals. This trail section is where Oak Creek Canyon begins to arch over you, its curved walls eroded into fantastic animal and object shapes. After 2 miles you'll be surprised to find several small patches of bamboolike plants growing near the water's edge. These are rushes, also known as horsetails, and they initiate the final mile of the maintained trail into the canyon. In summer many hikers refresh themselves here

On the trail

by diving into the trailside pools, and it's a great way to beat the heat.

Around the 3-mile mark the sheer canyon walls close in upon you, and in high water periods the creek swamps the trail. This is not the end of the trail, however, so wade the stream if it's not too high and continue on. After 0.25 mile of clambering over some rocky spots you come up to the canyon walls standing directly in front of you, with the creek pooled across the foot of the wall. This is the end of the West Fork Trail. If you're willing to wade and swim through the creek, however, you'll be rewarded with another 10+ miles of spectacular and solitary trail, all the way to Forest Road 231. (Don't hike this in high water periods!) Otherwise, turn around here and hike back to the trailhead, leaving Red and

Rocky where you met them, waiting to meet the next lucky visitor.

Nearby Trails

If the West Fork Trail is too crowded for your tastes when you visit it, drive south down the road a couple of miles and take on the more solitary Sterling Pass Trail (Hike 28). The alter ego to the easygoing West Fork Trail, this rigorous trail gains over 1,100 feet in its first 1.5 miles to Sterling Pass, providing open vistas rather than close-in canyon views. From the top of the pass you can hike down to one of Sedona's best-loved landmarks, Vultee Arch.

Camping

If you plan to camp in the canyon, you'll have to hike to the end of the West Fork

Trail and proceed into the backcountry for another 3 miles, because camping isn't allowed in the first 6 miles. Campgrounds line US 89A north and south of the West Fork Trail: Manzanita, Bootlegger, Cave Springs, and Pine Flat. Pine Flat and Cave Springs are often the last to fill up. For more details on these campgrounds, go to www .redrockcountry.org.

For more information, contact the Red Rock District, PO Box 300, Sedona, AZ 86336. Telephone: 928-282-4119.

High-Country Havens

30

Escudilla Mountain: Golden Bowl

Location: 5 miles north of Alpine in the Escudilla Wilderness of the Apache-Sitgreaves National Forest.

Total distance: 5 miles

Hiking time: 3 hours

Total elevation gain: 1,140 feet

Difficulty: Moderately difficult

Best months: May through September

Auto accessibility: Good. The last 0.5 mile is rock and requires slow driving in passenger cars.

Maps: USGS: Escudilla

Rules: Not recommended for horses. Pets on leash allowed. No bikes.

Comments: A meadow-filled trek up to statewide prospects on Arizona's third-highest peak. For all its elevation gain, this is a pleasant hike even for novice hikers, with a gradual incline along a well-marked trail. The fall colors make it a magnificent autumn hike.

After reviewing three different trail descriptions of the Escudilla Lookout Trail, I was prepared for a 7-mile round trip that would take me the better part of a day. Imagine my surprise when, after several stops for photos and elevation readings, I popped out onto Escudilla Mountain after two hours and 2.5 miles. The shorter-than-expected distance and time only gave me more time to walk around the summit's lookout tower and ogle the entrancing views of New Mexico and northern Arizona. With its wide-open vistas from every angle, you can spend as much time touring around the mountainside as you spent going to it.

"Escudilla" is Spanish for "wide bowl," and the massif's meadow-lined sweep is clearly evident as you hike through its aspen and spruce habitats to the summit's lookout tower. You'll also pass through golden meadows decorated with irises and butterflies, so there's plenty of eye candy to sweeten your journey into the user-friendly Escudilla Wilderness.

Getting There

From Springerville, drive south on US 191 for 25 miles to make a left near mile marker 420, heading east on Forest Road 25. Continue on the moderately rutted forest road for 4.5 miles to make a left and drive slowly along a rough dirt and rock road for 0.4 mile to the Escudilla Wilderness sign on your left.

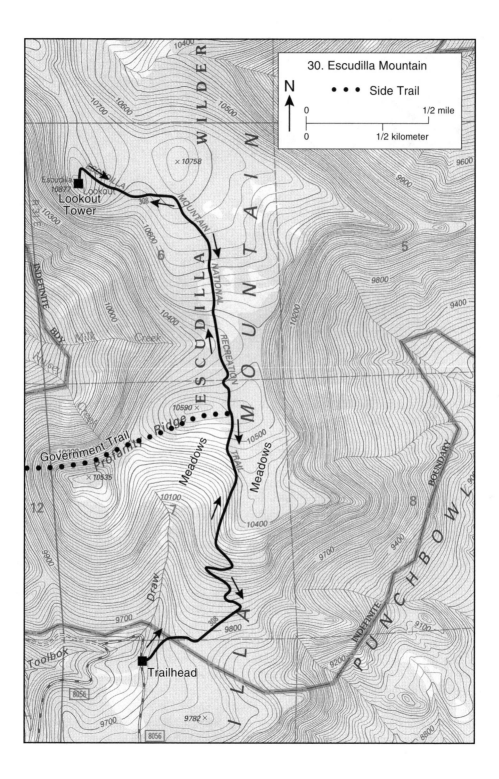

30. Escudilla Mountain

••• Side Trail

0   1/2 mile

0   1/2 kilometer

N

Escudilla Lookout Tower

Escudilla 10877

Government Trail

Profanity Ridge

Meadows

Meadows

PUNCHBOWL

Trailhead

Toolbox

8056

8056

Escudilla Mountain lookout tower

The Trail

Trailhead to Government Trail junction,1.2 miles, 780-foot elevation gain, moderately difficult with several difficult inclines.

The trail starts behind the Forest Service signboard next to the wilderness sign (elevation 9,720 feet). After a rocky start, the trail smooths out as it climbs up through several stands of dense aspens. There are several steep sections along the trail, but they are relatively short segments that don't require many rest breaks. You'll encounter your first meadow at the 0.5-mile point. The meadows provide you with westward glimpses of the vast plateau of the Mogollon Rim, with more sweeping views the higher you climb. In summer you'll see numerous bouquets of bluebells and Rocky Mountain iris gracing the open meadows, the feature flowers of the numerous blooms along the Escudilla Trail. It's a lovely, calming perspective that prompts many to plop themselves in the grass for a scenery break.

After 0.75 mile you'll dip down into a grove of statuesque Douglas firs and Engelmann spruce for 0.2 mile, to emerge into a large grassland named Toolbox Meadow. Heading up into the meadow, you come to a sign for the Government Trail on your left (elevation 10,500 feet). The junction is a great spot for a water break (pack your own, there's none on the trail) and to spot elk lounging around this wilderness pasture. The view westward down the meadow shows off the San Francisco Peaks and the craggy hump of Mount Baldy, the second-highest peak in the state (see Nearby Trails section). After a meadow break, continue up the clearly marked Escudilla Trail toward the lookout.

Government Trail junction to Escudilla Lookout, 1.3 miles (2.5 total miles), 360-foot elevation gain including top of lookout tower, moderately difficult.

There is little elevation gain the rest of the hike. That makes for a steady pace that lends itself to sightseeing, and there's plenty to see along this trail stretch. The track gradually winds through several more shady stands of Engelmann spruce and white fir, interspersed with summer meadows of irises and leopard butterflies. This entertaining grassland-to-forest pattern continues for the rest of the hike, until at 0.2 mile from the top you scale a few steep but short switchbacks to come up to the base of the Escudilla lookout tower at 10,880 feet.

The mountaintop views are very impressive, but they are even better if you climb the lookout tower, the highest one in the state, and walk around the tower's outside railing. Now you can see the Mogollon Rim's buttes and mountains ripple across the western landscape, highlighted by Mount Baldy to the northwest, Mount Graham to the southeast, and the neighboring Blue Range peaks and canyons just south of Alpine. If you look to the east you can study the Black Range peaks of New Mexico's nearby Gila Wilderness. Needless to say, there are a lot of Kodak moments up here near 11,000 feet. (The summit is officially listed at 10,912 feet.) An added hiking convenience is an outhouse located opposite the lookout tower.

Lookout to trail's end, 2.5 miles (5.0 total miles), 1140-foot elevation loss, moderately difficult.

The hike down is an even downhill almost all the way, but pay attention to where you step. There are lots of loose rocks on the trail in several of the shady forested sections, and you can turn an ankle if you are day dreaming too much. But even a sore ankle is worth this most beautiful of "bowling trips."

Nearby Trails

The popular West Baldy Trail leads you near the summit of the second-highest peak in Arizona. The summit itself is a sacred Apache site and is off limits to hikers. Be that as it may, the 7-mile hike up to the mountaintop guides you through some verdant streamside scenery on your way to panoramas of Escudilla Mountain, the Blue Range, and the White Mountain Apache Reservation. Route descriptions for this hike are on the web site at www.hike arizona.com, and at www.fs.fed.us/r3/asnf /recreation/trails/alpine_trails/trl_alp_ escudilla.shtml.

Camping

There are several primitive camping spots among the conifers near the top, if you bring enough water for a night's bivouacking. There are also several pull-in primitive campsites along FS 25 near the gemlike Hulsey Lake. Many hikers prefer to camp at Alpine Divide, 3 miles south of the Escudilla Trail turnoff on US 191. Campground information is at www.fs.fed.us/r3/asnf/recreation/camp grounds.

For more information, contact the Alpine Ranger District at 928-339-4384. Detailed topographic information on the trail is available at www.public.asu.edu/~bvogt/ 20-20/escudilla/in-escudilla.html.

31

KP Trail #70: Cross Creek in a Canyon

Location: Blue Range Primitive Area in the Apache Sitgreaves National Forest near Alpine.

Total distance: 18.8 miles

Hiking time: 12 hours

Total elevation gain: 2,810 feet

Difficulty: Difficult

Best months: May through October

Auto accessibility: Excellent. From US 191 it's a short drive along a well-paved highway.

Maps: USGS Strayhorse, Bear Mountain

Rules: Dogs on leash and horses permitted.

Comments: A summer wilderness trail that is surprisingly verdant, watery, scenic, and solitary. For a memorable overnighter, hike for 5 or 6 miles and camp in the canyon bottom next to its crystal creek. Wear high-top boots for the ankle-turning pebbles on this rock-and-roll (your ankle) trail.

Solitude, sweet solitude! After finishing a neighboring trail that was populated with two large groups of northern Arizona schoolchildren, I was prepared for lots of company when I headed out for the KP Trail. Surprisingly, when I pulled into the trailhead next to picture-perfect KP Meadow, I was the only weekend visitor there. In fact, no one had registered at the trailhead for six days! The solitude remained for the rest of my trip through the canyon. Not a single person crossed my path on a crisp June day that was as energizing as the trailside scenery.

The KP Trail is that rarest of birds, a highway-accessible wilderness trail that has retained its wilderness character and beauty. Why this route isn't filled with summer hikers is as big a mystery as the "KP" appellation given to it in the 1920s.

Antedating the wilderness designation movement, Arizona's Blue Range was designated a "primitive area" in the 1930s, to preserve its unsullied wildlands. Home to Mexican gray wolves and hordes of elk, the Blue Range Primitive Area is as wild as any wilderness, and is blessed with a 200-mile web of hiking trails so interconnected that a trail map of the area looks like a city street atlas. The KP Trail is one of my favorites because it shows off most of the area's outstanding features: wide grassy meadows, dense spruce-and-fir forests, canyon views above and below you, frenetic streams and waterfalls, maybe even a glimpse of a wolf. This is one of those memorable trails that had me planning my next summer visit to it before I had even finished the first.

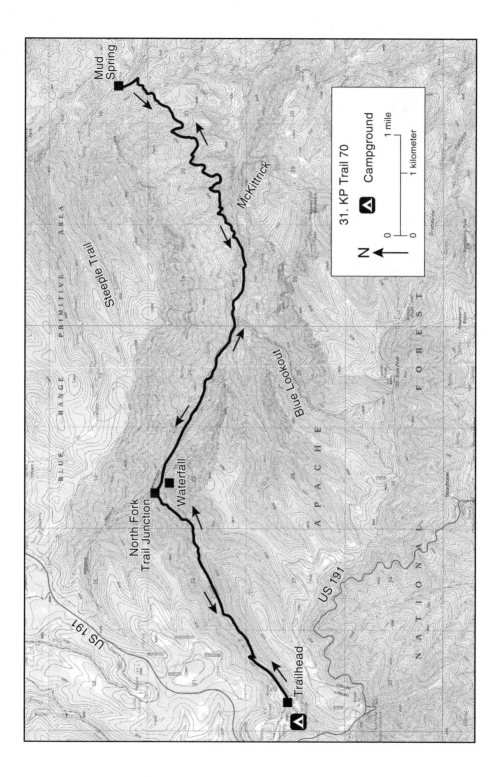

Campground

N

0
0

1 mile

1 kilometer

Mud Spring

Steeple Trail

PRIMITIVE AREA

BLUE RANGE

McKittrick

Blue Lookout

North Fork Trail Junction

Waterfall

APACHE

US 191

US 191

NATIONAL

FOREST

Trailhead

Getting There

From Alpine, drive south 26 miles on US 191 past milepost 227, turning left into the KP Cienega Campground road. Drive 1.3 miles down the well-maintained gravel road to the trailhead, 0.2 mile in front of the campground.

The Trail

Trailhead to waterfalls, 2.9 miles, 1,400-foot elevation loss, moderately difficult.

The trail starts behind the trail register (elevation 8,960 feet), cutting through a lush watered meadow to head toward a forest of tall Engelmann spruce and Douglas fir. After 0.5 mile, the South Fork of KP Creek joins you along the trail, and at the 0.9-mile point you cross the stream for the first of dozens of times along your hike. The rocky earthen trail weaves its way through the 80-foot firs, pines, and spruce that fill the shallow canyon, as it moves along a ridge next to the creek. This trail segment's feature wildflower is the bright, eye-catching red columbine. There are hundreds of these elegant flowers bordering the trail on your way to the waterfalls, which explains why hummingbirds zoom around this part of the trail. You'll also find a number of fallen trees blocking your path, so be prepared to clamber over them. Although the forest understory is blanketed with ferns and other low-lying plants, this creek-hugging trail is easy to follow.

At the 2.9-mile point of your journey into KP canyon, you to come to a junction (7,560 feet elevation) with North Fork Trail #93, leading left to US 666. After you pass the junction, some 50 feet up the trail you can spy two lacy waterfalls on your right, wafting down some 15 feet into the bush-lined creek. This spot is also a junction where the South and North Forks of KP Creek merge to become KP Creek, which follows you for the next 3 miles. It's surpris-

ing to find waterfalls in a high desert environment, but this trail has all sorts of scenic surprises. For example, as you hike over the next 0.5 mile you may spot some spiny claret cup cactus clinging to the trail's big basalt boulders, showcasing their scarlet summer sprays.

Falls to final creek crossing, 3.7 miles (6.6 total miles), 970-foot elevation loss, moderately difficult.

From the waterfalls, the trail climbs above the creek before dipping down to cross the stream dozens of times along the way, which is the reason I've nicknamed this trail "Cross Creek." Another 0.1 mile brings you to several primo campsites near the creek, level spots complete with fire rings. The path has become a bit wilder now because there are more fallen trees and large rocks on the path, but there isn't anything here that can't be stepped over. The small difficulties in hiking this trail section are compensated for by the scenery. There are a score of creek riffles and tumbles gushing over a rocky streambed fenced with alders, maples, and willows—there are so many types of trees on this trail!

The route continues along the creek as it cuts under several small red and gray bluffs that arch protectively above you. Bouquets of scarlet penstemon now appear, supplanting the red columbine as the boss bloom. There are even several caves etched into the limestone above the water. The trail continues to alternately rise above the creek and then descend to it, adding to your modest elevation gain. You'll also see several more streamside campsites along the way, and hordes of summer butterflies. With lots of flora and fauna to identify, you might want to bring a field guide along for this trek.

After 4 miles of hiking, you'll see the misty Blue Mountains rising on each side of you as the canyon opens up and becomes

The Blue Mountains

sunnier. The trail habitat changes from a shady spruce-and-fir environment to a drier and more open pine-and-juniper life zone thickly carpeted with pine needles. At the 5.6-mile point you arrive at a trial junction with the Blue Lookout Trail (6,810 feet) as you scramble along the rocky streamside trail. Near the 6.6-mile benchmark you cross the creek one last time at 6,590 feet to start switchbacking up the side of the canyon.

Last creek crossing to trail's end, 2.8 miles (9.4 miles total), 440-foot elevation gain, difficult.

After crossing the creek you begin to switchback steeply up the canyon side. Now the trailside habitat is a desert one of scrub oak and alligator juniper, dotted with yucca, nolina, and cactus. This sunny section can be quite hot, so you should pack plenty of water for this last stretch of the trail. As you climb up the canyon you are treated to spectacular views of the Blue Mountains around you, including Bear Mountain and craggy Sawed-Off Mountain. And the views down into KP Canyon hundreds of feet below you are just as entrancing.

Finally, at the 9.4-mile point of your journey, you come to the top of red rock KP Mesa and the junction with the Steeple Trail (elevation 7,230 feet). Mud Spring is a short jaunt from the junction, which is predictably muddy, but it may be flowing enough to refill your filtered water bottle for the trip back.

Trail's end to trailhead, 9.4 miles (18.8 total miles), 2,370-foot elevation gain, difficult.

If you've hiked to the end of the trail you'll want to camp somewhere for the night, and the best spots are back down the trail past the first stream crossing. The return up the canyon to your start is a steady, even grade that is easy to accomplish, especially with all the riparian scenery to distract you from your efforts. However far you hike into the KP Trail, you'll enjoy your journey along the little-used trail.

Nearby Trails

The 9.2-mile Raspberry Trail is just south down US 191 from the KP Trail, and like the KP it's a scenic riparian hike with lots of solitude. The trail meanders through piñon and juniper woodlands before it heads into Raspberry Creek Canyon. And guess what berry bounty you'll find here in summer?

Camping

The KP Cienega Campground is my type of camping spot. It's secluded and scenic, provided with bathroom facilities, flanks the trailhead, and it's free. If I didn't have to leave the area because a forest fire broke out, I might still be camped there. There are backpacker camping spots scattered along the first 6 miles of the trail. Most of them are shady, open spots near the stream, perfect for summer camping. Camping info is at www.fs.fed.us/r3/asnf/recreation/camp grounds.

For more information, contact the Alpine Ranger District at 928-339-4384.

32

Foote Creek and Clell Lee Cabin: Consider the Lilies of the Field

Location: Hannagan Meadows, 23 miles south of Alpine, in the Apache Sitgreaves National Forest.

Total distance: 2.5 miles (1.25-mile shuttle hike)

Hiking time: 1.5 hours

Total elevation gain: 50 feet

Difficulty: Easy

Best months: May through October

Auto accessibility: Excellent

Maps: USGS Hannagan Meadow

Rules: Pets on leash and horses permitted. No bikes or motorized vehicles.

Comments: An easy and attractive hike to an Old West homestead set in a picture-perfect meadow. This trail is part of the extensive Hannagan Meadows cross-country ski network.

If you ever want to take summer hiking vacation in Arizona, you can't do better than setting out along the Hannagan Meadows trail system. Set in the 8,000-foot elevations of the Blue Mountains, the KP Trail (see Hike 31) and a score of other routes guide you into the many streams, canyons, and summits of the 180,000-acre Blue Ridge Primitive Area. This is an untrammeled preserve, where there are regular sightings of wolf, bear, and elk. Solitude-seeking hikers revel in the area's backpacking bounty, venturing along a web of trails that routinely exceed a dozen miles in length.

The beautiful Hannagan Meadows plateau is not just for distance hikers, however. It also has some strikingly beautiful short trails, typified by the Foote Creek hike that starts opposite the Hannagan Lodge.

Getting There

Driving south from Alpine, go 23 miles along US 191, better known as the Coronado Scenic Byway. The Byway is often listed among America's top scenic motor routes, and the drive is almost as pretty as the hike. Turn left off US 191 just past milepost 232 and the Hannagan Meadows Lodge, at the road marker for trails 73 and 76. Drive 0.3 mile down the well-maintained gravel road to a large parking lot with several horse corrals, which is the trailhead for the Foote Creek Trail and Steeple Trails.

The Trail

Trailhead to Highway 191, 1.25 miles, 50-foot elevation gain, easy.

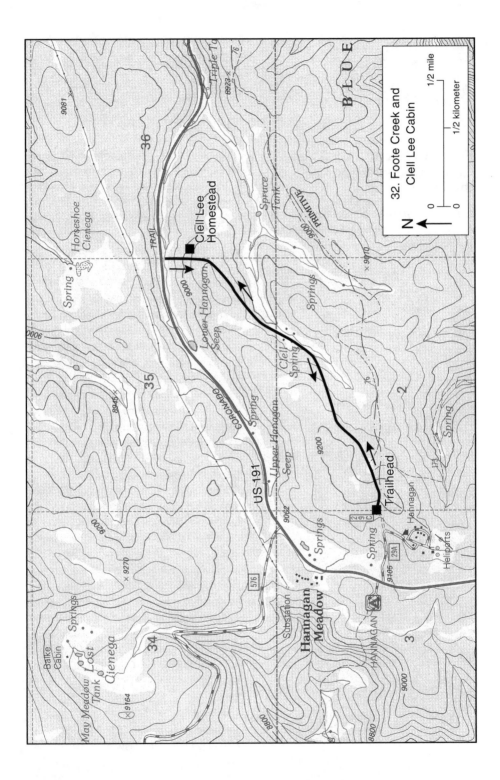

32. Foote Creek and
Clell Lee Cabin

The Clell Lee homestead, a remnant of the Old West

Walking past the trail marquee (elevation 9,110 feet), you move along a wide earth path that tours through a transitional forest, where young upstart conifers are replacing large, old aspens that nurtured them in their shade. Here the forest is densely packed with tall Colorado blue spruce, Engelmann's spruce, Douglas fir, and quaking aspen. You can actually hear the trees creak as they rub against one another in the wind.

At 0.2 mile you come to a trail sign indicating that the Foote Trail is to your right, but you continue straight ahead along the wide, straight path. As you continue, the Hannagan area's famous meadows emerge to sweep across your view. The meadow fields are awash with waves of thick green grass and are gaily daubed with clumps of wildflowers such as the violet-blue Rocky Mountain iris, also called the snake lily or fleur-de-lis. Squint your eyes and you might think you are gazing at the world's largest Impressionist landscape painting. This iris is rare in most of

Arizona, but it flourishes here in the cool, moist meadows. The trailside trees are blazed with notches set into the trunks, and there are diamond-shaped metal markers above them, so your route is easy to follow.

At 0.5 mile you come to the fenced border of the old Clell Lee homestead, a cabin with some log outbuildings from the bygone days of the Old West. Walk through the opening in the fence and continue past the homestead, perhaps pausing here for a nap or to explore the cabin grounds, or for a picnic in the lush meadow grasses.

From here, hiking past the cabin to trail's end is like walking through a wide green carpet runner, with the meadow carpet stretched some 30 to 100 feet on each side of you, walled by the gracefully bowed limbs of 8-story Engelmann spruce. If you are lucky enough to be here in late spring or early summer, you'll gape at the riot of iris and other wildflowers that enliven the meadow carpet. This is a place to take photos for those back home who think that Arizona is all cactus and desert!

Continuing on the trail, you'll pass one of the small marshy ponds that are characteristic of cienegas, or marshy meadows. This is a morning spot for elk and deer. You'll also find several campsites set in the meadows and back among the trees, nice overnight spots for first-time backpackers. At 1.25 miles you come the trail's end at US 191 next to a small asphalt pull-in spot (elevation 9,160 feet).

Highway 191 to trailhead, 1.25 miles (2.5 total miles), 50-foot elevation loss, easy.

From the highway it is an easy stroll back through the meadow to your car, a pleasant walk that leaves you with enough energy to explore more Hannagan Meadows attractions.

Nearby Trails

The Steeple Trail (#73) starts right from the Foote Creek trailhead and heads 13 miles into the Blue Ridge Primitive Area. This strenuous trail moves through a variety of habitats: thick conifer forests, boggy meadows, and arid piñon and juniper woodlands. Elk and wolves have been spotted in the nether regions of this trail, and it draws many backcountry wildlife watchers. The Steeple Trail also connects with five other trails in the Blue Ridge Primitive Area, making it a handy, off-highway starting point for extensive backpacking trips.

Camping

The Hannagan Meadows Campground, at 9,200 feet, is one of the highest in Arizona. That means it's also one of the coolest, in terms of temperature. The forested campground is opposite the highway from the Foote Creek trailhead, just past the Hannagan Meadows Resort. It has 8 sites that can accommodate vehicles to 16 feet, as well as tents. Well water and handicapped-accessible toilets are available, but there are no hookups. There is no camping fee. The campground is open from late spring to early fall. Check the web site at www.fs.fed.us/r3/asnf/recreation/camp grounds.

For more information, contact the Alpine Ranger District, PO Box 469, Alpine, AZ 85920. Telephone: 928-339-4384. The Apache Sitgreaves National Forest website is at http://www.fs.fed.us/r3/asnf.

Playing Above the Mogollon Rim

33

White House Ruins Trail: The Word for "World" Is "Canyon"

Location: Canyon de Chelly National Monument, near Chinle on the Navajo Reservation.

Total distance: 2.4 miles

Hiking time: 2 hours

Total elevation gain: 600 feet on the return

Difficulty: Moderately difficult

Best months: March through November

Auto accessibility: Excellent

Maps: USGS Del Muerto

Rules: No pets or horses on trails. Except for the White House Ruins Trail, you must hire a Native American guide ($15 an hour) to accompany you on a trail.

Comments: An easy hike into the spectacular canyon home of the Navajo. Start early on the trail to avoid the crowds that frequent it and pack your own water.

I've laced up my hiking boots, filled my water bottle, and strapped on my backpack—it's time to go to church. I'm hiking in Canyon De Chelly National Monument, a spiritual and geographic center of the Navajo nation. Although the Navajos regard all outdoors as holy ground, Canyon de Chelly is especially revered because its 130 square miles contain the remains of the mysterious Anasazi ("Ancient Ones"), the Navajos' fourth-century predecessors. Hiking the monument's three canyons is walking ground twice holied by place and heritage, with the sacred relics that are the Anasazi cliff dwellings ensconced in Canyon de Chelly's 500-foot sandstone walls like religious statues in the alcoves of a church or temple.

Many Western canyons are inhospitable environments, rocky gashes in the earth's crust with narrow rubbled bottoms, chasms where only a few hardy plants or animals survive. The wide floor of Canyon de Chelly, on the other hand, is an oasis of fruit trees, farms, and roaming livestock.

A descent along the White House Ruins Trail is a descent into another world, a world sheltered from weather and intruder by the soaring canyon walls around it. Small wonder that the Ancient Ones built their homes high up in the rock faces of these protective ramparts. This is the reason the Navajo call this place "Tseyi" which means "in the rock." The canyon floor is a world of living history, its sights and sounds documenting two millennia of Native American life, and the White House Trail is your entry point into it.

Getting There

Canyon De Chelly is near Chinle, Arizona, 345 miles from Phoenix via I-40 and US 191. From Chinle, drive 3 miles east on AZ 64 to the monument visitor center. From the visitor center drive 5.5 miles along South Rim Drive and turn left at the sign for the White House Trail. Drive 0.3 mile to the wide parking lot next to the canyon overlook, which is the start of the White House Ruins Trail (elevation 6,220 feet).

The Trail

White House Ruins trailhead to White House Ruins, 1.2 miles, 600-foot elevation loss, easy.

The trail starts along a wide concrete sidewalk that leads to a canyon overlook, veering left to wind down toward the valley floor. The first part of the trail is bordered with large rocks, making it easy to find the correct path across the open rock face that the trail traverses. At 0.2 mile you corkscrew around the trail to walk through your first tunnel. From here you can see the entire trail unravel at your feet, all the way to the bottom.

From the tunnel the trail gradually switchbacks down to the valley floor, on a distinct route channeled into the canyon wall. Although this trail segment is almost entirely solid rock, as you hike it morphs into a variety of textures beneath your feet. In some places you'll walk across shallow ridges of rock, as if you were traversing a sandstone grill.

In other places the trail rock is styled in smooth, shallow ripples, and it's like walking on a petrified ocean roller. Although the trail itself is entertaining, the real marvel unfolds in the canyon below you, with more canyon walls and rock formations revealing themselves as you descend.

Gazing at the valley floor, you can see the first tiny Navajo farm appear, with livestock and crops encircling the traditional hogan, a ceremonial dwelling built with no corners for spirits to hide in. At 0.9 mile you walk through another short tunnel in the rock to emerge next to the small farm you saw from above, backdropped by skyscraper canyon walls of terra cotta sandstone. But this pastoral scene is not a Kodak moment: There are signs requesting that you take no photos.

Turn left at the farm and walk along the sandy canyon bottom, where you may see several herds of sheep rambling by, jingling their collar bells. You'll then pass through two miniature groves of feathery-leafed tamarisk trees, arching over the trail like a miniature version of the South's canopy roads. The soft, sandy trail encourages you to walk slowly, as befits a hike on hallowed ground.

After 0.3 mile, at the 1.2-mile point, you walk past a set of rest rooms on your right to come to a sign explaining the White House Ruins (elevation 5,620 feet). The largest house is at the valley floor, an 80-room dwelling first inhabited by the Anasazi about a.d. 1100. A second house (for emergency security?) is enshrined in a small cave some 50 feet above the canyon bottom.

Built of the surrounding sandstone, these dwellings seem to have grown from the rock instead of being built, so deftly do they merge with their environment. In one of my previous careers I interviewed I.M. Pei, the world-famous architect. He remarked that his inspiration for designing the National Center for Atmospheric Research (NCAR) was the way that Mesa Verde's and Canyon de Chelly's dwellings magically merged with their environment. Their symbiotic "spirit of place" led him to use native stone for NCAR,

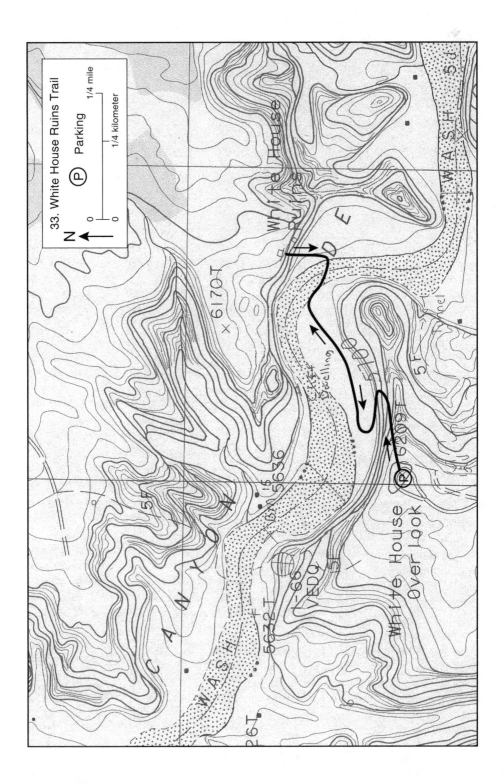

33. White House Ruins Trail

(P) Parking

N

0
0

1/4 mile
1/4 kilometer

Anasazi cliff ruins

so it would blend with its surroundings. Thus do the Ancient Ones still teach us today, if we will attend to their stories.

White House Ruin to trailhead, 1.2 miles (2.4 total), 600-foot elevation gain, moderately difficult.

On your return, make sure that you bear right and follow the canyon wall, so you don't continue down the road in the valley floor. You are now gaining back all that elevation you lost on your stroll down, so it may be a good time to sit on one of the benches placed along the trail, to study the canyon below.

Nearby Trails

To hike the other park trails you must hire a guide, and I thoroughly enjoyed my 4-mile (one-way) guided hike from the Tunnel Overlook across the valley floor. The guide pointed out several ruins and petroglyphs that I would have missed by myself, and filled me in on the history of the farms we passed. Once you learn to ignore the tour jeeps that rumble across the valley floor, abrading the timeless ambiance like a curse in church, you can enjoy the unique sights of this outdoor museum. You can arrange for guides at the visitors center. Here's a tip: For a one-way shuttle hike, you can have a friend of the guide (often a younger member of the family) meet you at one of many overlook spots along the rim and drive you back to your start.

Camping

The Cottonwood Campground is just south of the visitors center, providing easy access to the canyon rim. Within the 96-site, year-round campground there are rest rooms and a dumping station, but no hookups. Sites are filled on a first-come, first-served basis.

For more information, contact the Canyon de Chelly National Monument visitors center at 928-674-5500. Or check the web site at www.nps.gov/cach.

34

Buffalo Park Loop: Take a Walk on the Tame Side

Location: Eastern Flagstaff, 1.5 miles from city center.

Total distance: 2-mile loop

Hiking time: 1 hour

Total elevation gain: 40 feet

Difficulty: Easy

Best months: March through October

Auto accessibility: Excellent

Maps: USGS Flagstaff East

Rules: Pets on leash. Bikes permitted.

Comments: One of Flagstaff's prettiest little trails is also one of its easiest and most convenient, offering a causal stroll through a wide-open parkland bordered with mountains. This wide, flat, and solid trail is wheelchair accessible. There is a water fountain at the trailhead.

There are some days when you want to leave the mountain climbing to Sir Edmund Hilary, or let Lewis and Clark do the exploring. Maybe your mind and body are tired from one too many high-country travails, or maybe you have only a few hours to grab a slice of nature before you return to civilization. These are days when you just want... a walk in the park! The Buffalo Park Trail will fully satisfy such wants. This route has the open space and uncluttered scenery of a mountain trail, yet it has the ease and accessibility of a city park. So, when you are

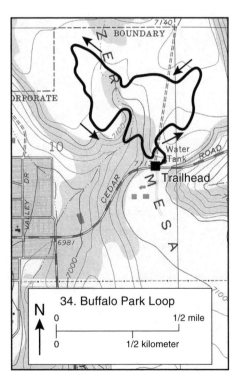

34. Buffalo Park Loop

On the Buffalo Park Loop

looking for a casual and social hike, leave your mountain boots at home and put on your sneakers—it's time to take the Buffalo Park Trail.

Getting There

Starting from the intersection of US 40 (66) and San Francisco Avenue in downtown Flagstaff, drive 1 mile north on San Francisco Avenue, heading toward the mountains, then make a right onto Forest Avenue. Follow Forest Avenue for 1.5 miles to turn left at the Buffalo Park sign and drive into the parking lot on your right.

The Trail

From the trailhead parking lot you can see the entrance to Buffalo Park, a roofed gateway that frames Mt. Elden and the San Francisco Peaks. Almost any time of day, you'll see knots of walkers and runners moving around this popular trail loop. Walk through the gateway to start on the Buffalo

Trail (elevation 7,150 feet), a 9-foot-wide gravel path that snakes across the perimeter of an open meadowland studded with ponderosa pines.

This is one trail where you won't need a GPS or a map. The trail is flat as a pool table and has mileage signs every 0.25 mile. For most of the trail you can see your starting point near a two-story green storage tank.

Trail distance is user-adaptable. If Uncle Harry from Queens is feeling a little overwhelmed by the 2-mile distance, he can bail out by using a cutoff back to the trailhead. If Cousin Serena feels the need to add some distance and altitude, she can join the Oldham Trail from this path and enter Flagstaff's extensive mountain trails system (see Nearby Trails section). Or she can use the workout stations placed along the route.

From the trailhead, custom dictates that you head right (counterclockwise) at the

Playing Above the Mogollon Rim

trail crossroads 300 feet from the start, strolling along toward tower-capped Mount Elden (9,699 feet elevation) directly in front of you.

Birds love Buffalo Park as much as Flagstaffians do, so you are apt to enjoy the sweet trills of the hermit thrush and other birds as you loop around the park.

At the 0.6-mile point junction (7,165 feet elevation) you continue straight ahead, or you can go right to enter the forest trail system or shortcut back along the utility access path to the trailhead. From the junction, Mount Humphreys (12,633 feet) and the San Francisco Peaks are very visible, and the ponderosa pines become larger and denser along the trail.

At 1.75 miles you enter a small forest of pines and Gambel's oaks as you top the high point of the trail at 7,190 feet, from which you will then amble back to your starting point. What a pleasant way to spend an hour in the city!

Nearby Trails

From the back loop of the Buffalo Trail, a 500-foot hike to your right takes you into the trailhead for the two Oldham trail loops, comprised of Oldham (5.2 miles round trip) and Easy Oldham (3.0 total miles). Using these trails you can scramble along the trees and rocks along the base of Mount Elden, or connect to a week's worth of trails that take you all the way up to Mount Humphreys. This is why you will see hikers loaded with three-day backpacks walking along the tame Buffalo Park Trail. The Buffalo is a handy gateway to all sorts of hiking and backpacking adventures.

For more information, contact the City of Flagstaff Department of Parks and Recreation at 928-779-7685.

35

Heart Trail: Hiking to be Above It All

Location: North Flagstaff, in the Coconino National Forest.

Total distance: 7.6 miles

Hiking time: 4.5 hours

Total elevation gain: 1,720 feet

Difficulty: Difficult

Best months: April through October

Auto accessibility: Excellent. A few forest road miles off US 89.

Maps: USGS Flagstaff East, Sunset Crater West. You can purchase a detailed Flagstaff trails map at area bookstores or at www.emmittbarks.com.

Rules: Pets on leash, bikes and horses permitted. No motor vehicles.

Comments: This mixed-habitat hike up the south side of Mount Elden gives you unobstructed views of Flagstaff's famous Volcanic Highlands. Bring plenty of water on this trail, as you won't see any after Little Elden Spring at the start of your hike. And wear high-top boots for the steep ascent and descent over the last mile of the Heart Trail (a.k.a. "Heart Attack" Trail).

There are times when you want civilization's social surround, and other times when you just want to be above it all so it can't get to you. The Heart Trail fulfills the latter objective for Flagstaff area hikers. This rigorous trail is just a few miles past Flagstaff's busy Mount Elden trailhead, but it's much less populous than the latter trek, appealing to those who want a bit of solitude on their journey to higher places. Yet the Heart Trail has much of the scenery that attracts hikers to crowd up to Mt Elden: overviews of the Flagstaff cityscape, glimpses of Sunset Crater and its volcanic surround, and en route studies of Mount Elden's own volcanic rock formations. At 8,810 feet in elevation, the Heart Trail is a good bet for those who want to be above it all, and away from most.

Getting There

From Flagstaff, drive north 8 miles along US 89 to pass mile marker 423, and turn left onto Elden Springs Road (Forest Road 556), driving another 2 miles along the dirt and gravel road to a brown sign that reads "Little Elden Springs Horse Camp." Park in the roundabout opposite the sign, and walk across the road past a Little Elden Springs sign to come to the spring itself, pouring from a hose into a metal drum set in the earth. Walk left from the spring to start along the Sandy Seep Trail.

The Trail

Little Elden Spring to Heart Rock trailhead, 1.7 miles, 220-foot total elevation gain, moderately difficult.

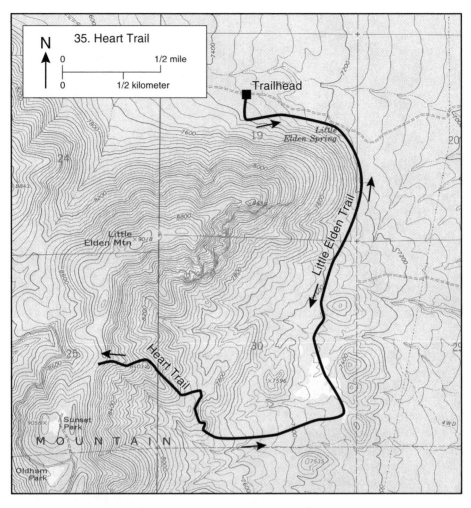

Trailhead

Little
Elden Spring

Little Elden Trail

Little
Elden Mtn

Heart Trail

Sunset
Park

M O U N T A I N

Oldham
Park

From Little Elden Spring (elevation 7,150 feet), go left to pass through a wire fence and start on the Sandy Seep Trail. This trail segment is the quintessential Arizona lowland ramble, undulating over some shallow gulches through a sunny landscape of piñon and ponderosa pines. Hiking in and out of the trail's shallow depressions, you'll gain another 60 or so feet in elevation. In spring you'll find many small patches of creamy white desert rose flowers, shrubby bouquets that are scattered among the Gambel's oaks and Arizona madrones.

Crowned with relay towers, Mt. Elden (9,295 feet) looms above you as you tramp along this well-marked dirt trail. The mountainsides above you are denuded of trees, victims of the 1977 Radio Fire that swept up Mount Elden and its neighboring peaks. The absence of trees, however, allows you to see more of the craggy mountainside rockscape than you can perceive from the many forested Flagstaff trails.

After 1.6 miles, you'll notice that the landscape is looking less like a desert and more like a transition forest, with 70-foot

---

Majestic view from the Heart Trail

ponderosa pines scattered around the gentle slopes of a grassy meadow. Another 0.1 mile among these shady pine giants takes you to the Heart Trailhead on your right (elevation 7,310 feet).

Heart Trailhead to trail's end, 2.1 miles (3.8 total miles), 1,500-foot elevation gain, strenuous.

As you start up the Heart Trail, you soon leave the large pines behind and return to the oak and madrone landscape of the arid chaparral. The first trail mile is a steady climb up toward the ridge leading toward Mt. Elden. Then, during the second mile of the hike, you begin to gain some serious elevation, switchbacking 20 times up the mountainside as you head toward the top of the Mt. Elden Ridge. This last mile of this dusty red trail can leave you gasping, so take some scenery breaks en route. The views of Flagstaff and the Coconino Plateau only become more expansive as you ascend. Looking left, to the northeast, you can

understand why they call this region the Volcanic Highlands: There lies the 1,000-foot-high cinder cone of Sunset Crater National Monument and the Bonito Lava Flow that surrounds it like a petrified river. These volcanic views are rare trail sights this side of Hawaii, so pause to enjoy them.

After 2 miles up the trail you'll notice it shading into a cream yellow color, a sign that you are less than 0.2 mile from the top. You'll then complete several more short switchbacks and pass a pair of pinnacles on your immediate right, to finish along a high ridge forested with some tall firs and pines that escaped the Radio Fire. A Heart Trail sign here tells you that you have reached the end of the trail (elevation 8,810 feet). If you spend any time at this junction, you are likely to meet either hikers coming down from the Mt. Elden lookout another 1.7 miles south of you or those climbing up from the Little Elden Trail. You can use the Little Elden Trail as an alternate return route.

Playing Above the Mogollon Rim

When you have rested up at the trail junction, return the way you came or loop back along the Sunset Ridge and Little Elden Trails (see Nearby Trails).

Heart Trail terminus to trailhead, 3.8 miles (7.6 total miles), 1,720-foot elevation loss, moderately difficult.

Descending the Heart Trail is all downhill, but that doesn't mean it's a walk in the park. Watch out for loose rocks underfoot, which can turn your hike into a skin-scraping slide. If you brought a hiking pole or walking stick you'll put it to good use on this trail segment, bracing your descent and taking a load off your knees. After a mile downhill the trail levels out as you jaunt down to the Sandy Seep Trail junction, going left to return to the spring and the start of your journey.

Nearby Trails

At the end of the Heart Trail, you can make an 8.4-mile loop hike out of your trip by going right (north) to take the Sunset, Little Bear, and Little Elden Trails (4.8 total miles) back to your start. You'll have lots of east valley views along this way, and views of 12,633-foot Mount Humphreys. Another alternative is to turn right at the end of the Heart Trail and follow the Sunset Trail another 1.8 miles and 500 feet up to Mount Elden's summit and its expansive east-west views.

Camping

Your best backcountry campsites would be near the start of the your hike along the Sandy Seep Trail, near Little Elden Spring, and at the shady but waterless junction of the Sandy Seep and Heart Trails. The Bonito Campground has 44 sites with places for tents and trailers up to 22 feet. The grounds have drinking water and flush toilets. The campground is 7 miles north of your trail turnoff on AZ 89, where you make a right to go 2 miles along FR 545 to Sunset Crater National Monument.

For more information, contact the Peaks Ranger Station, 5075 North Highway 89, Flagstaff, AZ 86001. Telephone: 928-526-0866. For trail and camping information, check the web site at www.fs.fed.us/r3/coconino/recreation/peaks/rec_peaks.shtml.

36

Kachina Trail: A Well-Known Secret

Location: North Flagstaff, in the Kachina Wilderness of the Coconino National Forest.

Total distance: 10 miles (5.2-mile shuttle hike)

Hiking time: 6.5 hours

Total elevation gain: 590 feet

Difficulty: Difficult round trip due to distance, moderately difficult as a shuttle hike.

Best months: May through September

Auto accessibility: Excellent, with paved roads all the way to the parking lot.

Maps: USGS Humphreys Peak. You can purchase a detailed Flagstaff trails map at area bookstores or at www.emmittbarks .com.

Rules: Pets permitted on leash. No bikes in the wilderness. Horses permitted.

Comments: An all-day, high-country ramble along the side of the San Francisco Peaks. Decked out in fir forests and aspen groves, this trail is both a shady summer hike and a glorious fall color walk.

Panoramic, more panoramic, most panoramic. The farther along the Kachina Trail I walked, the more expansive the views became. The path continually parted its cloaks of dark green conifers and golden aspens to reveal the sweep of northwest Arizona beneath it, from Flagstaff across the Coconino Plateau to the Grand Canyon. Although this scenic trail is easily accessed, out-of-town hikers often bypass it to tackle the more elevated trails that climb up to Mount Humphreys (Hike 37) and the other San Francisco Peaks. But their loss is your gain in solitude, as you roll along one of the locals' most popular day hikes, a secret to visitors, the vista-laden Kachina Trail.

Getting There

From Flagstaff, drive north 8 miles on US 180, making a right just before mile marker 223 onto Snowbowl Road (Forest Road 516). Drive up this twisty but well-paved road for 6.5 miles until the road dead-ends with a barrier across it. Turn right at the barrier and drive 300 yards down to the road's end and park your car in front of the trailhead.

The Trail

Kachina trailhead to twin aspens, 2.5 miles, 180-foot elevation loss, moderately difficult.

At the trailhead (elevation 9,340 feet) you begin a rolling ramble through groves of some of the largest aspens you'll see anywhere, counterpointed with huge firs and pines. The clearly marked trail is soft underfoot but veined with tree roots, so watch

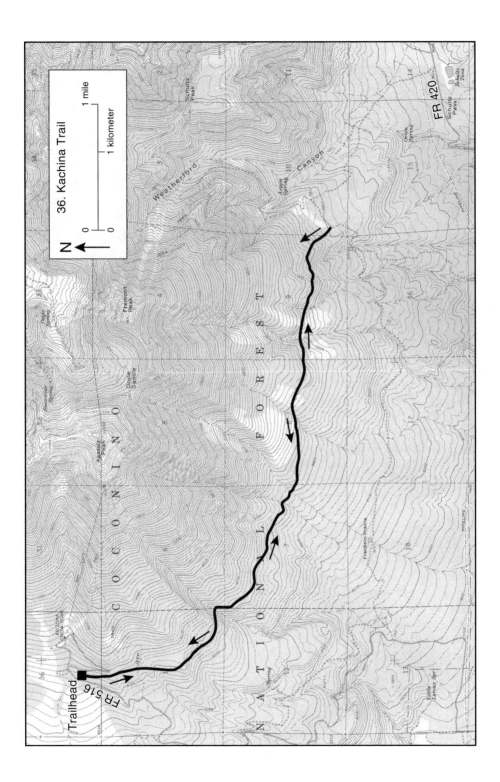

36. Kachina Trail

San Francisco peaks above the Kachina Trail

your step. At the 0.2-mile point, you arrive at the trail register and enter the Kachina Peaks Wilderness.

The trail alternates between shady and sunny habitats, adding to its visual variety. You will pass through shady stands of aspens and 80-foot firs floating in a sea of large ferns, characteristic of a Canadian Zone habitat. Then you'll pop out into sunny, open meadowlands carpeted with grass hummocks and spiked with stately ponderosa pines, typical of the Transition Zone. In many of these meadows you can look to your left and see the pointed tops of the San Francisco Peaks above you. Far below your right side you'll spy a northwestern Arizona landscape of small towns, buttes, isolated mountains such as Mount Kendrick, and, away in the distance, the rim line of the Grand Canyon. It's enough to keep your head constantly swiveling to catch all the sights.

Although the varied foliage is intriguing, the fauna is just as entertaining as the flora.

Along the first miles of the trail you will likely see one of the area's many herds of deer and elk. They like to roam among the small meadows that flourish along both sides of the trail. The trees are filled with the staccato hammering of woodpeckers working on the fallen aspens and firs that fill the forest understory. And there are scores of small birds adding their sweet trills to the woodpeckers' raucous cries. Throw in the rainbow of summertime butterflies that flutter among the trailside grasses, and you have a hike enlivened by the sights and sounds of life all along it.

After an hour or so you'll see a 3-foot-thick, twin-trunked aspen on your immediate left in an open meadow (elevation 9,160 feet), marking the 2.5-mile point of your hike.

Twin aspens to trail's end, 2.5 miles (5 miles total), 410-foot elevation loss, moderately difficult.

From the twin aspens the trail continues to undulate along the mountainside, alternating between meadows and copses of trees. On the way, you'll scramble across several rocky spots, but it's a straight walk for most of the trip. At 4.6 miles, you hike down through some thick groves of aspen trees and across another grassy meadow to arrive at trail's end at 5 miles (8,750 feet). You'll see a sign for the Kachina Peaks Wilderness here, at the trail junction with Freidlin Prairie Road (FS 522).

To make a shuttle hike out of the trip, go right and hike down the trail for 0.2 mile to join FS 522 where you would leave a car at roadside. For further trail explorations, take the trail junction to the left and hike 0.25 mile to another trail junction, where you will go left to follow the Weatherford Trail or right to go to Schultz's Tank. Otherwise, start back up into the wilderness to return to your starting point.

Trail's end to trailhead, 5.0 miles (10 miles total), 500-foot elevation gain, difficult.

Don't underestimate the return hike to your car. With another 5 miles to hike, the gradual elevation gain can be very tiring if you do not take some rest breaks and fuel up on food and water. The lovely trailside meadows almost beg you to sprawl among them and take a nap, so why don't you listen to them? This trail teaches you patience, the patience to enjoy the distant views and the patience to wisely negotiate its 10-mile distance in a single day.

Nearby Trails

From the end of the Kachina Trail you can hike an easy 1.6 miles over to Schultz Tank Road, where you will find water. This is a good spot to drop off a car for a 6.6-mile shuttle hike. Just prepare yourself for a bumpy 6-mile ride along Schultz Pass Road (FR 420) to drop off your car. The panoramic 8.7-mile Weatherford Trail can be used to loop back to the Kachina trailhead for a two-day hike. Trail descriptions for both trails are at www.fs.fed.us/r3/coconino/recreation/peaks/rec_peaks.shtml.

Camping

Dispersed camping sites are scattered along Snowbowl Road up to the trailhead. The sites nearest to the trail are off FS 522 between mile markers 2 and 3, on your right as you drive up to the trail. The FS 522 road has 14 tent sites with fire rings. There is no fee for camping. The nearest full-service campgrounds are the Bonito Campground next to Sunset Crater National Monument, and the Lake View Campground near Lake Mary. For campground specifics go to the web site at www.fs.fed.us/r3/coconino.

For more information, contact the Peaks Ranger Station, 5075 North Highway 89, Flagstaff, AZ 86001. Telephone 928-526-0866.

37

Mount Humphreys: Easy to be Hard

Location: Kachina Peaks Wilderness in the Coconino National Forest, 14 miles northeast of Flagstaff.

Total distance: 9.4 miles

Hiking time: 6.5 hours

Total elevation gain: 3,350 feet

Difficulty: Strenuous

Best months: June through September

Auto accessibility: Excellent. The trailhead is right off a paved road to the ski area.

Maps: USGS Humphreys Peak. A detailed topographic Flagstaff trails map is available at area sporting goods stores or at www.emmitbarks.com.

Rules: Dogs on leash permitted. No horses or bikes. No camping above 11,400 feet.

Comments: A day-long hike to Arizona's highest mountain and most expansive views. With its well-distributed elevation gain and clearly marked path, this is one of Arizona's "easiest" very strenuous trails. Hike early to avoid afternoon storms in the summer.

There you are, at the top. It's been a long hard trek, and that last mile to the Mount Humphreys summit added 20 years to your life as, huffing and puffing, you shuffled your way past the three false summits to plod up the shallow saddle to the top. But it was worth it, as you can see. And see, and see. Here at the pinnacle, a stunning geologic spectacle encircles you. Where else, this side of Hawaii, can you behold canyons, volcanoes, mountains, and plateaus in one turn of the head? And even Hawaii does not have the magnificent sweep of that lofty palisade of the gods, the Mogollon Rim, stretching off to New Mexico. Yes, it's a hard journey to the top of Mount Humphreys, but it's a peak viewing experience made easier by the trail's evenly distributed elevation gains.

Getting There

From downtown Flagstaff, drive 7 miles north on US 180 to milepost 222, to make a right at the Arizona Snow Bowl sign. From the turnoff, cruise uphill another 7 miles to arrive at a wide parking lot on the left side of the road, with the Mount Humphreys trail sign displayed next to the lot.

The Trail

Trailhead to Agassiz Saddle, 3.7 miles, 2,570-foot elevation gain, difficult.

Starting at elevation 9,280 feet, you begin by hiking through a wide grassy field (Hart Prairie) next to the ski lifts, soon to enter the spruce and pine forest of the Kachina Peaks Wilderness. The aspen forest has an understory of fallen trees, so you may have to scramble over a couple of na-

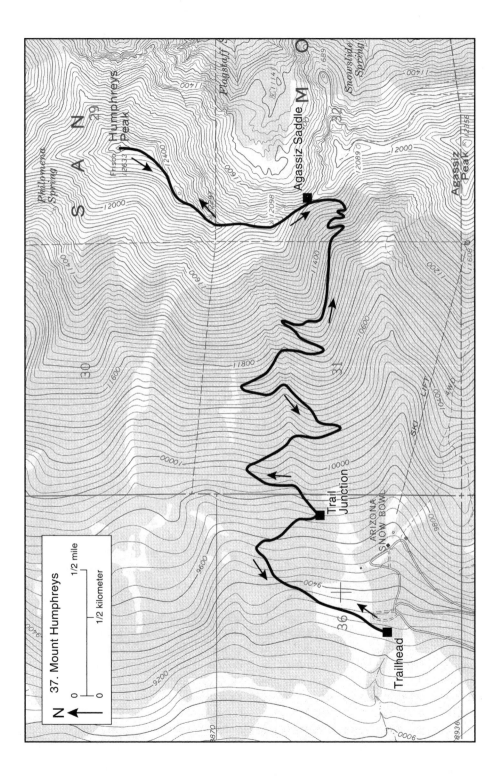

N

37. Mount Humphreys

1/2 mile
1/2 kilometer

Humphreys Peak

Frisco

Philomena Spring

S A N

29

30

11800

1600

11400

11600

12000

Flagstaff

Agassiz Saddle

Snowslide Spring

M O

32

12000

Agassiz Peak

31

10600

10000

Trail Junction

ARIZONA SNOW BOWL

SKI LIFT

9800

9600

9400

36

9200

Trailhead

9000

ture's "speed bumps" on the trail. At 0.9 mile (9,760 feet elevation), you pass a trail junction with a path leading to the ski lodge, as you continue the steady ascent up the mountainside via a series of long, looping switchbacks.

As you ascend, the aspen forest changes to a predominantly spruce-and-conifer habitat, and you can smell the trees' spicy fragrance on hot days. After 2.5 miles the trail opens a bit to show some expansive westside views of Kendrick Mountain and the Hochderffer Hills, as the environment gradually morphs into a Mutt-and-Jeff habitat of tall ponderosa pine and squat alligator junipers. Finally, after about 3.4-miles, you encounter a sign marking the trail's 11,400-foot elevation point, warning you that there is no camping allowed beyond this elevation.

From the sign, the gravelly trail coils steeply as it enters a life zone of bristlecone pine. This is Arizona's only preserve of these gnarly mountain "bonsais," some of which are more than 1,200 years old. After another 0.3 mile and you level off on top of the Agassiz Saddle (11,850 feet elevation) at the 3.7-mile point. You are now above a treeline that is the highest in North America (more than 11,000 feet!), owing to the warm Arizona location of this elevated peak.

Agassiz Saddle to Mount Humphreys Summit, 1 mile (4.7 total miles), 780-foot elevation gain, strenuous.

The panoramic saddle is marked by a trail sign for the Humphreys and Weatherford trails. Looking east from the saddle, you stare down some 2,000 feet into the mountains and cinder cones of the Inner Basin. The basin was likely formed when the giant stratovolcano that was San Francisco Mountain collapsed in a Mount St. Helen's–type eruption, creating the expansive Inner Basin valley and the three summits around its rim: Mount Humphreys, Agassiz Peak, and Fremont Peak.

You are now 1 hiking mile from the top, unsheltered in the treeless tundra. (Cell phone transmissions are very good here, by the way, so emergency calls are possible.) From here on, the trip to the true summit involves stairstepping up the volcanic rock piles that cobble the mountainside. The narrow path is marked with trail posts to guide you, and you have less than 1,000 feet of elevation gain remaining, so take heart and press on.

The first 0.25 mile of trail from the saddle is one of the most strenuous trail segments, as the breezy path ladders up the first of three false summits that hide Mount Humphreys. After passing the first false summit, you negotiate the shallow saddles between the next two peaks to arrive at the top of the third false summit at 12,450 feet, and you've hiked 0.7 mile from the saddle. The final 0.3 mile to the top can be exhausting because of the altitude, so take a break and hike slowly as you cross this final ridgeline. From the ridgeline you'll top off at Mount Humphreys (12,633 feet), identified by its summit marker and black registration box.

From the summit you receive a visual reward for all your efforts, an unparalleled prospect of Arizona's "rock stars." Every viewing angle has a spectacle, it's just a question of where you want look first. Peer south and you see the Verde Valley and Oak Creek Canyon, as well as neighboring Fremont and Agassiz peaks. To the northwest lies the maw of the Grand Canyon. Below you in the west sprawl Kendrick Mountain and some of the 600 volcanoes of the San Francisco Volcano Field, while the eastern views look off to the volcano field of nearby Sunset Crater National Monument. To keep track of all the sights, bring the Coconino and Kaibab forest maps to identify everything you see. But keep an eye out for clouds while you are up

Mount Humphreys

here, in case a summer afternoon storm is rolling in.

Humphreys Peak summit to trailhead, 4.7 miles, 3350-foot elevation loss, moderately difficult.

Pick your way carefully down the saddle, because rushing your rocky descent here can mean a turned ankle. From the Agassiz Saddle the even angle of descent allows for a brisk walk down the trail switchbacks, looping down through the trees until you emerge in the open meadow near your vehicle. You've just returned from your trip to Arizona's highest point—congratulations!

Nearby Trails

Just across the road from the Mount Humphreys trailhead is the Kachina Trail (Hike 36). This 10-mile (round-trip) trail is short on elevation gain but long on scenery, weaving through the forests and meadows of the Kachina Peaks Wilderness along the western side of the San Francisco Peaks. It receives fewer visitors than the Mount Humphreys trail, making it attractive to solitude seekers.

Camping

The open prairie surrounding the trailhead is the best place for primitive camping, because there are few spaces in the thickly treed understory along the trail. You'll also see several tent or trailer pull-in spots along Snow Bowl Road leading up to the trailhead. The nearest full-service campground is the Bonito Campground (44 units, vault toilets, trailers to 22 feet) near the Sunset Crater National Monument, 12 miles northeast of Flagstaff on US 89. Visit the Coconino National Forest web site at www.fs.fed.us/r3/coconino/recreation/peaks/rec_peaks.shtml.

For more information, contact the Peaks Ranger Station, 5075 North Highway 89, Flagstaff, AZ 86001. Telephone: 928-526-0866.

38

Sandys Canyon to Walnut Canyon: Playing the Baby Grand

Location: South Flagstaff, in the Lake Mary section of the Coconino National Forest.

Total distance: 7.6 miles

Hiking time: 4 hours, 15 minutes

Total elevation gain: 260 feet

Difficulty: Easy

Best months: April through November

Auto accessibility: Excellent, just a short turn off table-smooth Lake Mary Road.

Maps: USGS Lower Lake Mary, Flagstaff East. You can purchase a detailed Flagstaff trails map at area bookstores or at www.emmittbarks.com.

Rules: Pets and horses permitted. Bikes allowed only on Arizona Trail segment.

Comments: Tired of the Grand Canyon crowds? Take a hike through a small canyon that boasts the geology and features of its famous cousin. Bring your camera; this trail is relatively short on distance but long on scenery. Pack plenty of water, because Walnut Creek is often dry. For a pleasant change from hiking, you can rent a horse at the nearby outfitter and ride the canyon trails.

How'd you like your own personal Grand Canyon? Pint-sized Walnut Canyon has many of the Grand Canyon's intriguing geologic features, such as its multilayered, multicountoured, multihued sandstone layers capped with limestone from the ancient Kaibab sea.

Granted, this nanocanyon lacks the expansive grandeur and depth of its 270-mile-long counterpart to the northeast, but it's also missing the hordes of warm-weather visitors and vehicles that can give The Grand's South Rim a Disneyland atmosphere of crowd and bustle. Hiking Walnut Canyon via Sandys Canyon (as opposed to its busier canyon entrance off I-40) provides an up-close-and-personal tour of canyon walls that are only a few steps away from your hiking path. And the farther you go into this tiny canyon, the wilder and more solitary your hike becomes, so you can make this easy trek a bushwhacking adventure. So, if you find yourself near Flagstaff, do yourself a favor and play (in) the Baby Grand. You'll make beautiful music together.

Getting There

From downtown Flagstaff, drive three miles south on US 89 to turn left onto Lake Mary Road (Forest Road 3) and drive 6 miles south. After you pass mile marker 339, make a left into the Canyon Vista Campground. Drive 0.25 mile through the campground to the parking lot and trailhead at the left road branch.

Playing Above the Mogollon Rim

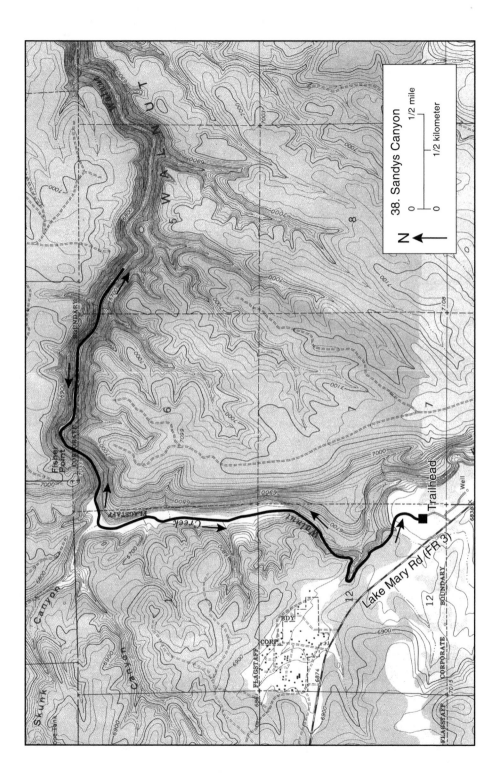

38. Sandys Canyon

N

0   1/2 mile

0   1/2 kilometer

Trailhead

Lake Mary Rd (FR 3)

Fisher Point

Skunk Canyon

Canyon

The Trail

Sandys Canyon trailhead to Arizona Trail, 1.4 miles, 190-foot elevation loss, easy.

The Sandys Canyon path starts out at 6,870 feet elevation, in a montane park of ponderosa pines scattered about open grasslands. As you start out along this well-marked dirt trail, you can see Sandys Canyon, the entry to Walnut Canyon, immediately in front of you, making it easy to find your destination. In the background of this parklike trail segment you can see snow-capped Mount Humphreys (Hike 37) and the other San Francisco Peaks soaring above the landscape, so you have the rare perspective of canyon views below you and mountain scenes above. It's a nice way to start a hike.

After 0.1 mile you turn left at a trail junction to follow the canyon rim and stroll up to another trail junction (6,920 feet) at the 0.5-mile point, where you turn right. From here you begin a gently curving descent into Walnut Canyon, cruising among 4-foot-thick pines. The canyon walls here are striated gray and salmon sandstone, the same colors and composition as the walls of its big brother canyon, the Grand. The trail is rocky in spots before it levels out to become an old road surrounded with aspens, so high-top boots come in handy.

At 1.4 miles you face a wooden sign indicating you are connecting to the Arizona Trail (6,680 feet elevation). The junction to the right leads to Marshall Lake at 4.7 miles, but you continue straight ahead along the old roadbed.

Arizona Trail junction to Walnut Canyon, 0.9 mile, (2.3 total miles), 40-foot elevation loss, easy.

From the trail junction, you stroll left (north) along the Arizona Trail, following the floor of Walnut Canyon toward Fisher Point. Mount Elden looms directly in front of you, with its dubious crown of microwave towers. The occasional drone of a logging truck reminds you that you are still not too far from highway civilization. At the 2.1-mile point you come to a fork indicating you go right to follow the Arizona Trail (elevation 6,640 feet). Bearing right, you soon come to another trail junction with the Fisher Point route on your left, but you continue right at this junction. You are now leaving the Arizona Trail and heading into the confines of Walnut Canyon, easing past an 80-foot canyon wall with a deep cave at its feet.

Walnut Canyon junction to trail's end, 1.5 miles (3.8 total miles), 30-foot elevation gain, moderately difficult.

Sculpted by erosion, the tan and cream canyon walls here have all sorts of shapes: many wall segments have a rounded liquid appearance like giant globs of melted wax, while others look like stacked piles of thick pancakes, and still others are formed into swooping curved arches. This is an intimate canyon; the 80-foot walls rise up close on either side of you, and the oaks, willows, and cedars crowd around you on what has now become a narrow, rolling trail. Keep an eye out for the poison ivy that also loves this trail segment.

Hiking here, you'll see lots of side trails leading to caves and groves of walnut and ash trees, handy spots for a cool break from the sun. Birds love to flit among the dense foliage along this canyon bottom, including black grosbeaks, hummingbirds, and hermit thrushes. All in all, the canyon sights and sounds make for an entertaining exploration, drawing you further into its depths.

The Walnut Canyon Trail has no specific end, and it becomes narrower and more obstructed as you go deeper into the canyon. After hiking some 1.5 miles into this canyon branch, (6,670 feet elevation) you will be bushwhacking over fallen trees more than walking, which may a good reason to head

Entering Walnut Canyon

back to the trailhead. This will be at about the 3.8-mile point of your hike.

Trail's end to trailhead, 3.8 miles (7.6 total miles), 200-foot elevation gain, easy.

With such a level route back to your start, it's easy to put your head down and motor back as quickly as you can. But keep your attention on the canyon walls, they will show you different shapes and perspectives on your way back from the Baby Grand, finishing a pleasant day hike.

Nearby Trails

The 0.3-mile Vista Loop Trail is at a trail junction near the start of the Sandys Canyon Trail, and the loop is well worth the short side trip to savor its attractive canyon views. On weekends you may see several climbers scrambling about the canyon walls in the climbing area here, a good show to watch after you have finished the Sandys Canyon route.

Camping

You'll find some backcountry sites at the end of some of the side trails in Walnut Canyon, and there's lots of open level space in Sandys Canyon. The Canyon Vista Campground adjoins the Sandys Canyon trailhead and has 11 units that accommodate vehicles up to 22 feet, as well as tents. It has vault toilets, fire rings, and drinking water, but no hookups. Fees are $8 a night in peak season (May through September) and $6 a night at other times. The Marshall Lake area, about 8 miles south of Canyon Vista Campground, has free dispersed camping sites along the lake road, wide flat areas that can accommodate everything from a tent to a full-size trailer.

For more information, contact the Mormon Lake Ranger Station, 4373 South Lake Mary Road, Flagstaff, AZ 86001. Telephone: 928-774-1147. The National Forest web site is at www.fs.fed.us/r3/coconino.

39

Bill Williams Mountain: Made in the Shade

Location: Williams Ranger District Office in the Kaibab National Forest, 32 miles west of Flagstaff in Williams.

Total distance: 6 miles (3-mile shuttle hike)

Hiking time: 5 hours

Total elevation gain: 2,300 feet

Difficulty: Difficult

Best months: May through October

Auto accessibility: Excellent, a few minutes' drive off Interstate 40.

Maps: USGS Williams South. A trail description and map are available at www.fs .fed.us/r3/kai/oldrecreation/trwc_bill.html.

Rules: Pets on leash and horses permitted. No bikes or motorized vehicles except on the forest road up to the mountain.

Comments: Hike up to the mountaintop's fire lookout to study the multifarious terrain of northern Arizona: plateaus, mountains, buttes, and canyons. This moderately used trail is shady enough to be a more comfortable summer hike than many trails in the area. Pack your own water; there's none on the trail.

This trail climbs 2,300 feet through dense forests? Cool! When I first hiked the Bill Williams Trail, it was late May and the Flagstaff-Williams area was having unseasonably hot weather. Manfred, my Blue Heeler hiking companion, was tired of the hot, dusty desert trails we'd recently explored, and balked at even leaving the car when we parked at the trailhead. Once we set out up the side of the mountain, however, his trepidations disappeared. The higher we went, the cooler it became and the faster Manfred loped, until he was happily dashing through snowbanks at the 2-mile sign.

Even though this solitary trail is a rigorous ascent, it is a more comfortable summer trek than most of its low-level, sun-washed companions. And the bird's-eye views of northern Arizona from the mountaintop are an eye-candy reward for all your efforts. Named after a nineteenth-century missionary turned trapper, the Bill Williams Mountain Trail was made in the shade, topping you off at the state's fifteenth-highest mountain.

Getting There

From Flagstaff, drive 32 miles west on I-40 to exit 161 in Williams, going left (south) for 0.25 mile to turn at the Williams ranger station sign. Drive 0.5 mile down the frontage road to make a left and drive 300 feet to the ranger station. The Bill Williams Trailhead parking lot is on the left next to the rest rooms.

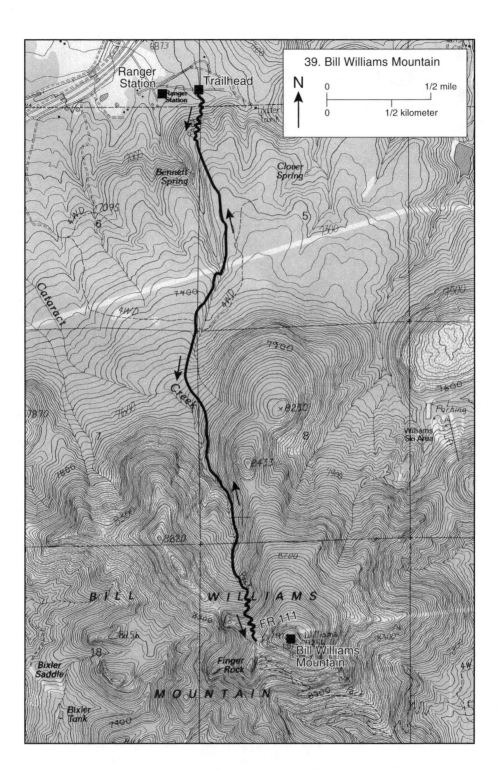

39. Bill Williams Mountain

N

| 0 | | 1/2 mile |
| 0 | | 1/2 kilometer |

Ranger Station

Trailhead

Ranger Station

Bennett Spring

Clover Spring

Cataract

Creek

Parking

Williams Ski Area

BILL   WILLIAMS

MOUNTAIN

Bixler Saddle

Bixler Tank

Finger Rock

Bill Williams Mountain

FR 111

View from the trail at Bill Williams Mountain

The Trail

Trailhead to 2-mile mark, 2.0 miles, 900-foot elevation gain, difficult.

From the outset at 6,960 feet, you'll switchback up through a piñon pine and alligator juniper habitat, accentuated with large basalt boulders scattered throughout the understory. Spring and summer bring a host of wildflowers to this sunny trail section, blooms such as orange-red Indian paintbrush, violet Arizona wild rose, and pink phlox. After 0.5 mile of moderately difficult hiking, you arrive at a junction with Clover Spring, a 0.5-mile jaunt over to this water source, and the Buckskinner Park Trail. Continuing up the Bill Williams Trail, the route becomes steeper and the forest habitat gradually changes from pine woodlands to a mixed conifer life zone. After an hour's hiking you'll climb up a short series of rocky steps among the tall shady firs, to arrive at the 2-mile trail signpost (elevation 7,860).

Two-mile mark to Bill Williams Mountain, 1 mile (3.0 total miles), 1400-foot elevation gain, strenuous.

The 2-mile point initiates the steepest section of this hike, as you push through several steep trail sections in the first 0.5 mile. The entire forest has become larger here, dominated by 4-foot-thick firs and 60-foot aspens. Fortunately, the huge trees provide some deep, cooling shade as you heat up from your steep ascent. (Hiking poles are helpful here.) Look down and you can view the northern Arizona countryside spread out far below you, showing how high you have climbed. Don't be surprised to see patches of snow here, even in early summer—this is one dark and cool trail segment.

At the 2.3-mile point you come up to a junction with the Bixler Trail at 8,640 feet. Another 0.2 mile of steep hiking brings you up to Forest Service Road 111 (elevation 9,060 feet) leading to Bill Williams

Mountain. Follow the forest road to the left, a gradual and comparatively easy hike after the thigh-burning ascent you have just finished. FS 111 is a sunny and breezy road that shows off all of the northern Arizona countryside from different directions, depending upon which part of the winding road you're hiking. Volcanic rock pinnacles decorate the overlooks beneath you here, the most notable being Finger Rock, which juts below you on the west side of the road.

Finally, at 9,260 feet, you come to Bill Williams Mountain, the high point of your hike. The summit is picketed with eight different microwave towers and a 1937 fire lookout. From the mountaintop you can study the enormous table of the Coconino Plateau to the north, Sedona's mountains and buttes to the south, and Mount Humphreys and the San Francisco Peaks to the west. The views are outstanding, but you have to work your way around the towers to get them. Your best bet is to go up the lookout tower so the microwave monsters intrude less on your vision. Or walk about the road, as I did, for equally impressive views. After filling your eyes and camera with overlook scenery, it's time to head back down the trail.

Bill Williams Mountain to trailhead, 3.0 miles (6.0 total miles), 2,300-foot elevation loss, easy.

The hike down is relatively easy, although you should watch out for slippery gravel underfoot during the first (and steepest) mile down from the mountaintop. If you want to make this 6-mile trek a shuttle hike, drive a vehicle up FS 111 off County Road 73 south of Williams, and park at the mountaintop.

Nearby Trails

From the Bill Williams trail junction at the 2.3-mile point, take a side trip over to Bixler Mountain via the Bixler Saddle Trail. This 2-mile trail loses some 700 feet in elevation as it descends along the forested side of Bill Williams Mountain to the Bixler Saddle. It's a good hike if you're looking for solitude. There is a trail description on the web site at www .fs.fed.us/r3/kai/oldrecreation/recreate.html.

Camping

You'll see several primitive campsites scattered along the left-hand side of the trail between the 0.5- and 2-mile marks, shady places to pitch a tent for the night. The Cataract Lake Campground is by Williams exit 161 off I-40. There are 18 campsites with tables and fire rings. Drinking water and pit toilets are also available at the campground, which charges $10 per night and accommodates trailers. The campground website can be found at www.fs .fed.us/r3/kai/oldrecreation/recreate.html.

For more information, contact the Williams Forest Service Visitors Center, 200 West Railroad Avenue, Williams, AZ 86046. Telephone: 520-635-4061. Check the web site at www.fs.fed.us/r3/kai.

40

Potato Patch Loop: Elevated Perspectives

Location: Hualapai Mountain Park, 12 miles southeast of Kingman.

Total distance: 4.3 miles round trip

Hiking time: 2 hours, 15 minutes

Total elevation gain: 1,000 feet

Difficulty: Moderately difficult

Best months: September through March

Auto accessibility: Good. The last mile of road is rutted but negotiable by any car.

Maps: USGS Hualapai Park. Free trail map available at Hualapai State Park entrance.

Rules: Dogs on leash. Mountain bikes and horses permitted on trails separate from hikers' routes.

Comments: This user-friendly trail shows off much of the northwest Arizona countryside as it circles the shady Hualapai Mountains. The trail's high elevations make this one of the best warm-weather hikes in northwest Arizona.

The Potato Patch hike is a pleasant sojourn along a shady trail provided with shelters, benches, and water fountains. Its gradual elevation gains take you to a half dozen mountain overlooks as you stroll beneath the craggy Hualapai Mountains. Even though the potatoes are long gone from its elevated croplands, this multiple-habitat trail still has appeal for everyone.

The Hualapai Mountains are named after the Native American tribe that inhabited them until the 1870s, when the US military relocated them to their present home at the South Rim of the Grand Canyon. The word "Hualapai" means "pine tree folk," and the tribe likely received that name because they lived in the coniferous Hualapai Mountains. Certainly, these granite-and-gneiss mountains were a sensible place to live in spring and summer, their cool, watered environs sharply contrasting with the arid lowlands of the surrounding Mohave Desert, one of the hottest places in America. In the 1930s the Civilian Conservation Corps created the Hualapai Mountain Park, building the cabins and trails that are used to this day. A haven for eagles, elk, foxes, and hawks, this accessible park is a frequent destination for Kingman residents, but rarely visited by Arizona's many Grand Canyon tourists, who drive right by its entry point on the interstate.

Getting There

From Kingman, drive 8 miles east on I-40 to turn off at exit 59, heading south along Mohave County Route 259 to Mount Hua-

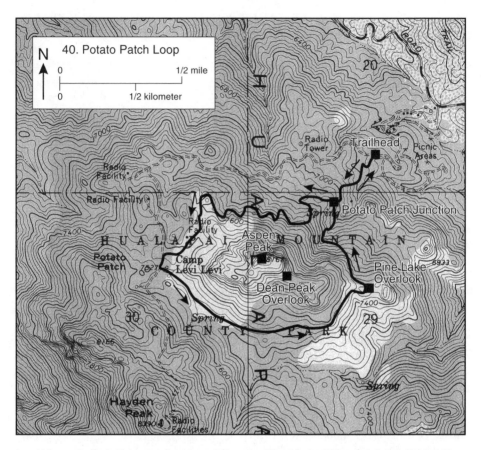

40. Potato Patch Loop

lapai Mountain Park. Drive 9 miles along CR 259, passing the ranger station in the last mile, and turn right at the park sign for hiking trails. Drive 1 mile up the park road until the road ends next to the unsigned trailhead on your right, in front of a blocked asphalt road with rest rooms on your left. Note: An alternate route from Kingman is to take Hualapai Mountain Road 14 miles to the ranger station.

The Trail

Trailhead to Boy Scout camp, 2.2 miles, 900-foot elevation gain, moderately difficult.

As you leave your car you will walk across an old asphalt road to head west up the dirt trail (elevation 6,720 feet) reserved just for hikers. You start by switchbacking up a wide and well-marked path, traversing a young pine forest with an open understory of pine needles. Adding to the entertainment and comfort of this shady mountain path, the Potato Patch Trail has a score of nature study signs scattered throughout its circuit, along with benches and water fountains.

After your fifth switchback you'll see the first of many overlooks, this one showing off wide views of the Aquarius Mountains southeast toward Prescott. After several more switchbacks you can savor the wide scope of northwest Arizona below you, with views of the Music Mountains out toward the South Rim of the Grand Canyon, and the Hualapai Indian Reservation that bor-

Awe-inspiring view from the Potato Patch Loop

ders it. You've barely hiked 0.5 mile, and already you have had vistas of several different areas of Arizona, a good return on your hiking investment!

At 0.6 mile you come to the junction with the Potato Patch Loop. Here you continue to the right, following the sign indicating that the Loop junction is 0.3 mile away. As you ascend, the pine habitat changes to one thick with New Mexico locust, Gambel's oak, and white fir. The trailside boulders here are awesomely large, as big as cabins, and are so close together that you have to squeeze between them to continue on the trail.

Nearing the 1-mile point, you come to another trail junction that you follow to the right, starting along a sunny, east-facing trail section where pines have reasserted dominance. The trail continues to climb, and the views open up to show sections of Arizona from the Grand Canyon south to the Sedona area. As you circle up the trail, you'll pass a rock formation called The Gossips, a group of turrets that look as if they are sharing a secret. You then arrive at the Music Mountains Overlook at 1.6 miles (7,510 feet elevation), where you can study the wide sweep of the mountains that front the Grand Canyon's South Rim. Leaving the overlook, you'll shortly top off near a storm shelter at 7,620 feet elevation, 1.7 miles from your start. From the shelter you'll pass a water spout, rest rooms, and the Dean's Peak Overlook (see Nearby Trails section), to troop down a wide earth road to a trail junction at the 2.2-mile point of your hike, with a Boy Scout camp on your left.

Boy Scout camp to trailhead, 2.1 miles (4.3 miles total), 100-foot elevation gain, moderately difficult.

From the Boy Scout camp you make a left to tramp 0.2 mile through its sprawl (water and rest rooms are here) along a wide dirt road, to turn left at the sign directing you off the road and up the ridge. From here the trail rolls up a wide, sunny, southeast-facing ridge with more open views. In warm weather the

Engelmann's hedgehog cactus, Echinocereus engelmannii

trail is daubed with colorful patches of scarlet, blue, and yellow wildflowers, micro beauties as alluring as the macro views. You'll pass a shelter at the 2.9-mile point of your hike (elevation 7,150 feet) to come full circle to the start of the loop junction at 3.3 miles. From the loop you follow the trail 0.9 mile down to your car. All in all, you should have had a pleasant ramble through a trail that has entertained you with its varied habitats, rock formations, and overlooks.

Nearby Trails

The Potato Patch Trail connects to a half dozen short branch hikes along its circuit, paths leading to neighboring peaks such as the Hayden, Aspen, and Hualapai mountaintops. The Dean's Peak Overlook is right off the Potato Patch Trail near the 1.7-mile point. If you are willing to chug the 700 feet up this 0.6-mile route to Aspen Peak, you can spy Getz and Dean's Peaks, two area

landmarks. From the overlook, a short scramble up another 100 feet will bring you to Aspen Peak (8,050 feet elevation) and its excellent views.

Camping

The best primitive camping spots are up near the junction of the Potato Patch and Dean's Peak Trails. The park has all types of camping available near the Potato Patch trailhead. There are 70 campsites at $8 a night and 11 RV sites at $15. Water and rest rooms are available at the campgrounds. The park also has a wide variety of cabins ranging from $35 to $70, with beds, stoves, refrigerators, bathrooms, and showers. Some have fireplaces or wood stoves.

For more information, contact Hualapai Mountain Park office at 928-757-3859. The Hualapai Mountain Park web site, with trail and camping information, is at www.mcparks.com.

Grand Canyon North and South Rims: Legendary Spectacle

41

Red Butte: 100-to-1 Return on Investment

Location: Kaibab National Forest near the South Rim of the Grand Canyon 70 miles northwest of Flagstaff.

Total distance: 2.4 miles

Hiking time: 1.5 hours

Total elevation gain: 900 feet

Difficulty: Moderately difficult

Best months: April through October

Auto accessibility: Fair. Passenger cars must drive slowly around some deep ruts over the last 1.5 miles of this otherwise excellent drive right off the highway.

Maps: USGS Red Butte

Rules: Pets on leash and horses permitted.

Comments: Invest a 1.2-mile hike to the top, and you'll be rewarded with 100-mile views of northern Arizona. This is a very good trail to introduce older kids to the exertions and rewards of hiking mountains. The trail is rigorous but short and has some Olympian views from the overlook at the top.

Barreling up US 180, most folks bullet right past Red Butte, intent on arriving at the Grand Canyon's South Rim playground as soon as possible, in a hurry to relax. Even the most task-oriented passersby can't fail to notice this roseate sky island rising from the pool-table terrain around it, but they don't know that there's a trail there that offers them a different perspective than they'll find when looking down into the Great Hole that is their final destination. For the price of a stiff 45-minute trek up to the butte's top, they could savor the best 360-degree views of northern and central Arizona this side of the Bill Williams Trail (Hike 39) with nary a visitor in sight. Now that's the way to start a vacation!

The only reason that Red Butte is not as flat as its surrounding terrain is because its basalt helmet has protected it from erosion. Eons of wind and rain have sanded away most of mudstone contours of the Coconino Plateau, leveling it down to its ancient limestone seabed. Red Butte, however, sports a maroon rock cap that has sheltered it from these reductionist elements, making it a butte out standing in its field, a prominent landmark among the sagebrush surround. So, if you find yourself heading to or from the South Rim, don't overlook this overlook, as you might be the only one visiting this room with a view.

Getting There

From Flagstaff, drive 28 miles west on I-40 to exit 165 in Williams for AZ 64 and the Grand Canyon. Drive 39 miles north on AZ 64 (also US 180) to mile marker 224, making a right onto Forest Service Road 320. Head east on

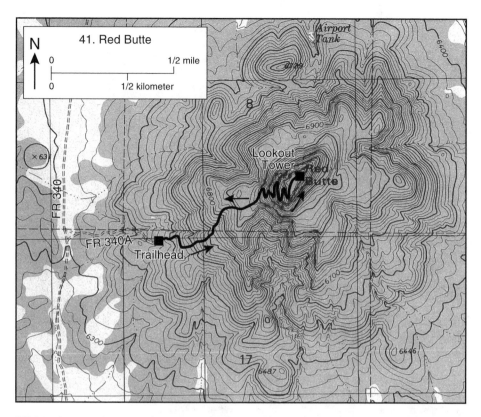

FS 320 for 1.5 miles, to make a left onto FS 340, driving this rutted dirt road for 1 mile to turn right at FS 340A and the Red Butte sign. The trailhead is 0.25 mile down the road, next to a prominent brown sign describing the geology of Red Butte.

The Trail

Trailhead to Red Butte, 1.2 miles, 900-foot elevation gain, difficult.

Starting along the trail at 6,470 feet, you begin by coiling up the well-marked dirt and rock trail, passing through a piñon and juniper forest with a shrubby but open understory. The trail continues as a series of wide, looping switchbacks that make the steep elevation gain relatively easy to handle. The trail breezes are cooling in spring and summer, but they are desiccating winds, so bring at least a quart of water per person.

After 0.25 mile up the trail, you can see the western portion of Arizona toward Kingman and the Hualapai Mountains. To the south and southeast stands the prominent volcanic trio of Mounts Williams, Kendrick, and Humphreys. As you continue up around the switchbacks you'll see north toward the Grand Canyon, with the northern Arizona views becoming more spectacular the farther up you go. (If you have binoculars, bring them.) Don't let the scenery totally distract you from watching the trail—rattlesnakes may be sunbathing along this path.

At the 0.8-mile point you can see Humphreys Peak near Flagstaff and the distant splay of Sedona's reddish mountains and buttes. You'll likely see helicopters sweeping beneath you, hauling Grand Canyon tourists. You have the odd perspec-

---

Red Butte: 100-to-1 Return on Investment

View from Red Butte. Snow-covered Humphreys Peak is in the distance.

tive of looking down upon a flying helicopter. Hike up another couple of switchbacks and you come to a jumble of large basalt boulders covered with lime-green lichen, signaling that you are almost at the top. Make one more turn and walk up to the large lookout tower at the top of Red Butte (elevation 7,350 feet). This lookout is on the National Register of Historic Lookouts at www.firelookout.net. For even better views, you can ask the lookout ranger if you can walk up on the lookout tower.

The butte is a good place for a picnic or rest break among the squat junipers and bright pink boulders. There is a rest room here, and several water tanks with a bowl that you can fill for your dog. Make sure you walk around the top of this level-headed butte. The views are engagingly different from each point of the compass.

Red Butte to trailhead, 1.2 miles (2.4 total miles), 900-foot elevation loss, easy.

The hike down is relatively easy. Just watch out for loose gravel underfoot on the few steep grades near the top.

Nearby Trails

There are no other trails around this solitary butte, but if you liked the views from Red Butte you might try the Bill Williams Mountain Trail (see Hike 39), which is only a few miles west of your turnoff from I-40 onto AZ 67. The Bill Williams Trail is longer and steeper, but it leads to another set of spectacular views of the northern Arizona terrain, and it's shady in summer. There is also a 23-mile Arizona Trail segment in the Grand Canyon's South Rim area. This alternate hike is described on the web site at www.fs.fed.us/r3/kai/oldrecreation/trwc.html.

Camping

You'll find pull-in primitive campsites along FS 340 and FS 340A leading to the trailhead, as well as several sites along the first 0.5 mile of the trail. The Cataract Lake

Campground is in Williams, 40 miles south-west of Red Butte. This lakeside camp-ground has rest rooms and water. You can find it on the web at www.fs.fed.us/r3/kai/oldrecreation/rec_campgrounds.html. There are several campgrounds around the South Rim, but they can be extremely crowded in high season. For details, go to www.nps.gov/grca/pphtml/camping.html.

For more information, contact the Tusayan Ranger District, Tusayan AZ 86023. Telephone: 602-638-2443.

42

Bright Angel Trail: Heaven Can Be Hellish

Location: South Rim in Grand Canyon National Park

Total distance: 19.2 miles round trip

Hiking time: 12 hours

Total elevation gain: 4,890 feet, with 4,680 feet of it on return trip

Difficulty: Strenuous

Best months: March to May and September to November

Auto accessibility: Excellent

Maps: USGS Bright Angel, Grand Canyon, Phantom Ranch. Alan Berkowitz's Bright Angel–Grand Canyon trail guide ($2.95) is available at Kaibab ranger stations.

Rules: No camping outside of designated campgrounds. No pets or bikes. Horses permitted. $20 per vehicle for a seven-day park pass.

Comments: The world-famous Bright Angel Trail has a bit of everything: spectacular Grand Canyon scenery, Native American petroglyphs, geologic studies, wildlife—and hordes of hikers! Visitors often underestimate the rigors of this two-day trek's steep return trip; allow twice as much time for the return as for the initial descent. Hike early in the morning or late in the afternoon on warm days.

For over a century, the Bright Angel Trail has been one of the most popular hiking trails in North America. Since 1903, when Ralph Cameron made this ancient Native American route a tourist trek tollway, millions of the world's hikers have crunched down The Angel's wide, level face, lured by the trail's international reputation for its non-stop display of mind-boggling canyon panoramas.

For all its longstanding fame, however, this is still a trail of surprises. Expecting a dusty tramp down the side of a barren rock face, many first-time hikers are surprised by The Angel's verdancy: Creeks run along much of the trail, ancient Native American farmlands sprawl out near the hike's midpoint, and Douglas fir microforests pop out along the way. Veteran hikers are often surprised by the trailside amenities; there are few backcountry trails that boast The Angel's en route toilets, water stands, and phone booths, giving this two-day hike the aura of a parkland stroll. For all its amenities, however, this is not a trail to be taken lightly: The Angel's return trip from trail's end is a bare-knuckle, 5,000-foot climb through a hot and dry climate. For the unfit or unprepared, The Angel will be heaven on the way down and hell on the way back up.

Having given you these warnings, I urge you to take this once-in-a-lifetime trail. Take a two-day journey to complete the trail, or day hike to the Three-Mile House or Indian Gardens turn-around points. Either way, the Bright Angel Trail will take you to your heavenly reward, a paradise of scenery.

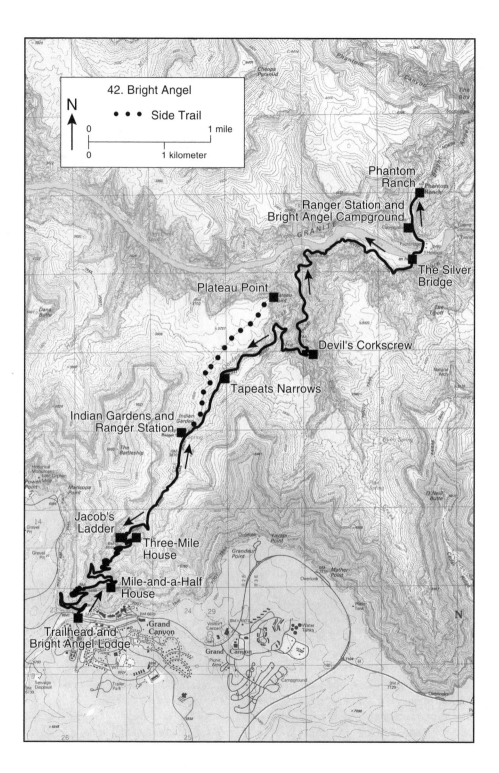

42. Bright Angel

• • • Side Trail

N

0   1 mile

0   1 kilometer

Phantom Ranch

Ranger Station and Bright Angel Campground

The Silver Bridge

Plateau Point

Devil's Corkscrew

Tapeats Narrows

Indian Gardens and Ranger Station

Jacob's Ladder

Three-Mile House

Mile-and-a-Half House

Trailhead and Bright Angel Lodge

Getting There

From Flagstaff, drive north on US 180 for 52 miles to intersect with AZ 64, going right (north) on AZ 64 for 28 miles to Grand Canyon Village. From the village, take the Village Loop Road for 3 miles to bear right at a Y-shaped junction with a Bright Angel Lodge sign. Drive 0.5 mile past the junction to West Rim Drive, going left (south) along West Rim for a few blocks to the public parking area. Walk up to the signed trailhead, which is a few hundred feet west of the Bright Angel Lodge, near the mule corral on West Rim Drive.

The Trail

Trailhead to Three-Mile House, 3.1 miles, 2,230-foot elevation loss, easy.

Starting out from the trailhead (6,780 feet), you descend along the wide flat trail through the piñons and junipers that surround the canyon rim, moving past the 100-year-old Kolb photography studio on your right. Awe-inspiring canyon views present themselves immediately, and become more spectacular as you descend—you can see the trail snake down between the canyon massifs all the way down to Indian Gardens 4 miles away.

After 0.2 mile you pass through a rock tunnel exhibiting a number of graffiti-scarred Native American pictographs, to loop down to a small stand of Douglas firs, a shady serendipity among its stark rock surroundings. This trail section's bright canyon walls are composed of Kaibab and Toroweap limestones, ancient seabed layers that are only part of the multilayered geologic formations you'll see all along the Bright Angel Trail.

After you leave the fir microforest, you loop down through a second tunnel that is carved through a wave of light yellow Coconino sandstone, and hike down some ten switchbacks before you cruise over to the Mile-and-a-Half Resthouse (1.6 miles, 5,710 feet). This 1930s stone-and-wood oasis has water available from May to October, with toilets and a phone.

From the resthouse, the trail moves through some more shady Douglas firs and Gambel's oaks to pass by a boulder with more Native American pictographs. It's on your left just before you reach Two-Mile Corner. From the corner you switchback down to an impressive gallery of red and black Supai shale cliffs, to stop at Three-Mile Resthouse (elevation 4,750 feet), a large shelter with the style and amenities of the earlier resthouse. Many day hikers turn around at this point, especially in the hot summer months, to complete a 4- or 5-hour trek. In cooler weather, Indian Gardens, at the 4.6-mile point, is another turning-point option.

Three-Mile House to Colorado River, 4.6 miles (7.7 miles total), 2,450-foot elevation loss, moderately difficult.

Leaving the Three-Mile House, you'll switch down through cave-riddled walls of ochre redwall limestone, a vivid addition to the Grand Canyon's earth-color pastiche. This 1-mile series of 15 trail loops is called Jacob's Ladder. After climbing down the Ladder, you are rewarded with a 0.75-mile stroll across the flat shale bed of the Tonto Plateau, to arrive at verdant, spring-fed Indian Gardens (elevation 3,800 feet). With a ranger station, campground, toilets, and year-round water, this scenic stop is a better rest area than you'll find on most highways. It's also a good place to turn around to complete an extended day hike of 9.2 miles. The maximum-spectacle Plateau Point Trail (see Nearby Trails) branches off from Indian Gardens, offering a memorable 1.5-mile (one-way) side trip.

From the Gardens you'll find the descent (and subsequent ascent) more moderate,

There are eye-popping Grand Canyon vistas all along the world-famous Bright Angel Trail.

as you follow Garden Creek through narrow walls of creamy Tapeats sandstone. The trees of the Indian Gardens' riparian habitat will catch your eye: alders, redbuds, and cottonwoods—not what you'd expect halfway down a stony canyon.

After 0.5 mile, the trail plummets down The Devil's Corkscrew, a series of steep schist switchbacks, to flatten out as you arrive at the Colorado River (elevation 2,300 feet) and a resthouse with phone and toilets. At 7.7 miles, the Colorado River is the end of the Bright Angel Trail. If you are this far down the path you're likely to stay the night, so you'll bear left to continue on the River Trail to the Phantom Ranch Campground, or the Phantom Canyon Lodge.

River Trail to Bright Angel Campground, 2.1 miles (9.8 total miles), 210-foot elevation gain, moderately difficult.

After the River Trail trailhead, you chug up and down several short but steep ascents as you follow the river for the next 1.6 miles, moving through 10-story walls of black schist striped with pinkish granite. The trail turns left (south) as you cross the Silver Suspension Bridge. The bridge is a wondrous modern anomaly in this land of billion-year-old rock, as if someone had sent the Brooklyn Bridge back to the age of dinosaurs. From the bridge you'll take a 0.5-mile walk over to the ranger station and the Bright Angel Campground (2,510 feet elevation, with year-round water) or continue to the Phantom Canyon Lodge (see Camping).

Bright Angel Campground to trailhead, 9.8 miles (19.6 total miles), 4,680 feet, strenuous.

Count on a 7-hour journey back to the top, taking your time for water and rest breaks. Jacob's Ladder can be a particularly tough climb on the way back out, made easier by pausing to enjoy the spectacle that surrounds you and conversing with the many hikers you are bound to meet on your way. Once you finally climb out to the top, you'll have a hiking story you can tell for the rest of your life, filled with the sights you have savored, the people you have met, and the pains you have endured.

Nearby Trails

After arriving at Indian Gardens, many experienced canyon hikers ignore the second half of the Bright Angel Trail to tramp 1.5 miles over to Plateau Point. This moderately difficult trail boasts calendar-perfect views of the Grand Canyon and the Colorado River. Don't be surprised to see several photographers trekking along this route with you.

Camping

The Bright Angel Campground is parked alongside Bright Angel Creek near trail's end, 0.5 mile north of the Colorado River and 0.5 mile south of Phantom Ranch. The facility has 31 sites with faucet water and toilets. The lovely Indian Gardens Campground, shaded with tall cottonwoods, is an option for those who hike to the Colorado River and push back up the trail for 3 more miles before retiring. Indian Gardens has faucet water, toilets, and a ranger station. The Phantom Ranch Lodge has both cabin and dormitory rooms available, with meals. Reservations should be made well in advance for any of these locations.

For more information and advance reservations, visit Grand Canyon National Park's South Rim web site at www.fs.fed.us/r3/kai/oldrecreation/camp_dem.html. Bob Ribokas has an excellent web site for hiking Grand Canyon trails, complete with situation-specific hiking advice and war stories. It's at www.kaibab.org/home.htm.

43

Rim Trail: A Scenic Cruise

Location: South Rim in Grand Canyon National Park

Total distance: 23.8 miles (11.9-mile shuttle hike)

Hiking time: 11 hours

Total elevation gain: 825 feet

Difficulty: Moderately difficult

Best months: September through November and March through May

Auto accessibility: Excellent

Maps: USGS Phantom Ranch and Grand Canyon. A route map is in the Grand Canyon Guide, a free newspaper available at park entrances and visitors centers.

Rules: $20 per vehicle for seven-day park pass. Pets allowed. No horses or bikes.

Comments: One of North America's most spectacular overlook trails is also one of its most user friendly: flat, painstakingly signed, and accessible by free bus from a number of points. It's a scenic cruiser's dream. You'll find a United Nations spectrum of languages and dress among the many trailside visitors. For a one-way shuttle hike, leave one car at Bright Angel Lodge and start out at Pipe Creek Point, returning to Bright Angel Lodge via the trail's end bus shuttle at Hermit's Rest.

Relentlessly beautiful, that's the Rim Trail. Each of its dozen segments exhibits a trailside gallery of Grand Canyon panoramas. Hiking the entire route, you run the happy risk of beauty overload. You meander from one canyon overview to the next, staring at the scores of parti-colored pinnacles and buttes that rise from the mile-deep gorge beneath you, until your numbed mind must stare at a nearby tree, or boulder—anything without spectacle—to relieve your eyes' attempts to absorb a hundred square miles of grandeur. Small wonder the Park Service has placed benches along the trail—you might need to sit down and refocus!

The Rim Trail is a trail network that parallels a transportation network across the Rim. The many eastern trail sections can be accessed by car or free shuttle bus, and the more solitary western segments are serviced by park shuttles. So it's very easy to build your own hike along this route.

For handy reference, the Rim Trail segments are summarized in the trail table on pg. 222, moving from east to west.

Getting There

From Flagstaff, drive 51 miles northwest on US 180 and make a right at the intersection with US 64–US 180, continuing north for 32 miles to Desert View Drive, pausing at the Grand Canyon entrance station ($20 entry fee). From the intersection of Desert View Drive and US 64, drive 1.5 miles east on Desert View Drive to the Pipe Creek overlook on your left.

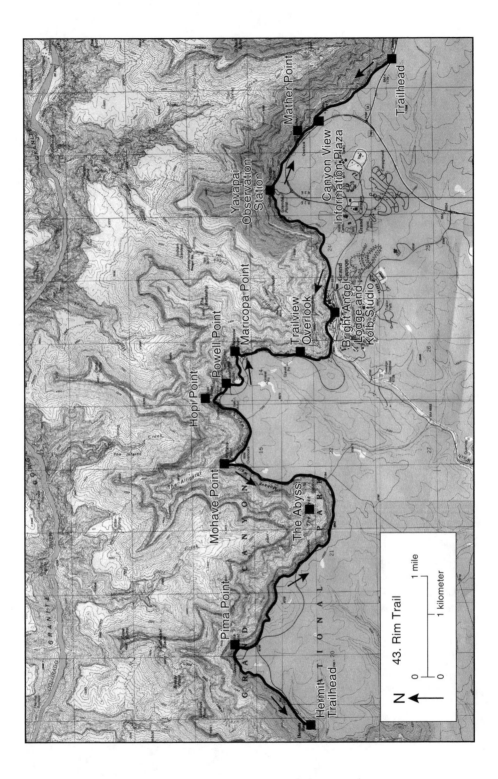

N

43. Rim Trail

0   1 kilometer

0   1 mile

Trailhead

Mather Point

Yavapai
Observation
Station

Canyon View
Information Plaza

Maricopa Point

Trailview
Overlook

Bright Angel
Lodge and
Kolb Studio

Powell Point

Hopi Point

Mohave Point

The Abyss

Pima Point

Hermit
Trailhead

GRAND CANYON NATIONAL PARK

From the Rim Trail, you can see forever.

The Trail

Pipe Creek trailhead to Mather Point, 1.5 miles, 55-foot elevation loss, easy. This trail segment is paved and wheelchair accessible.

The trail begins at one of the most dramatic canyon viewpoints, Pipe Creek Vista (7,175 feet elevation). In this section you'll hike through much of the vegetation typical to this area, including piñon pine, juniper, scrub oak, and yucca. There are several fine overlooks of the narrower, eastern portion of the canyon that heads toward Page. The thrum of nearby traffic reminds you that you are not too far from the highway.

As you hike past the 1-mile point you'll be treated to some open views of the eastern canyon narrows. This is a fine photo spot at sunset, especially by the water tank and relay tower near trailside. The trail ends at the rest rooms and water provided at Mather Point (elevation 7,120 feet).

Mather Point to Kolb Studio at Bright Angel Lodge, 2.5 miles (4.0 total miles), 270-foot elevation loss, easy. This trail segment is paved and wheelchair accessible.

If you are hiking at sunset or sunrise near Mather Point, you'll likely encounter some of the deer or elk that frequent this remote section of trail. After hiking 0.7 mile you arrive at the Yavapai Point observation station and overlook. This boulder-lined trail segment is dotted with wind-sculpted piñon pines that make a great foreground for sunrise canyon shots. There are several benches along the way for rest stops.

After hiking along the rim for 1.5 miles past Yavapai Point, you'll pick up the first sights and sounds of Grand Canyon Village. You soon stroll past the Bright Angel Lodge to end at the renowned Kolb Studio (6,850 feet elevation). From here you can view the precipitous drop of the Bright Angel Trail (Hike 42) below you and see much of the

From	To	Distance
Pipe Creek	Mather Point	1.3 miles
Mather Point	Yavapai Observation Station	0.75
Yavapai Observation Station	Shrine of the Ages	0.75
Shrine of the Ages	Kolb Studio	1.0
Kolb Studio	Trailview	0.7
Trailview	Maricopa Point	0.7
Maricopa Point	Powell	0.5
Powell	Hopi Point	0.3
Hopi	Mohave Point	0.8
Mohave Point	The Abyss	1.1
The Abyss	Pima Point	2.9
Pima Point	Hermit's Rest*	1.1
TOTAL		11.9 miles

* = Bus stops on its return from Hermit's Rest, heading to Hermit's Rest Transfer Station near Bright Angel Lodge.

north canyon rim opposite your vantage point. It's a good spot to look out for the California condors that ply the air currents in this wide-open section. If you want a break from hiking, the Bright Angel Lodge has all sorts of food and refreshments.

Kolb Studio to The Abyss, 4.1 miles (8.1 total miles), 150-foot elevation gain, moderately difficult.

This trail segment has a several overlooks that are bus pickup points, so you can stop and catch a ride back to the Bright Angel Lodge. There's no water available at the lookout points, however, so pack your own.

From Kolb Studio, the trail gradually climbs, showing you more of the Bright Angel Trail as you arrive at the Maricopa Point overlook at 7,020 feet. From Maricopa the route flattens out, but several branch trails make it difficult to follow—just remember to stay close to the rim. Before arriving at Powell Point, you'll walk out on the road

for 0.1 mile (you'll do this a dozen times more before the trail's end), and turn right to go to the Powell Overlook.

Around Powell Point the views are wide-open, 180-degree views of the opposite rim, more panoramic than the narrower canyon views at the beginning and ending trail segments. The roseate pinnacles near you contrast with the mellower buff colors of the opposite rim walls, with the emerald-green Colorado River below it all for contrast. Beyond Powell Point the trail becomes rockier and more primitive. This section is quieter than most—you can hear the beating of birds' wings as they circle the rim edge in front of you. As you head to Abyss Point (elevation 7,000 feet) you can hike right to the edge of the fenceless rim where the earth plummets directly beneath your feet.

The Abyss Point to Hermit's Rest, 3.8 miles, (11.9 total miles), 350-foot elevation loss, moderately difficult.

Starting from The Abyss overlook, you'll skirt a branch canyon, where the views of the opposite canyon wall are much closer than at most of the other overlooks. Here you'll again be hiking at rim's edge with some dizzying but stupendous views of the canyon beneath you. At the 1.7-mile point of this section, the trail becomes a flat dirt road until at 2.6 miles you pop back down to hug the rim until you reach the Pima Point overlook. From Pima Point you can hear the raucous Granite Rapids of the Colorado River below, as you jaunt the last mile to trail's end at Hermit's Rest (6,650 feet).

Hermit's Rest has rest rooms, water, even pop and snack machines, so you can refresh yourself while you wait for one of the shuttle buses to pick you up for your return. Or, if you are feeling ambitious, turn around and hike the 11.9 miles back along this user-friendly trail, taking another scenic cruise along the Grand Canyon rim.

Nearby Trails

After skimming the Rim, the perfect trail complement is one that delves deep into the canyon itself, offering you the perspective of the massive canyon walls looming above you rather than below you. The Bright Angel Trail (Hike 42) is right off the Rim Trail near the Bright Angel Lodge and the Kolb Studio.

Camping

There is no camping along the rim, but the very popular Mather Campground is nearby in Grand Canyon Village, and the more solitary Desert View Campground is near the east park entrance.

For more information, call Grand Canyon National Park's visitor information phone at 928-638-7888. Comprehensive Grand Canyon information is also available at www.nps.gov/grca, and the web site should be consulted before calling the staff for information.

44

East Rim, North Canyon, and Arizona Trail Loop: Terrific Trail Trio

Location: 70 miles southeast of Fredonia in the Saddle Mountain Wilderness of the Kaibab National Forest, near the North Rim of the Grand Canyon.

Total distance: 6 miles

Hiking time: 3.5 hours

Total elevation gain: 1,400 feet

Difficulty: Difficult

Best months: May through October

Auto accessibility: Excellent

Maps: USGS Dog Point, USFS Kaibab National Forest (North)

Rules: Pets on leash and horses permitted. Mountain bikes allowed on Arizona Trail.

Comments: This three-trail loop route guides you down into the scenic confines of North Canyon before looping back up to a spectacular rim tour of Northeast Arizona. With the shade provided by the cool canyon bottoms and tall trailside trees, this watered path is one of the Kaibab Plateau's best summer hikes. Wear high-top hiking boots to ease the steep descent into North Canyon.

"Now where does this trail go?" I asked myself this question as I stood next to frenetic North Canyon Creek at the canyon bottom. Coming down from the East Rim Trail (#7), I had intended to pursue the North Canyon Trail (#4) northwest to its terminus. But a sign at the trail junction indicated that the southeast branch would lead to a spring, promising more riparian pleasures if I went opposite my intended direction, straight into the mouth of this high-walled canyon.

Acting on a hunch that this would be a cooler hike that the rest of my route, I ventured along the lush canyon bottom to eventually wind my way up a steep switchback that led me along a panoramic Arizona Trail segment back to my starting point. Because there's nothing I like better than a loop hike, a decided I'd share this cobbled-together route with you. It's an exhilarating day hike in which you'll experience the highs and the lows of the scenically diverse North Canyon environs.

Getting There

From Fredonia, drive 30 miles southeast along US 89 to its intersection with AZ 67 at Jacob Lake. Drive south on AZ 67 for 27 miles, to make a left just past the De Motte Campground onto FS 611. Head 1.3 miles up FS 611 and bear left at its intersection with FS 610, following the sign for the East Rim Viewpoint. Drive 3.5 miles further on FS 611 to the spacious parking lot for the Arizona Trail, at 8,880 feet elevation.

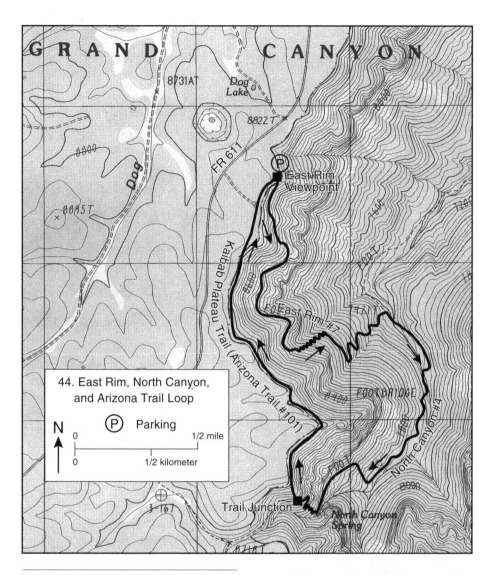

The Trail

East Rim trailhead to North Canyon Creek, 2 miles, 1,400-foot elevation loss, moderately difficult.

Walk along the Arizona Trail's paved entryway for 0.1 mile, and you'll find a signed junction for the Arizona and North Canyon Trails. Follow the trail branch to the right, which is East Rim Trail #7, and you immediately descend into the magnificent maw of

North Canyon. Even at the start of this trail, you have see-forever views of the Kaibab Plateau, House Rock Valley below it, and North Canyon's opposite wall in front of you. On this hike, you don't have to wait long for vistas to appear.

You'll switchback down North Canyon's wide rock shelves along a well-cleared earthen trail, surrounded by the Kaibab Plateau's mixed habitat vegetation of

A fabulous vista on the North Canyon Trail

manzanita, aspen, blue starflowers, and scarlet gilia. Opposite you, North Canyon's salmon-colored ridge faces jut from their dense pine masks, a long ridge of knurled abutments called Cock's Comb. As you descend, keep your eyes to the sky; you may see a pair of the California condors that patrol the north plateau. The condors have a distinctive white underlining across their 9-foot wingspan—they're as awesome a sight as the canyon spectacle beneath you.

At 1.3 miles you'll enter a shaded habitat of tall pines and firs (7,740 feet) to continue down the soft earthen trail to the canyon bottom. At 2.0 miles, you arrive at North Canyon Creek and a trail junction with trails #4 (North Canyon) and #7 (East Rim) at 7,480 feet. You head right, following the sign that indicates that North Canyon Spring is 1.5 miles farther along.

North Canyon Creek to East Rim Trail sign, 2.0 miles (4.0 total miles), 1,360-foot elevation gain, difficult.

From the creek you roll along a low-lying ridge that parallels the stream, trekking west into North Canyon. The trail is shady and cool under its canopy of bigtooth maples and conifers, a welcome respite for summer hikers and hikers' dogs. In several places you'll see the tiny creek pouring down wide rock shelves, as placidly energetic as a Japanese water garden. The creek is also a refuge for the native Apache trout, if you're inclined to incline down here for some fishing.

Just before the 3-mile mark of your hike, the trail begins to switchback out of its shady surround. Because this trail section is less frequented than other Kaibab routes, it's very quiet—you can hear the whisper of the aspens around you and the gushing stream beneath. Several five-story sandstone monoliths loom around you like trailside statues, adding to this section's audiovisual appeal. It's a pleasant place to take a break before you hike up to the rim's top.

At the 3.3-mile point you'll arrive next to photo-op North Canyon Spring, with its stream of water crashing 100 feet down onto the creek boulders below. Hiking on to your 4.0-mile point, you pass a stock gate to arrive at a multi signed trail junction (8,860 feet) for Kaibab Plateau Trail #101, Crystal Spring, and the East Rim Viewpoint. Head along the East Rim route, which leads you back to your starting point via the Arizona Trail.

East Rim Trail sign to trailhead, 2.0 miles (6.0 total miles), 40-foot elevation gain, easy.

As you wend along the level canyon rim, you'll find this section to be sinuous, smooth, and spectacular. The first forested mile has a score of overlooks that gift you with hundred-mile prospects that the windshield tourists never see. Hiking along, you'll view the stupendous red and yellow wall of the Vermilion Cliffs to the north, stretching out for a score of miles. The particolored walls of Marble Canyon rise to the east in front of you, bordered by the silver ribbon of the canyon-carving Colorado River. The solitary hump of Navajo Mountain rises from the Navajo Reservation flatlands near Glen Canyon Dam. But my favorite attractions here are the otherworldly "butte islands" and volcanoes of House Rock Valley in front of the Vermilion Cliffs. These prominences float in a milky sea of low-lying fog and clouds. Over the last trail mile, these views just become more open and inspiring—it's demands a strolling pace just to savor all the sights.

Finally, you arrive at a sign indicating the East Rim Viewpoint is only 0.25 mile away as you return to your paved trail entry point, finishing a loop hike you'll pass along to others.

Nearby Trails

If the Arizona Trail whets your appetite for more spectacular rim hiking, drive a little farther south on AZ 67 to the Widforss Trail in Grand Canyon National Park. The Widforss is a moderately difficult, 10-mile round trip, but if you hike even a few miles of it you'll find a host of panoramic overlooks between the trailside aspens and conifers. Trip details at www.nps.gov/grca/grandcanyon/dayhike/nr-day-hike.htm.

Camping

There are several flat and shaded primitive campsites in the North Creek Canyon bottom, with more along the Arizona Trail. The De Motte Campground, on AZ 67 by the trailhead, has 23 sites for tents and motor homes. The campground has water, telephones, and toilets, but no utility hookups. If this campground is full, seek out the Jacob Lake Campground near your entry point at the US 89–AZ 67 junction.

For more information, contact the Kaibab Plateau Visitors Center, Jacob Lake, AZ 85051. Telephone: 928-643-7298. You can find good North Kaibab campground information and trail descriptions on the web site at www.fs.fed.us/r3/kai/oldrecreation/camp_dem.html.

45

South Canyon: Wild!

Location: Saddle Mountain Wilderness in Kaibab National Forest near the North Rim of the Grand Canyon, 70 miles southeast of Fredonia.

Distance: 5 miles round trip (2.5-mile shuttle hike)

Hiking time: 3.5 hours

Total elevation gain: 2,030 feet

Difficulty: Difficult

Best months: May through October.

Auto accessibility: Good

Maps: USGS Little Park Point, Point Imperial, Buffalo Ranch. USFS Kaibab National Forest (North)

Rules: Pets on leash permitted. Only experienced trail horses are recommended for this trail. No bikes.

Comments: Take this precipitous and overgrown primitive trail for solitude and a true wilderness experience. It is one of the Kaibab Plateau's most solitary and least developed trails; you'll feel like an explorer when you hike this one! GPS signals do not pick up near the trailhead, where there is a relay tower. Bring bug repellent and water.

What was the South Canyon Trail like? After inquiring at two Kaibab ranger stations, I still didn't have an answer; none of a half dozen staffers had been down it. None of my hiking web sites posted a trail description. My only clue was a general trail summary and map provided by the receptionist at the Kaibab Plateau Visitors Center. Promising I would send the staff more details, I drove over to explore the South Canyon Trail.

"Explore" would turn out to be an accurate term for my adventure. It was a busy fall weekend, and the North Kaibab Plateau was swarming with hikers imbibing the luminous fall colors around the Grand and Marble Canyon rims. But I met no one along the South Canyon Trail, nor were there any signs that anyone had recently been there. Perhaps no one had been there because there are so many other plateau pathways, or perhaps it's because this nonmaintained route is difficult to find and to hike. Whatever the reason, you'll likely find yourself hiking alone, enjoying the route's chuckling little stream and enormous forest overgrowth. But the solitude comes at a price. Be prepared to go skidding down some steep and crumbly portions of trail, ducking through dense overgrowth, and gasping your way back up the sections you had skidded down. If you're like me, you'll find the trip more exhilarating than frustrating, tangling with a tangled trail that puts the "wild" back into the popular "wilderness."

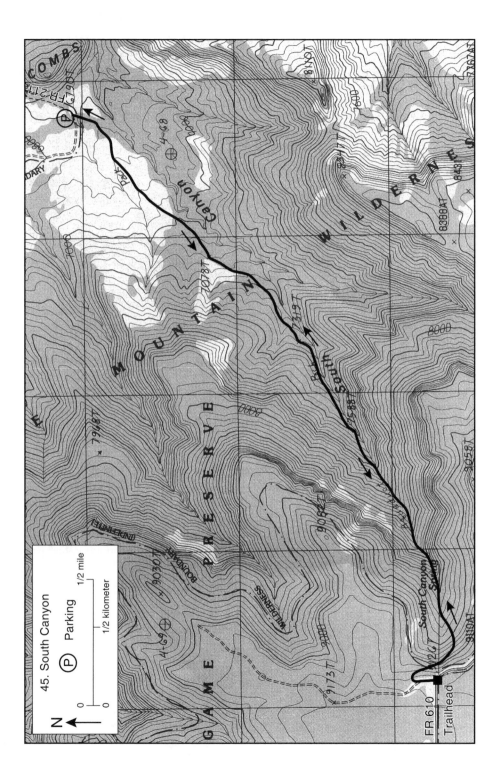

45. South Canyon

ⓅＰarking

N

0   1/2 mile
0   1/2 kilometer

COMBS

FR 211

FR 190

BOUNDARY

DECK

Canyon

MOUNTAIN

PRESERVE

GAME

WILDERNESS

WILDERNESS

BOUNDARY

South Br.

FR 610

South Canyon Spring

Trailhead

x 8167T

x 8211T

8388T

8438T

8000

x 7958T

9036T

9173T

9058T

8169T

7964T

7868T

8000

10787T

7319T

7588T

Getting There

From Fredonia, drive 30 miles southeast along US 89 to its intersection with AZ 67 at Jacob Lake. Making a right, drive 27 miles south on AZ 67 to turn left onto FR 611 just past the DeMotte Campground. Drive 1.3 miles on FR 611, and then turn right onto FR 610. Go 7.5 miles along FR 610, driving 0.6 mile past the sign for the Marble Canyon Overlook, and make a left into an unmarked dirt road. Bear right for 0.3 mile to come to the trailhead marker on your right, barely visible among the trees and brush surrounding it.

The Trail

Northern trailhead to Trail 6 sign, 2.5 miles, 2,030-foot elevation loss, difficult.

Pushing your way through the brush around the trailhead (9,120 feet elevation), you soon pass a wilderness marker, at which point you bear right and begin your descent into the canyon. You'll pass through several groves of tall aspen that make this a glorious autumn hike, when the sun backlights the aspen leaves into molten gold. This verdant trail segment is overgrown with several types of brambly little bushes; unless you're into self-flagellation you should wear long pants on this hike. The pines and firs grow so close together here that you can hear them groan as they rub against one another in the wind—it's a haunting sound in the dead quiet of this trail. The soft dirt path is crumbly underfoot, making is easy for you to slide on the steeper sections, so walk carefully.

This jungle-gym workout continues for the first trail mile. You'll corkscrew down this tricky trail, climbing over a half dozen snags (fallen trees) that straddle it, some of them 4 feet high. Although there are several spots where water usually trickles across

the trail, you should pack your own to be safe. And pack a gallon, because you'll work up a sweat!

After a mile, the trail leaves behind its densest undergrowth, and you are treated to views of rock outcroppings on both sides of the trail. After 1.5 miles, you can glimpse the pale walls of South Canyon on your right, as the trail becomes more a steady decline. Along this trail segment you'll spy hosts of scarlet gilia and many other wildflowers, accompanied by the many birds that flit and twitter among the trees and brush. As the trail levels out over its last mile, you'll find yourself cruising along, enjoying the wildlife and the scenery.

At 2.5 miles you pass a trail 6 sign (for the number of the South Canyon Trail) and several backcountry campsites at 7,090 feet. This is a good spot to turn around if you are hiking back up to the trailhead. If you are doing a shuttle hike, you'll leave your car near this trailhead at the end of Forest Road 211. If you hike another 0.5 mile or so along FS 211, you'll see more open canyon views and find lots of shady and level campsites.

Trail 6 sign to northern trailhead, 2.5 miles (5.0 total miles), 2,030-foot elevation gain, difficult.

The return trip has several steep sections over the last mile up to the trailhead, so you might want to take a couple of breath breaks on your way back.

Nearby Trails

If you continue along FS 610 past the South Canyon Trail entrance, you'll come to the Nankoweap Trail (#57), a busy but spectacular 14-mile entrance into the depths of the Grand Canyon. The first 6 miles are a pleasant hike through the Saddle Mountain Wilderness.

South Canyon vegetation is rich and varied.

Camping

The first backcountry campsites appeared near the 2.25-mile point on my descent into the canyon, with more cropping up as the trail went along. The Demotte Campground, which you pass on AZ 67 on your way to the trailhead, has 23 sites for tents and motor homes. The campground has water, telephones, and toilets, but no utility hookups. If this campground is full, seek out the Jacob Lake Campground near your entry point at the US 89–AZ 67 junction.

For more information, contact the Kaibab Plateau Visitors Center, Jacob Lake, AZ 85051. Telephone: 928-643-7298. You can find more North Kaibab Plateau campground information and trail descriptions on the Forest Service web site at www.fs.fed.us/r3/kai/oldrecreation/camp_ dem.html.

46

Mount Trumbull: Remotely Attractive

Location: Mount Trumbull Wilderness in the Grand Canyon–Parshant National Monument, 60 miles southwest of Fredonia.

Total distance: 5.2 miles

Hiking time: 2.5 hours

Total elevation gain: 1,550 feet

Difficulty: Difficult

Best months: March through November

Auto accessibility: Acceptable. The bumpy, primitive road requires 20- to 30-mph speeds.

Maps: USGS Mount Trumbull NW, NE, and SE

Rules: Dogs on leash permitted.

Comments: A solitary hike to the top of a basalt mesa that rules over one of Arizona's remotest regions.This is one of those rare mountaintop climbs that becomes easier as you approach the summit. Pack at least a quart of water per person for the trip, and double that amount in summer.

"Solitude, I reflected, is the one deep necessity of the human spirit to which adequate recognition is never given in our codes. It is looked upon as a discipline or a penance, but hardly ever as the indispensable, pleasant ingredient it is to ordinary life; and from this want of recognition come half our domestic troubles."

–Freya Stark, from *The Journey's Echo: Selections from Freya Stark* (1934)

After an hour of bouncing across the primitive roads of the million-acre Grand Canyon–Parshant National Monument, I almost turned tail back to the paved and posterior-pampering smoothness of AZ 389. But the mystery of the Mount Trumbull Trail lured me on. Because this trail is situated in one of Arizona's remotest regions, there were few trail descriptions of Mount Trumbull, and my inquiries of local forest rangers produced only sketchy details. And so I wondered: What was this hike like? Why didn't anyone know about it?

I discovered that this trail is protected from casual visits by the long and winding road that leads to your goal, one that tests your driving patience but rewards you with grade-A solitude and scenery. After a visit to this wide-open tableland of buttes and mesas, I was grateful that I had persisted in my solitary pilgrimage to the Mount Trumbull summit. At the top I gaped at tri-state views of pristine buttes, mesas, and mountains, set in a deserted desert landscape that looks much the same now as it did to its first human visitors over ten thousand years ago. So, if you find remoteness attractive,

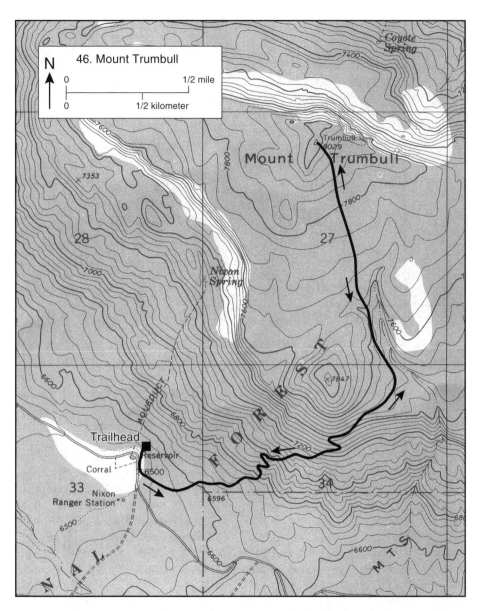

take a trip back to the land that time (and developers) forgot, with a climactic trek up the Mount Trumbull Trail.

Getting There

Created in 2000, the Grand Canyon–Parshant National Monument is a biological and geologic sanctuary that abuts Grand Canyon National Park and envelops the junction of Arizona, Utah, and Nevada. To reach the monument from Fredonia, drive 7 miles west on AZ 389 to turn left just past the National Park sign for Toroweap, starting along Mount Trumbull Road. Proceed

---

Mount Trumbull: Remotely Attractive

The view from Mount Trumbull

46 miles at a slow pace (25 to 35 mph) along this road, to make a right at the sign for Mount Trumbull. Drive another 7 miles to the well-marked trailhead, passing a simple Mt Trumbull sign about a mile before you reach the parking lot, and turn into the parking lot on your right. You'll park in a small valley surrounded by mountains and buttes.

The Trail

Trailhead to Mount Trumbull summit, 2.6 miles, 1,550-foot elevation gain, difficult.

Setting out from the trailhead at 6,520 feet, you immediately begin climbing up to the summit. Along the first half of the trail you'll wend through a mixed dryland habitat of piñon pine, agave, prickly pear cactus, and manzanita. The open woodlands here provide many glimpses of the undeveloped countryside around you, featuring the nearby humps of Mount Logan and other summits.

The higher up you go, the better the views become, which should motivate you to push through this steep trail segment. In spring and summer the path is sprinkled with the bright colors of cactus blossoms, red penstemon, and sunny yellow asters, glowing against the spongy basalt pebbles that surround them. The pebbles are rocky remnants of Mount Trumbull's past life as a lava-spewing volcano, a reminder that these arid wild lands were once a tropical swamp replete with dinosaurs, a fascinating chapter in the monument's billion-year history.

Near the 1.4-mile point of your hike (elevation 7,540 feet), you'll notice that the piñon woodlands are giving way to a ponderosa pine habitat, signaling your entrance into a different life zone. The trail now levels out to become a foot-friendly earthen path, carpeted with pine needles and dappled with the shade of the surrounding 40-foot conifers—it's as pleasant as a walk in the park. Farther on, the trail narrows and becomes a bit more difficult to follow, but there are several rock cairns to lead you along the righteous path, as the final trail segment winds and rolls up the side of the summit.

As a layer of scrub oak replaces the open understory of the pine woodlands, you'll know you're near the top. During the last 0.2 mile you'll step up through a short, steep section to top off on a narrow, woodsy ridge lined with pines and oaks. A wide, flat boulder at the top contains a geodetic marker from 1953, a sign that you are standing at the summit (8,070 feet elevation). From the summit you can walk around and glimpse an impressive geologic scene that only Mount Trumbull's few visitors ever see. Off to the north, past the Utah border, lie the legendary monoliths of Zion National Park, with the great wall of the Grand Staircase–Escalante Monument sweeping off to its right. To the south march row upon row of buttes and small mountains, down toward Lake Mead, and to the east sprawl the flatlands of the Coconino Plateau and the Grand Canyon, with Flagstaff's San Francisco Peaks visible in the distance. No matter where you look, chances are you won't see any people, vehicles, or construction. Enjoy your unique perspective—it's a rockscape unlike any other in Arizona, a fitting reward for the work you've done to reach the top.

Summit to trailhead, 2.6 miles (5.2 miles total), 1,550-foot elevation loss, easy.

On your return, make sure you don't rush the final 1-mile descent to the trailhead. The pebbles underfoot can turn into marbles if you don't step down firmly. As you head toward your car, likely the only visitor to this trail, be grateful that the long and winding road that took you here is part of the reason you can feel that your hike has been a step back in time, where you can wander through an unspoiled landscape.

Nearby Trails

The Grand Canyon–Parshant National Monument is seamed with fascinating canyon labyrinths, and there are many trails and sights to explore near Mount Trumbull. One of the best is the Lava Falls Trail, a difficult, 1.5-mile hike to the roaring falls near the Colorado River. This slippery hike is also the shortest route from the Grand Canyon rim to the river. For more information on the Lava Falls Trail, consult the web sites at www.arizonahandbook.com/toroweap.htm and www.americansouthwest.net/arizona/grand_canyon/lava_falls_trail.html.

Camping

There are several backcountry campsites past the 1.5-mile point in the hike, in the soft earth underneath the pines. Nixon Spring, located near the base of Mount Trumbull, has permanent water and a primitive campground that is easily accessible.

For more information, contact the Bureau of Land Management (BLM), which manages the Grand Canyon–Parshant area. For more information, visit the BLM's web site, www.az.blm.gov, or contact the BLM Arizona Strip Field Office, 345 East Riverside Drive, St. George, UT 84790-9000. Telephone: 435-688-3200.

Hidden Treasures of Northeast Arizona

47

Horse Crossing Trail #20: Pooled Assets

Location: Mogollon Rim country in the Coconino National Forest, 35 miles northeast of Payson and 70 miles southeast of Flagstaff.

Total distance: 2.8 miles, with additional trail miles along the creek

Hiking time: 2 hours

Total elevation gain: 1,230 feet

Difficulty: Moderately difficult

Best months: May through October

Auto accessibility: Poor. High-clearance vehicle required for the last 1.8 miles of rutted and rocky Forest Road 513B.

Maps: USGS Blue Ridge Reservoir. A general trail description and map are on the web site at www.fs.fed.us/r3/coconino /recreation/mog_rim/horse-crossing-tr .shtml.

Rules: Dog and horses permitted. No motorized vehicles on the trail. FS 95 is closed to vehicles in winter.

Comments: This hidden gem is perfect for a family hike to the creek, followed by a fun exploration of its calendar-pretty creekside pools. If you plan to bushwhack along the creek trails, wear long pants to protect your legs from the canyon bottom's brambly bushes.

How about this for a camping idyll? Waking up to the sound of the creek chuckling along outside your tent, you crawl out to see the sun lighting up the striated sandstone walls in front of you, your back shadowed by the 10-story canyon ramparts behind. You've slept soundly in your solitary campsite, so you already feel energetic enough for a swim. Kicking off your sandals, you walk across the sandy little beach that curves beneath your camping spot, and take a running dive into a huge emerald pool. Then you paddle over to the black-and-tan rock ledges that arch over your quiet pond, hanging onto a ledge while you watch the sun set their craggy faces aglow.

Sound like a scene from some private tropical resort? Nope, it's just one of several idyllic spots at the end of the little-known Horse Crossing Trail. For the price of a half-hour hike down to East Clear Creek, you can enjoy the creek's deep pools and gin-clear waters, all set in a lush riparian habitat at the bottom of a rugged and colorful canyon. And if you are in the mood, you can explore several unnamed creekside trails that reveal more scenic surprises. It's hard to believe that this is a relatively unexplored trail, but there are few authentic trail descriptions of this Mogollon Rim gem.

Getting There

From Flagstaff, at the intersection of Forest Service Road 3 (Lake Mary Road) and AZ 87, drive north 9 miles on AZ 87, passing mile marker 299 to turn right onto FS 95, just past the Blue Ridge Ranger Station. Drive 4 miles down gravelly but level FS 95,

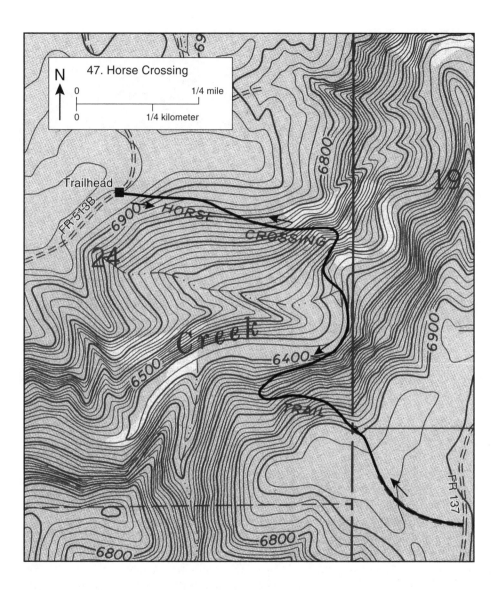

passing milepost 4 to turn left at the sign for Horse Crossing Trail #20 and onto FS 513B. Drive 1.8 miles on this dirt road, taking care to slowly negotiate the 2-foot-deep ruts that lie in wait, and turn into the parking lot next to the trailhead sign on your right.

The Trail

Trailhead to creek, 0.7 mile, 630-elevation loss, moderately difficult.

As you walk past the old wooden trailhead sign (elevation 6,960 feet) you start your continuous descent down the wide Horse Crossing Trail. The path is rocky and steep in some spots. You have to pick your way down carefully, but it is not dangerous. The trail threads its way down among a classic Mogollon Rim forest of huge pines and junipers, with an open understory carpeted with pine needles and dotted with

Clear Creek

miniature white and yellow wildflowers. As you descend, you will glimpse the sandstone skywalls of Clear Creek Canyon, awaiting your entrance.

At the 0.6-mile point you come past the ruins of a tiny cabin, complete with stone fireplace. This is one of the many old cabins that grace the trails of this area, remnants from the nineteenth-century ranchers and settlers who called the Mogollon Rim home. After passing the cabin, it's less than 0.1 mile down to the creek at 6,330 feet elevation. In spring and summer the creek habitat is filled with life: Trout swim in the deep pools, bushes bloom among the tall cedars and pines that dwell along the creek bottom, and birds and butterflies flutter among the flowers. Insects also swarm around here, so bring some bug repellent in case they get too personal.

Creek to trail's end 0.7 mile, (1.4 miles total), 600-foot elevation gain on return from the creek, moderately difficult.

From the creek you can switchback up another 0.7 mile to trail's end at FS 137, gaining some 600 feet in elevation. The trail reprises the piñon and juniper environment you enjoyed on your way down to the water from the trailhead. From FS 137, you return to the creek (2.1 miles total).

However, if you follow the creekside trails instead of going to trail's end, this is where the fun starts. Hike the unnamed trail upstream, which mostly hugs the shallow canyon walls on your right, and you will keep discovering new creek and canyon scenes as you move along the watercourse. Less than 0.2 mile along this trail, on the opposite side of the creek (which is usually shallow enough for wading) you will see a pretty campsite on a small knoll above the stream.

If you hike downstream from the trail crossing, you will find several deep green pools endowed with their own little beaches, scattered underneath the multicolored canyon walls that shelter the creek. You will have to crisscross the creek to find these scenic gems, however, and following the overgrown trail can be a challenge. But it's a safe challenge, the trail is flat albeit gravelly, and the rewards of discovering these off-trail oases will lure you ever farther into the canyon. (I know they had that effect upon me.) Just make sure you're prepared for wet feet!

After you have your fill of exploring these creekside wonders, bushwhack your way back to the beginning of the Horse Crossing Trail for your return to the trailhead.

Creek to trailhead, 0.7 mile (2.8 total miles), 630-foot elevation gain, moderately difficult.

The return trip is uphill all the way, so I hope you saved some energy after playing around near the creek. The gain is gradual, however, and an unhurried pace should prevent the return trip from being too breathtaking, after all that breathtaking scenery.

Nearby Trails

If you like Horse Crossing's riparian attractions, try the neighboring Kinder Trail for more aquatic enjoyments. This 6-mile (round-trip) trail is a cross-creek journey from one forest road to another, so you can make it a full-day hike or a shorter shuttle hike. Rumor has it that you can join the Horse Creek Trail from the Kinder Trail by following the unmarked creek trail upstream.

Camping

As you may have guessed by now, the Horse Crossing Trail has excellent back-country camping along the unnamed creek trails. There are also many pull-in, primitive campsites on the roads up to the trailhead, large enough to accommodate 20-foot trailers. The Blue Ridge campground is near the Blue Ridge Ranger Station on your way to the trail. The campground has 10 sites that can hold trailers up to 16 feet, with water and toilets. Fee is $8 per night.

For more information, contact the Blue Ridge Ranger Station, HC 31 Box 300, Happy Jack, AZ, 66024. Telephone: 928-477-2255. Nearby trails and campgrounds are described on the web site at www.fs.fed.us/r3/coconino/recreation/mog _rim/rec_mogollon.shtml.

48

Rim Lakes Vista Trail: Keeping a Constant Lookout

Location: Apache Sitgreaves National Forest, 31 miles east of Payson

Total distance: 6.6 miles (3.3-mile shuttle hike)

Hiking time: 3 hours, 15 minutes

Total elevation gain: 50 feet

Difficulty: Easy

Best months: March through November

Auto accessibility: Excellent, with paved roads all the way.

Maps: USGS Woods Canyon SW

Rules: Pets on leash; bikes and horses permitted.

Comments: You can't get any closer to the edge of the Mogollon Rim than hiking along this see-forever trail. The views are constant and spectacular, particularly when the morning light illuminates all of southern Arizona below you. The trail has a 0.8-mile wheelchair-accessible portion. Bring your own water.

The rim . . . the view . . . the rim with a view. These are the outstanding features of this edgy trail. Walking along the Rim Lakes Vista Trail is like walking along the edge of the world. Up on this windswept rock plateau, the rolling green Arizona country-side unfolds over a thousand feet below you, so distant it seems part of another country—and so it is. "Rim Country," as the Central Highlands are often called, has its own iden-tity, an on-the-level pine and juniper land-scape that shelters its many springs and creeks. Far below it lies the densely conifer-ous landscape of north-central Arizona, cor-rugated with mountain ranges that stretch all the way to the deserts of Phoenix and Tucson. The Rim Lakes Vista Trail, so named for its views and its proximity to several lakes, is a unique trail that is essentially one continuous overlook, as you stroll from one vista point to the next. If you like playing above the Rim, this trail is for you.

Getting There

From Payson, at the base of the Mogollon Rim, drive 31 winding, scenic miles east on AZ 260 to turn left at the Woods Canyon Lake sign. Drive into the rimtop parking area on your immediate right. The trailhead is di-rectly across the road from the rimtop kiosk and the rest rooms. It is marked by a plastic sign that just says TRAIL. If you look at the trees behind the sign, you will see the first of the many white diamonds that mark the Rim Lakes Vista Trail. (If you see white chevrons, they are for the General Crook Trail, and you are in the wrong place.)

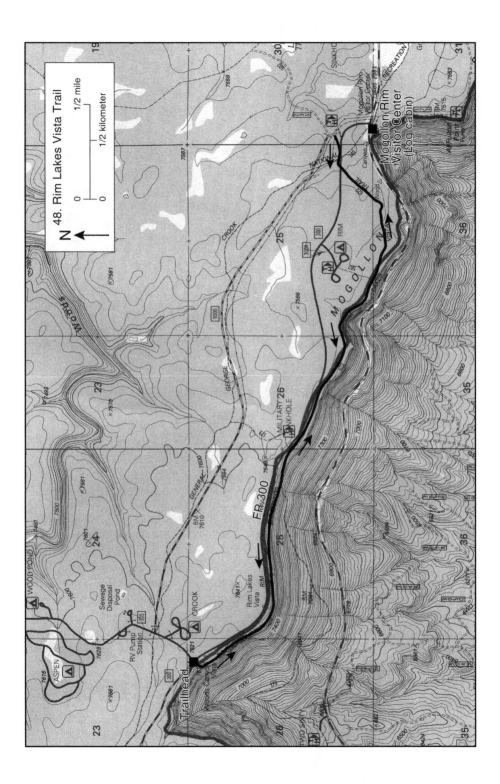

48. Rim Lakes Vista Trail

N

0   1/2 mile

0   1/2 kilometer

Mogollon Rim
Visitor Center
(Log cabin)

Mogollon Rim
Visitor Center

M O G O L L O N

RIM VISTA

FR 300

Rim Lakes
Vista RIM

GENERAL 7600

MILITARY 26

SINKHOLE

CROOK

NATIONAL

Trailhead

Sewage
Disposal
Pond

RV Pump
Station

ASPEN

WOODS POND

CROOK

On the Rim Lakes Vista Trail

The Trail

Rimtop parking lot to rock cairn, 0.8 mile, 10-foot elevation gain, easy.

As you walk past the trail sign (elevation 7,590 feet), you start through a wide grassy swale to encounter a trail sign at the 0.1-mile point, directing you to cross FS 300. After you cross the road you'll meander across an open landscape dotted with the pines, junipers, and aspens that populate much of the Mogollon Rim. I have spotted several small herds of elk roaming the trailside here in the morning, so watch for wildlife. You might also keep an eye out for summer thunderstorms here; the Mogollon Rim is the world's second-most-thunderstruck area!

After strolling along 0.8 mile you come to a 4-foot rock cairn (7,600 feet) and you veer right here to join the Mogollon Rim your level-headed companion for the rest of the trip.

Rock cairn to trail's end, 2.5 miles (3.3 total miles), 40-foot elevation gain, easy.

The breezy rim trail is very flat and very visible, so it's easy to concentrate upon the views to your left instead of the path. And what views they are! With your Olympian perspective you can gaze down at ant-sized farms and villages along AZ 260, and at the waves of mountains marching south, row upon row, all the way down to Mexico. At the 1-mile point, you'll reach the Rim Campground (you can use the campground as a starting point if you camp there), and continue along the flat rock shelf that the trail follows.

Birds love the rim area, and you might glimpse (as I did) one of the splendid western tanagers that visit the overlook area. With a bright red top and a brighter yellow body, the tanagers are a vivid color splash amid the green forest backdrop, so they are easy to spot. You'll also hear the occasional car or RV passing by on the nearby Rim Road (FS 300), reminding you that civilization is not too far away.

At 1.5 miles you join the first of several highway pull-in overlooks, each with sight-seeing benches near the edge of the rim. The benches are a sign that there is a particularly good view here. (I hope you brought your camera.) At the 2.5-mile point you start to cruise along on the wheelchair-accessible portion of the trail, passing the Rim Vista Overlook pull-in spot, to end the trail at the Meadow Trail kiosk and parking lot (elevation 7,640 feet).

Trail's end to trailhead, 3.3 miles (6.6 total miles), 50-foot elevation loss, easy.

The end of the trail is a parking lot off FS 300, 3 road miles from your trailhead parking lot, so it's easy to leave a second vehicle there if you want a shuttle hike. You can also start your hike from this point, but I found the path markers easier to locate by going in the direction I've described in this chapter. The return trip should be relatively easy, as long as you have brought enough water to replenish your precious body fluids. Make sure you don't wear down your fingertip (as a Grand Canyon guide once remarked) by pointing at all the scenery!

Nearby Trails

If you continue east on FS 300 past the Rim Lakes Vista trailhead for about 7 miles, you'll come to the See Canyon Trail entry point. This 3.5-mile (one-way) trail descends the Mogollon Rim by following a creek through See Canyon, providing Mogollon Rim overlooks as well as a verdant riparian environment of maples and aspen. The trail ends at the famous Highline Trail (See Hike 21) and the Christopher Creek community.

Camping

I noticed several primitive campsites in the first mile of the trail, but after that you are too near the forest road to pitch a tent. There's no shortage of campgrounds near the trail, however. You can even access the trail from the Rim or the Mogollon Campground right off FS 300. Each of these campgrounds has 26 sites that take tents and small trailers, and each has water. Fees are $10 per night, and neither accepts reservations.

For more information, contact the Black Mesa Ranger District, PO Box 968, Overgaard, AZ 85933. Telephone 928-535-4481. The trails list for the ranger district is on the web site at www.fs.fed.us/ r3/asnf/recreation/campgrounds.

49

Buena Vista Trail: A Peek at the Peaks

Location: 5 miles south of Show Low, in the Apache–Sitgreaves National Forest.

Total distance: 7.5-mile loop

Hiking time: 4 hours

Total elevation gain: 600 feet

Difficulty: Moderately difficult

Best months: April through October (hike early in the day in summer)

Auto accessibility: Excellent; trailhead is a short drive off of US 60.

Maps: USGS Show Low South

Rules: Dogs on leash. Mountain biking permitted. Horses permitted.

Comments: An easy ramble through the Mogollon Rim countryside, providing high-point peeks at the mountains of northern Arizona. This is one of the most clearly marked trails in the state, making it a secure hike for solitary or novice hikers.

As I left Show Low for Tucson, I drove past a Forest Service sign for the Buena Vista Trail. Acting on a whim, I pulled off the highway into the trailhead parking lot to explore this route. And I'm glad I followed my impulse. The Buena Vista Trail must be named for the four "buenas vistas" (Spanish for "good views") that pop up along different parts of this easy half-day ramble among the pines and junipers, providing glimpses of many of Arizona's highest pinnacles. Next time you are in Show Low, explore this little-known forest trail, and enjoy a peek at the peaks.

Getting There

From Show Low, go south on US 60 (AZ 77) toward Globe for 5 miles. Make a left just past mile marker 637 onto Forest Road 300, going 300 yards east to make a left into the trailhead parking lot.

The Trail

Trailhead to trail junction, 3.7 miles, 300-foot elevation gain, moderately difficult.

From the trailhead (elevation 6,550 feet), you'll start off on a level, sandy trail that snakes through a scattering of 80-foot pines and squat alligator junipers. After 0.5 mile you come to a trail junction that starts the loop portion of the trail. Bear right at the junction. The trail is clearly marked with light blue diamonds, indicating it is part of the White Mountain Trail System. Be sure to keep your eye on the diamonds as you hike, because there are a number of false trails and roads off both sides of this trail. In dry

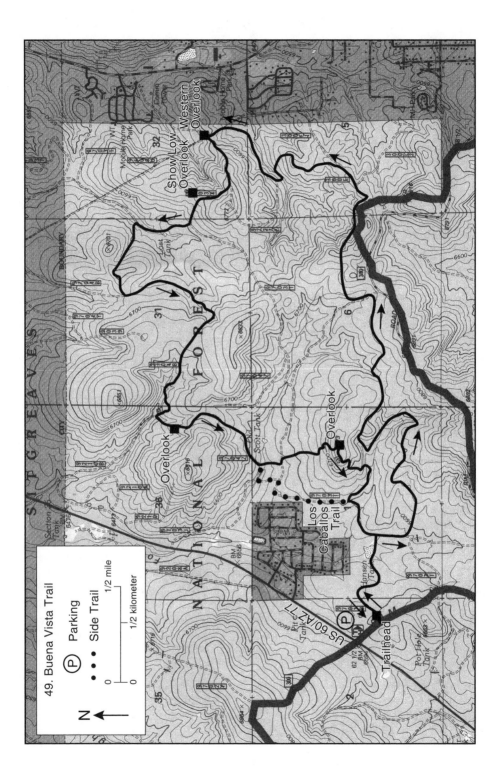

49. Buena Vista Trail

(P) Parking

• • • Side Trail

N

0   1/2 mile
0   1/2 kilometer

SITGREAVES

NATIONAL

FOREST

Western Overlook

Show Low Overlook

Overlook

Overlook

Los Caballos Trail

Trailhead

US 60/AZ 77

Mobile Home Park

Hansen Trail

Section Trail

On the trail

weather the trail terrain is a joy to walk: The soft and bouncy earth makes you feel as if you could hike all day on it. In wet weather the path morphs into a muddy morass, troweling your boot soles with half a foot of clay-like soil. For the sake of the trail and your legs, don't make this a rainy-day journey.

At 1.3 miles the trail takes on an Ozark character, with shallow rocky ridges jutting out of the hillsides, and rounded boulders bubbling out of the open forest floor. Then, at 1.6 miles, you encounter another junction (elevation 6,730 feet). Bear right to follow the trail sign marked #637. From here the trail rises gradually, and the route is now lined with the ceanothus bushes and small junipers that are parked under its pine steeples.

When you reach the 2.5-mile point, the trail ceases to be a forest road as it veers to the right and disappears into the trees, becoming a narrow trail that wends its way up to a high ridge. At 2.7 miles (6,830 feet elevation), the trail finally opens up into views of Timber Mesa to the west, with glimpses of the nearby White Mountains to the south, and the distant San Francisco Mountains near Alpine. From the overlook, the trail follows the boundary of the White Mountain Apache Reservation.

Another 0.1 mile brings you to an eastern overlook that shows Show Low below you. You can also spy highest-point Humphreys Peak in the distance near Flagstaff, and the sprawling Phoenix area off to the left—quite a variety of scenes. From here the trail is a forest road ramble down through manzanita and pines, flavored with some highway noise, until you come to another trail junction at the 3.7-mile point.

Trail junction to trail's end, 3.8 miles (7.5 miles total), 300-foot elevation gain, moderately difficult.

From the junction at 6,580 feet, you fork to the left and leave the forest road to ascend a narrower trail. At the 4-mile mark the trail emerges into more views of western Arizona at 6,730 feet. Just 0.5 mile farther along at 4.5 miles, you start up a short rocky ridge to discover 270-degree views of eastern, northern, and western Arizona. From here you can perceive the outlines of Mount Escudilla and Mount Baldy, two of Arizona's highest peaks, off to the east.

Trooping along from the lookout, you come to a junction of the Buena Vista and Los Caballos Trails (elevation 6,640 feet) near the 6-mile point, and continue along the Buena Vista Trail. After another 0.5 mile you mount a manzanita-lined ridge for the fourth and final overlook (elevation 6,790 feet) of Show Low and western Arizona. Walk another 0.5 mile and join the original trail junction at the 7-mile point of your hike, to stroll the final 0.5 mile to the trailhead. It's been a pleasant forest ramble with several arresting views, a fine way to spend a day in the forest.

Nearby Trails

If you are looking for a longer or more difficult hike than the mellow Buena Vista Trail, consider the trail that joins it, the Los Caballos Trail. This 14-mile trail has some steep ascents as it rolls through the pine and juniper woodlands of the Mogollon

Rim to show off overlooks of the White Mountains and the White Mountain Apache Reservation. You can reach the Los Caballos Trail from the Buena Vista Trail, or via FS 136 near Show Low. To learn more about the Buena Vista Trail, visit www.fs.us/r3/ansf.recreation/trails/lakeside_rd/tr_lak_buena_vista.shtml. For more about Los Caballos Trail, visit www.fs.fed.us/r3/asnf/recreation/trails/lakeside_rd/trl_lak_los_caballos.shtml.

Camping

There are many opportunities for backcountry camping along the forest road sections of the trail, and near the overlooks. Fool Hollow Lake Campground is a large campground parked among the shady pines and piñons alongside (well, duh!) Fool Hollow Lake. There are 92 sites for RVs under 45 feet and 31 developed campsites. The fee is $15 a night for hookup sites, $10 a night for sites without hookups. Go to the Forest Service web site at www.fs.fed.us/r3/asnf/resources/devcamp_hollow.htm for details.

For more information, contact the Lakeside Ranger District at 928-368-5111. For trail and camping info, visit the White Mountains Online website at www.fs.fed.us/r3/ansf/recreation/campgrounds.

50

Long Logs and Agate House Trails: A Monumental Journey Back in Time

Location: Petrified Forest National Park, 23 miles southeast of Holbrook.

Total distance: 2.2 miles

Hiking time: 1.5 hours

Total elevation gain: 50 feet

Difficulty: Easy

Best months: March through November

Auto accessibility: Excellent. The trail is right off the paved highway that runs through the national monument.

Maps: USGS Agate House. Free park map at visitors center.

Rules: Pets on leash permitted. Bikes only on paved roads. Don't take away any pieces of the Petrified Forest. $10 entry fee per vehicle.

Comments: The longest trail combo in the Petrified National Forest is an easy hike to an up-close study of the park's petrified logs and sandstone formations. The Long Logs Trail has the greatest concentration of petrified logs in the entire monument.

Tropical Arizona? Believe it. During the Triassic period, some 225 million years ago, the Holbrook area was a vast swampy floodplain, fed by streams that flowed northward off the Mogollon Rim. Dinosaurs roamed groves of gigantic trees such as that granddaddy of all conifers, 200-foot *Araucarioxylon*. As the trees died, they fell into groundwater filled with silica-laden volcanic ash. The groundwater gradually "petrified" these logs by converting the wood to quartz. Today, the swampy forest has turned into an arid highland awash with the multicolored remnants of fossilized trees, many of which are on display in Petrified Forest National Park. If you stroll the park's Agate House and Long Logs Trails, you'll see fossils and hills painted in a rainbow of earthtone hues, monuments to a time when dinosaurs roamed the earth.

Getting There

From Holbrook. drive 20 miles east on US 180 to the park entrance, and make a right to drive 0.5 mile to the park entrance station ($10 entry fee), and proceed another 2 miles to park in the Rainbow Forest parking lot, the start of your hike.

The Trail

Parking lot to Agate House trailhead, 0.6 miles, 20-foot elevation gain, easy.

Starting from the museum parking lot (elevation 5,505 feet) you walk along the museum gift shop's sidewalk across a small bridge over the Jim Camp Wash, and turn right to pass through a concrete entrance

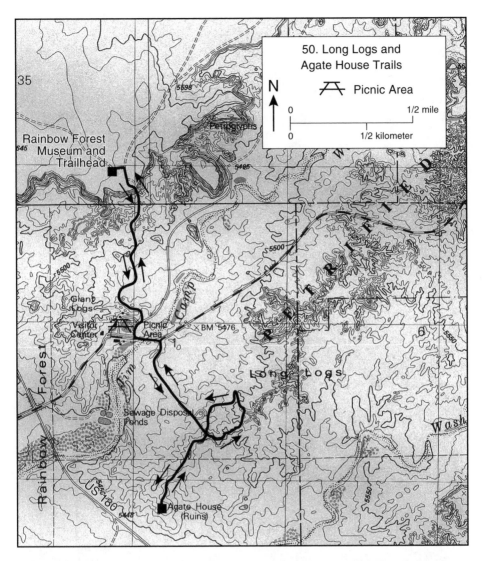

50. Long Logs and
Agate House Trails

N

⬆

🛆 Picnic Area

0   1/2 mile

0   1/2 kilometer

gate onto a black asphalt walkway. Stroll up the blacktop walkway for 0.5 mile and you'll enter a now-abandoned parking lot. There are small petrified logs sprawled around you at this spot, with many more to come. At the far end of the parking lot you'll see a sign for the Agate House and Long Logs Trails. Take the Agate House Trail on the right, to start along a pebble-and-concrete sidewalk.

Agate House trailhead to Agate House and back, 0.5 mile (1.10 miles total), 50-foot elevation gain, easy.

Walk 500 feet up the pebble trail and bear right past a concrete shelter, heading to Agate House directly in front of you. On this trail segment you'll see many petrified logs colored with black and rust layers. Along other parts of the trail you'll see petrified wood with milky, ruby, and jasper-

Petrified wood on the Long Logs Trail

brown hues. The hue and texture variations in the stone wood are subtle but beautifully distinctive to those who pause to study them. Some petrified logs are 5 feet in diameter and look like large, tree-shaped chunks of multihued agate—which they are!) It's tempting to pick up a souvenir here, but resist the temptation; you might also pick up a hefty fine for violating federal law.

After 0.25 mile of touring this rock garden, you end the trail at Agate House (elevation 5,555 feet), a 1930s re-creation of the house constructed there in A.D. 1000. This humble ruin is built of materials a shah would envy: darkly gleaming blocks of multicolored petrified wood, solid enough to last through the millennia of sun and storm these fossilized rocks have endured. From the house you stroll back down the trail to join the Long Logs trailhead and return to the Agate House trailhead and start the Long Logs Loop Trail.

Long Logs Loop to Agate House–Long Logs trailhead, 0.5 mile (1.6 total miles), 300-foot elevation loss, moderately difficult.

The Long Logs Trail (not to be confused with the Giant Logs Trail next to the museum) has one of the largest concentrations of petrified logs in the national park. As you start up this loop you'll see many 6-foot-long, marbleized tree trunks along your path, precursors to even larger examples farther along the trail. On warm days you may also see coteries of prairie dogs scampering about in the plain, keeping a watchful eye out for the golden eagles that soar above them.

As you move along the trail, you'll approach some gray and chocolate-brown mounds toward the north, 25-foot hillocks that are next to the trail. These sandstone and clay formations have been eroded into distinctive shapes that children would enjoy searching—one has a face complete with wind-sculpted eyebrows and teeth. Bring one of the free park maps along, and you can identify the various stone layers by their colors and levels. When you're done studying the hillocks, loop around past some more fossilized logs to rejoin the Agate House Trail and head back to the parking lot.

Agate House–Long Logs trailhead to parking lot, 0.6 mile (2.2 miles total), 20-foot elevation loss, easy.

From the Agate House trailhead, retrace your steps back to the museum parking lot, as you leave this prehistoric landscape to return to the trappings of civilization.

Nearby Trails

Want to walk on the wild side, but not get too wild? Explore the Painted Desert Wilderness and you can make your own wilderness trail in a low-risk environment. This 43,000-acre wilderness sprawls around the north entrance to the Petrified Forest National Park, by the Painted Desert Inn. Although the wilderness does not have any maintained trails, there are plenty of unsigned trace trails to follow. The landscape is relatively flat, so it's easy to keep your bearings. No matter where you are, just hike over to prominent Pilot Rock (elevation 6,234 feet) and from there you can see the park headquarters and restaurant. Some park rangers take an after-work stroll by themselves into this wilderness, knowing it's safe to go it alone. That said, you should still exercise caution in this wild land: Bring water, look back to remember the way you came, and let someone know where you have gone.

Camping

There are no campgrounds in the park, but you can backpack into the Painted Desert

Wilderness and camp overnight. The nearest campgrounds are in Holbrook, 23 miles northwest of the national park.

For more information, contact Petrified Forest National Park, PO Box 2217, Petrified Forest, AZ 86028. Telephone: 520-524-6228. The park web site is at www.nps.gov/pefo/index.htm.

References

Books

Abbey, Edward. *Confessions of a Barbarian: Selections from the Journals of Edward S. Abbey, 1951-1989.* Boston: Little, Brown, and Company,1994.

Chronic, Halka. *Roadside Geology of Arizona.* Missoula, MT: Mountain Press Publishing Company, 1988.

Dollar, Tom and Sieve, Jerry. *Guide to Arizona's Wilderness Areas.* Englewood, CO: Westcliffe Publishers, 1998.

Epple, Anne and Lewis. *A Field Guide to the Plants of Arizona.* Guilford, CT: The Globe Pequot Press, 1995.

Leavengood, Betty. *Tucson Hiking Guide, 2nd Ed.* Boulder, CO: Pruett Publishing Company, 1997.

Warren, Scott. *Exploring Arizona's Wild Areas.* Seattle: The Mountaineers Books, 1996.

Warren, Scott. *100 Classic Hikes in Arizona.* Seattle: The Mountaineers Books, 2000.

Web Sites

The state's best trail web site is www.hikearizona.com. This free trail info site has some entertaining trail narratives by locals who have hiked all over the state. Included are links to topographic maps for the trail area.

You can find hiking information about Arizona's 20 tallest peaks and 20 deepest canyons at Arizona State University's 20-20 Challenge web site at www.public.asu.edu/~bvogt/20-20/challenge.html.

The Tucson chapter of the Sierra Club has a trails website with Tucson-area trail details and photos. It's at www.arizona.sierraclub.org/trail_guide.

Index

Let Countryman Guides Take You There

Our experienced backcountry authors will lead you to the finest trails, parks, and back roads in the following areas:

50 Hikes Series

Northeast
50 Hikes in Connecticut
50 Hikes in the Maine Mountains
50 Hikes in Coastal and Southern Maine
50 Hikes in Massachusetts
50 Hikes in the White Mountains
50 More Hikes in New Hampshire
50 Hikes in the Adirondacks
50 Hikes in the Lower Hudson Valley
50 Hikes in Central New York
50 Hikes in Western New York
50 Hikes in Vermont

Mid-Atlantic
50 Hikes in Maryland
50 Hikes in New Jersey
50 Hikes in Central Pennsylvania
50 Hikes in Eastern Pennsylvania
50 Hikes in Western Pennsylvania
50 Hikes in Northern Virginia
50 Hikes in Southern Virginia

Southeast
50 Hikes in Kentucky
50 Hikes in Louisiana
50 Hikes in the Mountains of North Carolina
50 Hikes in the Tennessee Mountains
50 Hikes in Central Florida
50 Hikes in North Florida
50 Hikes in South Florida

West & Midwest
50 Hikes in Colorado
50 Hikes in Michigan
50 Hikes in Ohio
50 More Hikes in Ohio
50 Hikes in Wisconsin

Hiking, Climbing, Fishing & Travel
Crossing Arizona
Arizona Trout Streams and Their Hatches
Fly-Fishing the South Atlantic Coast
Alaska on Foot
American Rock
Backwoods Ethics
The California Coast
The Pacific Crest Trail
Shawangunks Trail Companion
Switzerland's Mountain Inns
Weekend Wilderness: California, Oregon, Washington
Where the Waters Divide

Bicycling

Northeast
Backroad Bicycling in Connecticut
25 Bicycle Tours in Maine
25 Bicycle Tours in Vermont
Backroad Bicycling on Cape Cod, Martha's Vineyard, and Nantucket
25 Mountain Bike Tours in Massachusetts
Backroad Bicycling in Western Massachusetts
Bike Rides in the Berkshire Hills
Backroad Bicycling in New Hampshire
25 Bicycle Tours in the Adirondacks
25 Bicycle Tours in the Lake Champlain Region
25 Mountain Bike Tours in the Adirondacks
Backroad Bicycling in the Finger Lakes Region
25 Bicycle Tours in the Hudson Valley
The Mountain Biker's Guide to Ski Resorts

Mid-Atlantic
25 Bicycle Tours on Delmarva
25 Bicycle Tours in Maryland
30 Bicycle Tours in New Jersey
25 Mountain Bike Tours in New Jersey
Backroad Bicycling in Eastern Pennsylvania
25 Bicycle Tours in and Around Washington, D.C.

Southeast
Backroad Bicycling in the Blue Ridge and Smoky Mountains
25 Bicycle Tours in the Savannah & the Carolina Low Country

West & Midwest
Bicycling America's National Parks: Arizona & New Mexico
Bicycling America's National Parks: California
Bicycling America's National Parks: Oregon and Washington
Bicycling America's National Parks: Utah and Colorado
25 Bicycle Tours in the Texas Hill Country and West Texas
Backroad Bicycling in Wisconsin
25 Bicycle Tours in the Twin Cities & Southeastern Minnesota

We offer many more books on hiking, fly-fishing, travel, nature, and other subjects. Our books are available at bookstores and outdoor stores everywhere. For more information or a free catalog, call 1-800-245-4151 or write to us at The Countryman Press, P.O. Box 748, Woodstock, Vermont 05091. You can find us on the Internet at www.countrymanpress.com.